BLACK REBELS
AFRICAN-CARIBBEAN FREEDOM FIGHTERS IN JAMAICA

The author with Nana Rowe, the last living authority on the Kromanti songs of Accompong

BLACK REBELS

African-Caribbean Freedom Fighters in Jamaica

BY

WERNER ZIPS

TRANSLATED FROM GERMAN
BY SHELLEY L. FRISCH

 Markus Wiener
Publishers

PRINCETON

 Ian Randle
Publishers

JAMAICA

THE PUBLICATION OF THIS BOOK IN ENGLISH WAS SUPPORTED BY THE
AUSTRIAN FEDERAL MINISTRY FOR RESEARCH AND TRAFFIC, VIENNA.

FOR INFORMATION WRITE TO:

MARKUS WIENER PUBLISHERS
231 NASSAU STREET, PRINCETON, NJ 08542

LIBRARY OF CONGRESS CATALOGING-IN-PUBLICATION DATA
ZIPS, WERNER, 1958–
[SCHWARZE REBELLEN. ENGLISH]
BLACK REBELS: AFRICAN-CARIBBEAN FREEDOM FIGHTERS IN JAMAICA /
WERNER ZIPS; TRANSLATED FROM GERMAN BY SHELLEY L. FRISCH;
FOREWORD BY FRANKLIN W. KNIGHT.
INCLUDES BIBLIOGRAPHICAL REFERENCES.
ISBN 1-55876-212-4 HARDCOVER
ISBN 1-55876-213-2 PAPERBACK
1. MAROONS—JAMAICA—HISTORY.   2. MAROONS—JAMAICA—WARS.
3. JAMAICA—RACE RELATIONS.   I. TITLE.
F1884.Z5613   1999   972.92'00496—DC21
99-16568   CIP

FIRST PUBLISHED IN JAMAICA 1999 BY
IAN RANDLE PUBLISHERS, LTD.
206 OLD HOPE ROAD, BOX 686, KINGSTON 6, JAMAICA

ISBN 976-8123-66-4 PAPERBACK

A CATALOGUE RECORD FOR THIS BOOK IS AVAILABLE FROM THE
NATIONAL LIBRARY OF JAMAICA.

MARKUS WIENER PUBLISHERS BOOKS ARE PRINTED IN THE UNITED STATES OF AMERICA
ON ACID-FREE PAPER, AND MEET THE GUIDELINES FOR PERMANENCE AND DURABILITY
OF THE COMMITTEE ON PRODUCTION GUIDELINES FOR BOOK LONGEVITY
OF THE COUNCIL ON LIBRARY RESOURCES.

TABLE OF CONTENTS

"Often in interviews the question has been asked of me: 'What does it mean to you to be a Maroon today?' When it is considered that Grandy Nanny, Kojo, Accompong and others of our leaders prevailed against the forces of a kingdom that ruled more than a quarter of all the lands on earth, then the pride of their Maroon posterity can be understood and appreciated. Yet these physical victories gave rise to other victories of deep moral, psychological and spiritual significance which increased that pride and its concomitant thankfulness a hundredfold. If the Maroons had been defeated, meaningful black resistance to the indignity and cruelty of African slavery would have ended—at least for a season—and so even today the cries of the tortured might still have been heard on the plantations, in the dungeons and from myriad village squares across the world. The knowledge that the Mother of my fathers, from her base in little Jamaica, burst asunder the prison bars of black bondage means more to me than life itself. It is like a sacrament taken daily as I kneel in humanity at the feet of Nyankipon (The Creator) in the peaceful evening hour. Nyame adom (Thank God), I would not change my Maroon Heritage for occupancy of the White House nor the grandeur of the British Throne."

Colonel C.L.G. Harris (1992:73)

vi

FOREWORD

BY

FRANKLIN W. KNIGHT

The history of the Caribbean prior to political independence has always consisted of two contrasting, yet interwoven threads. One thread represented the formal and legally constituted structure of the European colony, often alternating between settler and plantation societies. Although never operating in tranquillity, this formal thread included the various sorts of imperial bureaucrats, boisterous settlers, exasperated planters, persevering merchants, aspiring free persons of color, long-suffering slaves, and odd hangers-on of every description. What held them together was a vague notion of the state and social order, often communicated violently and inconsistently. The other thread represented the heterogeneous social by-products of the constant, invariably tumultuous changes that accompanied the evolution of the Caribbean systems. Different socio-political situations engendered miscellaneous social types, generally considered under the generic rubric of transfrontiersmen. Among this category were found hermits, mountain men, pirates, buccaneers, and maroons.

Perhaps the most interesting, the most durable, and maybe the most important types were the communities of Maroons, found wherever the Europeans established colonies. Maroons were organized communities of escaped slaves and their descendants. The word derives from an original Iberian description for cattle that had escaped to the high peaks beyond the range of care and culture, and proliferated—*ganado cimarrón*—and the description still prevails in parts of South America, as in Colombia and Venezuela. Like so much else, the word *cimarrón* became Americanized after 1492, being applied rapidly to indigenous people who rejected docile subordination to the early Spanish colonists, and subsequently to the African slaves who aggressively refused to endure perpetual servitude and escaped from their masters. By the nineteenth century the term Maroons connoted almost exclusively the communities of ex-slaves and their descendants living in symbiotic relationship with the geographically contiguous colony.

The incessant flight of slaves from servitude—*marronage*—represented an intrinsic aspect of the history of the American slave society. There were two types of *marronage* reflecting the presumed intention of the individual, or individuals, or the actual accomplishment: *petit marronage* and *grand marronage*. Both represented the autonomous decision of the slaves to alter their condition or their social relationship by themselves. *Petit marronage* was transient, the desire to avoid unpleasant or inconvenient labor, to procrastinate, to manifest oblique disobedience to the master, or to engage in social activities such as visiting distant family or friends or participating in dances or rituals. Invariably a personal conflict between masters and slaves, *petit marronage* was eventually accepted as an unavoidable dimension of the constantly negotiated world of punishment and incentives that shaped the cruel and coerced relationships of the American slave systems. *Grand marronage*, a case study of which is done by Werner Zips in this book, represented fully organized attempts to establish autonomous communities politically and socially independent of the colonial authorities. Their success and longevity provided their indelible nomenclature.

Although established as an alternative organization to the colonial societies of the European New World, Maroon societies were not intrinsically a threat to the principal, settled, or organized sphere. Maroon communities were designed to fulfill the slaves' inherent desires to be free, and to secure that freedom for their offspring. Economically, most Maroon communities depended on reciprocal commerce with the surrounding non-maroon communities, local and international. During the nineteenth century some Cuban *palenques* (as Maroon villages were called in the Hispanic Caribbean) like *El Frijol* in Oriente even traded with the neighboring island of Jamaica. Nevertheless, Europeans fearfully recognized Maroon villages as potentially subversive to the entire socio-economic complex of conventional colonial life and attacked them relentlessly. Maroon villages encompassed varying numbers of individuals. Some Maroon communities such as Cupey, El Frijol, Colunga, Todos Tenemos, Guarda Mujeres, La Palma, Quema Sol, and Palenque Viejo so extensively described by Gabino La Rosa Corzo in his book *Los palenques del oriente de Cuba* (Havana: Editorial Academia, 1991) were relatively short-lived. Others, like Accompong, Maroon Town, and Nanny Town in Jamaica, Le Maniel in French Saint-Domingue, Palmares in Brazil, and Esmeraldas in Ecuador, endured for centuries, fighting the colonial powers to repeated military stalemates, signing treaties of peace, and gradually consolidating themselves.

Only in Jamaica did the Maroon communities survive until the political independence of the colony. This was no small feat, given the odds—

and the history of such communities elsewhere throughout the hemisphere.

The success or failure of any Maroon community depended on time, place, circumstances, and local leadership. Large communities established before the nineteenth century had a better chance of long-term success than those established in the nineteenth century. The balance of military forces between attackers and defenders was not then as uneven. This partly explains why Maroon communities survived in Jamaica—where the Maroons signed peace treaties with the English in 1739 and 1796—but failed in Cuba, where marronage seems to have disappeared about the same time as the abolition of slavery in the 1880s. Location was also a major consideration for initial success. Most Maroon villages that survived for any significant length of time in the Caribbean were found in relatively inaccessible mountainous areas: the densely forested slopes of the Sierra Maestra in Oriente, Cuba; the rugged Cockpit Country of western Jamaica or the precipitous slopes of the eastern Blue Mountains in Jamaica; the formidable *massifs* of northern and southern Saint-Domingue; or the almost impenetrable *cordilleras* of Santo Domingo. Leadership also played an important role, as Zips examines in this book. Maroon communities, especially in the formative stages, required extraordinary leadership to combat the constant assaults by superior military forces with superior military resources.

Yet, the assets of initiation could be detrimental handicaps over the long run. Inaccessible locations with often poor soils condemned Maroon communities to economic marginality. The treaties signed with the surrounding societies often undermined rapid population growth and the timely introduction of fresh blood and fresh ideas, thereby restricting cultural development. And non-meritoriously selected leadership eventually led to mediocre statecraft, frequently jeopardizing the continuity of the community. But these characteristics were not peculiar, nor even exclusive, to Maroon communities. It is all the more remarkable, therefore, that so many such communities existed in so many places for such long periods in the history of the Americas.

Altogether the history of marronage still remains a neglected aspect of Caribbean and New World history. There are some reasons for this paucity of good studies. The research is unusually difficult, with extremely limited documentation, and even more limited opportunities for ethnographic exploration. Fortunately for the reader, in this case the author persevered and produced a very important contribution to the historiography.

Black Rebels is richly documented, impressively thoughtful, occasionally provocative, and invariably sensitive. An apt sequel to Barbara Kopytoff's unpublished study of the Jamaica Maroons (which in any case ends at the beginning of the twentieth century), Zips has produced an excellent study that stands as a powerful contribution to the growing literature on Jamaican and wider Caribbean marronage. He blends standard ethnography with conventional history, often vividly capturing the musical voices of the Jamaica Maroons. Throughout he questions many assertions by past reporters and current scholars on the culture, economy, and politics of Maroon society. In addition, *Black Rebels*, with its outstanding bibliography, nicely examines the Jamaica Maroons within the broader Caribbean and Atlantic context. Scholars everywhere will find this a very useful study.

Baltimore
July, 1999

PREFACE

After two unsuccessful attempts to reach the Maroon settlement of Accompong, I finally found my way there. My earlier trips were foiled by motorcycle mishaps, bad weather, and my lack of geographical orientation. I was quite anxious to meet the descendants of the first black freedom fighters in Jamaica. Their reputation as a militant group has survived into the present. When I arrived, however, I had the impression that my hopes would be dashed. Nothing seemed to distinguish this "rebel enclave" from other Jamaican villages.

That first visit took place in the summer of 1985. In the course of several subsequent visits over the next few years, Maroons helped me discern the distinctive features of their culture and history. This book depicts the special nature of Maroon life and its place within Jamaican society. My particular debt of gratitude goes to my friends in Accompong, Moore Town, and Maroon Town (formerly known as Kojo's Town). They entrusted me with their knowledge and their convictions without exercising direct control over the end product. I therefore hope that it meets with their approval. Many "co-authors" contributed to my plan to write a "history of resistance" rather than a "history of domination." I have attempted to weave their voices into the whole text and visualize them as directors of my interpretations.

A series of institutions lent financial and logistical support to my research over the years. In this context I would like to thank the Austrian Science Fund, the Akademische Senat of the University of Vienna, the Austrian Federal Ministry of Science and Transport, the Phonogrammarchiv of the Austrian Academy of Sciences, the Austrian Federal Institute for the Scientific Film (which enabled me to make twelve documentary films in Jamaica), and the Institute for Social and Cultural Anthropology (Ethnology) of the University of Vienna.

Of the many individuals who helped create this book, my special thanks go to Karl R. Wernhart, who established a focus on Caribbean research at the Institute of Ethnology and Cultural and Social Anthropology back in the late 1970s, when this area of study had not attained its current prominence as a result of reggae, Rastafari, and other popular forms of expression. His scholarly expertise, unflagging support, and constructive criticism were always at my disposal. Together with Manfred Kremser and other colleagues of the Institute for Social and

xi

Cultural Anthropology (Ethnology), he created a wonderfully stimulating and instructive context in which to discuss the fruits of my research.

I wish to thank the translator of this book, Professor Shelley Frisch, for her dedication and enthusiasm in capturing the precise meaning of the text without sacrificing the rhetorical flavor of the original German, and for her energy in preparing the publication.

Blue Mountain range

Introduction

Enslaved Africans on their "Trail of Tears" to the slave ship

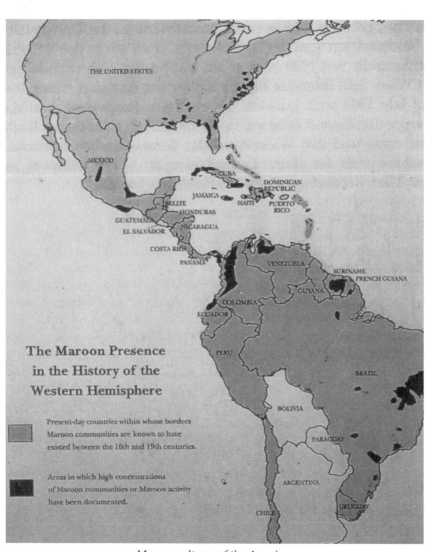

The Maroon Presence in the History of the Western Hemisphere

Present-day countries within whose borders Maroon communities are known to have existed between the 16th and 19th centuries.

Areas in which high concentrations of Maroon communities or Maroon activity have been documented.

THE UNITED STATES

MEXICO

CUBA

DOMINICAN REPUBLIC

JAMAICA

BELIZE

HAITI

PUERTO RICO

GUATEMALA

HONDURAS

EL SALVADOR

NICARAGUA

COSTA RICA

PANAMA

VENEZUELA

SURINAME

FRENCH GUIANA

GUYANA

COLOMBIA

ECUADOR

PERU

BRAZIL

BOLIVIA

PARAGUAY

ARGENTINA

CHILE

URUGUAY

Maroon cultures of the Americas

"A *people without a history is like a tree without roots."* This common comparison is of central importance for the conception of this book. Like many others, I first developed an interest in Jamaica and the Caribbean by listening to the reggae texts of Bob Marley and Burning Spear in the 1970s. The fragments of Rastafarian philosophy found in these songs impelled me to probe their historical context. In the spirit of the Rasta imperative "Seek and you will find," I began the journey that culminated in this book. According to Rasta reasoning, which entails communicative dissemination and cultivation of philosophical foundations, references to the past are an ongoing component. The capture and enslavement of Africans in the so-called New World and centuries of oppression and cultural expropriation are crucial experiences, as is the recollection of ancestral resistance.

Reggae texts both reflect Rasta reasoning and serve to bring it into the public arena. Rasta reasoning is built on particular discursive elements, notably the element of resistance. A call to opposition against the backdrop of historical experience drives numerous reggae texts about recalling the days of slavery and standing up and fighting for one's rights. My initial personal interest in this discourse was rooted in the present. Bob Marley, Peter Tosh, Burning Spear, and others allow audiences the option of reshaping the discourse to reflect current political relevance. In my view, this option explains why young people around the world use reggae music as a form of protest. Japanese teenagers rebel against their society's overreliance on technology, young Maoris protest colonial structures, young Swiss give voice to their resentment of restrictive policies on youth, adolescents from Zanzibar register objections to the strict code of conduct of Islam, and young Americans combat the ecological catastrophe by means of reggae. But for participants in this discourse who share their Jamaican outlook with the artists, there is yet a further dimension of common historical experience.

Reggae texts themselves are defenseless against selective listening, but direct communication partners can resist this tendency. During my first research trip to Jamaica, in 1984, Rastafari contextualized and thereby historicized my original understanding. Their basic message was that

Rastafari roots are in Africa. Whites sought to sever these roots to insure African transformation into slaves. The result was a crippling of opposition over the course of centuries. In the words of the Rasta social scientist Jah Bones (1985:5, 12): "So in effect, Rasta was a slave but Rasta rebelled hard and gradually fashioned a substantial 'contracultural' system that produced heroes and warriors such as Paul Bogle, Alexander Bedward, Marcus Garvey, Leonard Howell, and all the Rasta Youths. . . . Rasta is the totality of a life's experience which is reflected in history and projected into the future."

It was this historical perspective that steered my research interests to the experience of Africans who were brought to the Americas in captivity (using the example of Jamaica) and their resistance to enslavement. I also felt a philosophical and political obligation to participate in preserving the memory of the actual historical connections between whites and blacks.

A line from the reggae song "Slave Master" by Gregory Isaacs, in which the singer threatens to set fire to the plantations if he does not get his desire, describes a common historical practice of slaves. African resistance to slavery commenced at the very beginning of the slave trade on the west coast of Africa by the Portuguese in the mid-fifteenth century. Historical research has shown that the stereotype of the docile slave was nothing but a myth. Enslaved people reacted to the violence of the Europeans with diverse and creative acts of resistance. Once slave trade had extended across the Atlantic into what Europeans called the "New World," a dialectic of oppression and resistance characterized the following five hundred years. In older historical scholarship about this time period, Eurocentric, often racist biases on the part of the authors painted a skewed picture. To get beyond their one-sidedness, I chose an emancipatory approach that is gaining considerable currency in the social sciences.

The history of the enslavement of Africans by Europeans has been told from multiple perspectives. A wide array of ideological, theoretical, and methodological assumptions is manifest in how the various "histories" are told. An overtly critical approach has advanced the type of historical inquiry that investigates the relationship between Europeans and Africans as a struggle for power, thereby redressing previous oversimplifications. Many a study of slavery left the victims where the slaveholders wanted to capture them: as objects of the rulers; despite or in the face of their criticism of historical power relationships. Lopsided scholarship that focuses solely on the ruler—whether the intent is to defend or to criticize—reduces the existence of the suppressed people to their subservience and the sufferings born of this situation. Shifting the paradigm from the history of domination to the history of conflict (in this case, between Africans and Europeans) should provide a corrective to a serious imbalance.

If we are to attempt a multilayered historical reconstruction of the struggle for power, we must turn first to the complex relationships between oppressors and oppressed. Within this interpretive framework, my interest has been directed primarily to the active accomplishments of the resisters. This book, which stresses the actions and experiences of the Africans as historical agents, aims to contribute to a revision of the conflict between the claims to rule of the Europeans and the resistance of the Africans. It is a conscious departure from earlier presentations that reduce the people and societies victimized by slavery and colonialism to passive victims. Yet, the attempt to demarginalize cultural practices (including acts of resistance) in no way clashes with a categorical indictment of genocide of the ("Indian") First Nations[1] as well as the oppression, exploitation, and physical annihilation of millions of Africans.[2]

The active accomplishments of opposition and self-assertion are or have been at least as constitutive for the sociocultural development and identity of African-Caribbean societies as their experience of centuries of injustice. The conviction is growing, among black activists and others, that the essence of black history in the diaspora is not slavery and colonialism, but resistance to systematic oppression. Whereas the Africans who were treated as commodities or objects according to ancient notions of law proved by creative acts of resistance that they were subjects, not objects, the laws and practices of the whites placed their humanity in doubt. Their attempt to reduce people to work machines by institutionalizing slavery ultimately failed because of the resolute opposition and rebellion of those people.

Acts of resistance in Africa, as well as armed battle against slave hunters, revolts in the workplaces controlled by whites, and flight from trading centers, were continued in mutiny during the so-called Middle Passage of the triangle of trade between Europe, Africa, and America as well as in organized rebellions in the plantation colonies. They never allowed the colonial institutions and profiteers of the economic system of slavery to let down their guard. Right from the arrival of the first slave ships from Africa in the Caribbean, in the early 16th century, the newcomers threatened the exclusive claim to rule of the Europeans, which had scarcely been endangered by the subjugated First Nations. The severity of these threats varied, of course, according to the concrete conditions of each colony.

Outright battle exposed only the tip of the iceberg. Under the surface of the conduct that was visible to slaveholders, the enslaved people practiced their everyday resistance. The stereotype of the servile Uncle Tom as pictured by Hollywood (and other modern subsystems of white cultural domination) is not only distorted; it is an ideological construction to legitimate the social hierarchy. By contrast, black activists like Malcolm X invoke the term of loyal "house niggers" to motivate themselves and their fellow combatants to more decisive action. While many a slave may have acted in a style consistent with "Uncle Tom" or "house niggers," this mode of action was not a character trait. Their apparent assimilation to the system of slavery was a reaction to a set of circumstances and did not reflect a general passive psyche of Africans, as some ideologically loaded depictions would have us believe. The very same person who answered the white master at lunch with "yes massa, sure massa, thank you massa" may well have added a pinch of rat poison to the evening soup; or perhaps he merely oversalted it to upset the white master. Because he had to fear appalling recriminations for this sort of misstep, however, he might even prepare the soup according to the wishes of the "massa" until something jolted him into action and he finally did add the poison or at least the extra salt.

The third chapter of this book provides an overview of the forms resistance took against the backdrop of such considerations. A central question is whether the classification of resistance into dualistic categories such as passive versus active resistance should be rejected in favor of a more flexible analysis of the term "resistance." With these observations on the bases and modes of expression of resistance in a thematic context and following some basic observations on the slave system, the inquiry leads up to an examination of marronage, a form of self-organization and opposition that has been aptly called the antithesis of slavery.

"Free and unbroken." These were the connotations of the term Maroon. Today, at least in the African diaspora, the term is used as a synonym for freedom fighter. The English word Maroon derives from the Spanish word *cimarrón*, which in turn has etymological roots in an expression of the Arawak–First Nation of Hispaniola, which was the first Caribbean island to be occupied by Spain. Originally it referred to runaway farm animals, mainly cattle. Soon the term spread throughout the region to refer to enslaved members of First Nations who had successfully fled the plantations of the whites. This etymology sheds light on the historical

attitude of the Europeans upon encountering residents of territories they had "discovered": "The Europeans regarded the people whom they encountered in North and South America more as natural objects— another form of the fauna to be discovered and explored—than as human beings with histories as rich and ancient as their own" (Viola 1992:12).

Their attitude toward Africans was essentially the same. The European settlers imported a greater and greater number of slaves from Africa to labor as human beasts of burden to replace the "First Nations," whose ranks were quite decimated after just a few decades of war, ruthless exploitation, and disease. The word *cimarrón* was retained to describe a plantation runaway. In the English colonies it began to be used, in the translated form Maroons, as a general term for runaways, irrespective of ethnic affiliation (Price 1992:62).

The meaning of this term evolved as elaborate strategies of resistance developed. Runaways did not merely flee plantations to hide beyond the reach of the slaveholders in inaccessible areas; they also banded together, as small groups that gradually expanded in size, built up a military organization, and began to construct new social units based on various African traditions. These societal bands were, and still are, called Maroons or Maroon communities. Immense obstacles needed to be surmounted in developing structures of solidarity or "ethnicity." The Windward and Leeward Maroons of Jamaica exemplified the issues involved in cultivating ethnicity despite the difficulties of constantly integrating new runaways.

In the wake of military successes by the freedom fighters, the term Maroons attained respectful connotations, including proud, free, wild, unbroken, and untamed; however, these connotations did little to quell comparisons with the animal realm. Since Maroons had escaped "domestication" on the plantations, historical accounts treated them as uncivilized savages; some considered them noble savages (see Dallas 1803). From the perspective of colonial rulers and plantation owners, they posed a permanent threat to the white claim to rule and therefore of the whole system of plantation economy by means of slavery. Their determined struggle for liberation would also decisively alter their legal status within the colonial system of (unjust) law.

"Dead or free." There was essentially no third option. Flight from plantations and armed battle against the whites meant courting death. Virtually all colonial legislation required capital punishment, usually following unspeakable torture, for *grand marronage*—life in a Maroon community. Even *petit marronage*, which was a relatively brief absence from

the plantations, resulted in the severest possible corporal punishment, such as castration, amputation of limbs (especially of one or both feet), and public flogging. Many other forms of torture were implemented to forewarn potential runaways. Nonetheless, men and women in all slave colonies risked their lives for the reward of freedom. Only flight from the slave ships and plantations could achieve this inalienable ideal.

In 1502, the first slave ship to the "New World" reached the shores of the Caribbean island of Hispaniola. The advent of this ship also marked the arrival of the first Maroon, who jumped ship and fled to the interior of the island to join up with a First Nation. This tradition survived the entire period of slavery. During the 350 to 400 years of European tyranny by enslavement (from the early 16th century on), independent communities sprang up and remained in practically all (slave) colonies. These communities had been founded by Africans and their descendants born in the diaspora. Their size ranged from small groups to mighty states with thousands of people—as, for instance, Palmares in Brazil. Several factors influenced their membership numbers and the consequent likelihood of success of a given Maroon community. These factors included the natural conditions of the region, especially whether it included inaccessible places of retreat, the military strength of the colonial government, and the strategic and creative accomplishments of all societal members, especially the talents of their leaders. Their duties included maintaining order in addition to coordinating offensive and defensive strategies (Bilby and Baird N'Diaye 1992:54ff; also Price 1992:62).

Of the hundreds of Maroon communities during the nearly 500 years following the beginning of trans-Atlantic slave trade, few survived to the present day, among them the Maroons of Accompong, Moore Town and Scott's Hall in Jamaica, the Saramaka, Ndjuka, Paramaka, Matawai, and Kwinti of Suriname, the Aluku of French Guiana, the Seminole Maroons of Texas, Oklahoma, Mexico, and the Bahamas, the Palenqueros of Colombia, the Garifuna in Central America, and the Maroons of the Costa Chica region in Mexico. Most Maroon communities in the British North American colonies, which later became the United States, the European colonial territories in the Caribbean and Central America, as well as the South American regions occupied by Spaniards, Portuguese, and Dutch, came to a violent end. Often the colonial troops succeeded in exterminating the freedom fighters only after decades of bloody military battles.

However, even the great powers of the time had met their match in several Maroon communities. In some instances, colonial rulers exhausted their military means battling the impressive guerrilla tactics of the

The Middle Passage of human cargo

Maroons, then changed course to a path of peaceful co-existence. In 1739, nearly 40 years before the United States achieved independence from England, the Maroons in Jamaica had won their wars of independence. Peace treaties with agents of the British government have since guaranteed their quasi-state autonomy. They were, however, by no means the first free black communities in the western hemisphere. As early as 1579, the Spanish signed two treaties with runaway groups in Panama, and in 1609, yet another treaty with a Mexican community (Campbell 1990:8f.).

9

Other colonial powers such as England, France, the Netherlands, Portugal, and the United States followed this example. Unfortunately for the rebels, however, many peace treaties were not worth the paper on which they were written. Ratified in order to pacify "the black rebels," these treaties were often nothing more than an imposition by the whites. Once peace was in place, the European governments violated the agreements according to the criterion of *raison d'état*—without a trace of legal or moral scruples. Rights that had been agreed upon had to be defended again and again by diplomatic efforts, and, whenever necessary, with force. Some historians (most recently Campbell 1990:250ff.) have argued that Maroon diplomacy was nothing but collaboration with colonial power and therefore a sellout of the old ideals of the freedom fight. This issue will be addressed in the fourth chapter after an exploration of the issues concerning the military success of the Maroons of Jamaica as a prerequisite for the peace treaties.

In Jamaica, the regional focus of this book, several Maroon communities lasted through the entire period of British colonial rule, namely from 1655 to 1962. This endurance indicates more than a military success. Social, political, cultural, and economic achievements constituted the basis of their survival. Even at present, these independent black communities face pressure from the outside. Now that European colonial rule has come to an end in most regions of the African diaspora, the governments of the independent countries show little enthusiasm for the existence of additional claims for sovereignty on "their" territory (see Zips 1997 and van Rouveroy van Nieuwaal/Zips 1998b). In 1986, this conflict situation erupted into a war between the government and the members of the Maroons of Suriname.

The elected governments of Jamaica (since 1962, the year of independence from Great Britain) have pursued a policy toward Maroons that could be summed up as separate but equal. This expression recognizes the Maroons' implicit right to autonomy and other entitlements, such as tax-free status, although these rights are not stated in the Constitution, while allowing them their full citizenship rights as Jamaicans. The Maroons enjoy a virtual dual nationality. They elect their own government but are also entitled to cast their votes in general parliamentary elections. Chapter V examines the internal organizational form of their political, social, and economic relations and their historical evolution. It is also necessary to clarify questions of the cultural distinction of the Maroon communities from other Jamaicans. For one thing, which cultural practices "demarcate" them from outsiders and thereby affirm their

10

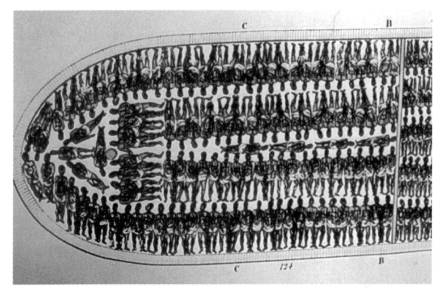

Stowage of British slave ship

historical identity as Maroons; for another, which interactions or relations make it possible to overcome this distinction between Maroons and non-Maroons in particular situations?

In my view, the African-American struggle for freedom in the diaspora cannot be limited to the Maroon communities. I see instead a continuum of widely varying modes of resistance, ranging from malingering often misperceived as laziness to refusals to work staged by feigning illness to acts of sabotage that are misconstrued as imbecility to flight from plantations and armed battle against the whites. Numerous interactions between practitioners of opposition with varying means underscore the inadequacy of rigid categories for the essentially common pursuit of resistance by the enslaved. For instance, how are we to categorize house slaves who acted subserviently to the white master while secretly eavesdropping and passing on information to the rebels? Were they practicing passive or active resistance? Were they servile or rebellious? If we bear in mind that a house slave could at any time opt to risk flight and cast his lot with the Maroons, such categories would appear to lose their analytical value.

Marronage—social independence defended by armed struggle—is ideologically linked by refusal to subjugate oneself to other practices of opposition and insubordination of enslaved Africans, as well as their descendants born in the diaspora. This paradigmatic assumption is not undermined by any evidence of breaks in solidarity, collaboration with the oppressors, and treachery within the ranks. Instead, it substantiates the varied interests, mentalities, and ad hoc decisions of the enslaved in connection with the structures of the system of slavery. In historical reality, the slaveholders did everything to prevent the dreaded consolidation of the enslaved. For a long time, their divide-and-rule strategies successfully upheld slavery and colonialism. Haiti was the major exception. In Haiti, unification of the blacks—with the participation of the Maroons—resulted in national emancipation from (French) tyranny in the early 19th century. For this reason, breaks in solidarity are as revealing as any intermittent harmonization of differing views; failures as much as successes and divergences as much as alliances.

The very individual and collective willfulness of individual slaves as well as larger ethnic or political communities that thwarted collaborative action was also in the long term the most effective weapon against the many forms oppression took. By sticking to their own powers of interpretation, expression, and strategic action, they resisted the ruthless exploitation of their work and of internal colonization. The physical and psychic battle for existence of the blacks in the diaspora was directed against the attempted destruction of their religious, social, cultural, political, judicial, and philosophical values and forms of expression by whites; it is continued today by resistance to perpetual missionary attempts, economic manipulation, indoctrination with European and Euro-American cultural imperatives, and other issues of that sort. The struggle for self-determination may be considered *the* integrative element of African-American experiences in the diaspora for manifestations of determination today. The Europeans failed at their attempt to deprive the Africans of their rights because they met with creative forms of opposition: "The revolt against slavery thus emerged as the basic assertion of human dignity and of humanity itself" (Genovese 1981:xiii).

Reading the present into the past. The communicative experiences of living in a Maroon society necessarily influence how one views the past. During my research stays in Jamaica, which began in 1984 and totalled well over two years, I spent a great deal of time with Maroons of Accompong as well as with residents of earlier Maroon territories (especially Maroon Town and Shaw Castle), to gain insight into their historical perspective. An idea and concept for a film about the social history of the Leeward Maroons in the Cockpit Country was beginning to take shape in my mind. The resulting documentary film, *Accompong—Black Freedom Fighters of Jamaica*, produced by the Austrian Federal Institute for the Scientific Film, came out in 1992. This film is based on contemporary Maroon views of their history and current situation (Zips 1991a). Their demand for recognition and their historical reasoning go to the foundation of this book. My intention is to reconstruct the historical development, transmitted by the dialectic between (power) structures and the practices of the historical social actors who both reproduced and transformed the colonial structures; however, my selection of topics as well as a particular mode of representation leads to a version of Maroon history informed by my actual encounters and developing relationships with living Maroons.

In the process of (ethno-)historical writing, our tempocentric rootedness (see Textor 1980:35f.) has a significant effect on how we interpret the past. In a foreword to his experimental narration on the resistance of the Maroons of Suriname, Price (1990:xviii) makes explicit reference to his conditioning by ethnographic experience in Saramaka: "While taking the greatest pains not to read the present backward into the past, I nonetheless am constantly trying to understand the records left by the past in terms that are unavoidably colored by the present." Not only the scholarly author, but also the people interviewed for the book mold their historical views to contemporary requirements; hence, tempocentricism works in two directions. I attempt to counteract this tendency by keeping the current political and social situation of the Maroons transparent and identifying the use of historical references for the formulation of current claims to validity. Moreover, the inclusion of secondary literature on the Maroons should serve to broaden the interpretative scope for the reader.

Even if the historical perspectives and visions of living Maroons do not provide direct access to the past, they create a tension with the written sources of the Europeans, which reflects the "real" conflict. Instead of trying to piece together diverse representations to form one coherent historical narration, I opted for a multivocal (re)construction of the conflict. In other words, I exploit the collision of the sources to uncover new ways to interpret them. Nurtured by the guidelines of a theory of practice (see Bourdieu 1972), this approach emphasizes (historical) action over positivist descriptions in the sources.

Positivistic readings of sources, even if the sources are approached with a critical eye, leave a weighty deficit because the European accounts are limited by a fixed interpretative framework. The bias of representations recorded during the period of slavery and colonialism requires a

more deconstructive gesture in dealing with these texts than conventional criticism is able to provide. I therefore opted to devote more attention
to the context of these European written sources. By widening the interpretative dimension, this methodology should clarify the actual quality
of texts by "colonial historians" and participating observers of the time.
Their reports do not reflect historical reality, even after critical correctives.
Instead, they express perspectives and values predicated on political and
economic interests, projections, fears, wishes, levels of information, etc.
Taking their descriptive contents at face value results in a scholarly transformation of attitudes to historical facts. A revision of the social history of
black resistance must therefore establish the contexts and proclivities of
written sources to disclose the information they leave unstated.

In the First Time, during the battle for emancipation, a critical defense
tactic of the freedom fights was to mislead military opponents by providing false information. Confession statements of captured Maroons
need to be analyzed in the context of their oppositional intention as a conscious maneuver, or at least to leave open the possibility of interpretation
along these lines. The Maroons of Suriname dispatched "secret agents"
who were deliberately captured by whites so as to provide false information under interrogation by the enemy (Price 1983b:39). Similar strategies
may also be assumed for other Maroon communities, but the literature on
the freedom struggle of the Jamaican Maroons has not given sufficient
consideration to this possibility (cf., for example, Campbell 1990; Patterson 1983; Robinson 1969).

On the basis of several "key sources" (especially military reports)
available in the London Public Record Office, some historians concluded
that the Leeward Maroons pursued a policy of accommodation, seeking
an arrangement with the colonial power. Following this logic, under the
leadership of Captain Kojo, the current cultural icon of Accompong, they
would thus have sought a compromise with the British in the early 18th
century, transformed themselves into loyal subjects of the British after the
peace treaty of 1739, and finally succumbed to the "colonial dependency
syndrome" in the late nineteenth century, losing their cultural values in
the process (Campbell 1990:254ff.). In discussing the military conflicts
and the internal organization of the Maroons, I hold up the following
questions as correctives to this type of inference: Can we not regard the
pejorative personality sketches of Kojo from the "enemy pen" of white
military reports as an expression of their need to rationalize racist attitudes? Is it not the case that the descriptions of the Leeward Maroons as
servile accommodationists—keeping in mind the numerous military

14

defeats of the Europeans—more likely served the legitimation of the claim to rule and the self-corroboration of their own superiority? Can we not interpret the confessions and other information provided by the Maroons as conscious "misleading of the colonial authorities"? Also, doesn't the alleged eagerness to concede to agents of the colonial administration after the conclusion of peace also point to diplomatic efforts to obtain and retain the right to autonomy? Could the confirmation of well-known white prejudices have been a mere pretext by the Maroon representatives with a devious (and opportunistic) intention? Even if there are no definitive answers to these questions, they do challenge the plausibility of many a conclusion of archival research.[3] These questions should help to develop a new approach to the so-called primary sources, which investigates the underlying interests, attitudes, and emotions in extant descriptive accounts.

The oral history of the Maroons bore virtually no resemblance to the archival sources, which should not surprise us, since the chroniclers of the time were themselves slaveholders, colonial officials, or close affiliates of officials. In addition to military and administrative reports, other historical sources such as diaries, letters, and conference minutes of the legislative and administrative agencies paint the same one-sided picture of the "Wild Negroes"—as the Maroons were called in the parlance of the day—as a thorn in the flesh of the whites. For the whites, the Maroons, as runaway slaves, were a kind of "rebellious property." By contrast, the earliest history of the Maroons, which was handed down orally, denies even the fact of their descent from slaves: "Accompong is a state within Jamaica. This is the Maroon land on which they lived before the British came. When the British came they found the Maroons here already. And these were the people the British tried to enslave. But they were not successful" (Colonel Cawley, interview of January 12, 1989). Other "oral histories" describe the first Maroons as African mercenaries in the service of the Spanish to ward off the

Harris N. Cawley

15

English occupation of Jamaica. Mann O. Rowe, the historian of Accompong, depicts Nanny, the supreme cultural heroine of the Jamaican Maroons, as the daughter of an African woman named Nyankipong and an English pirate (interview of January 1989).[4] Others derive the first Maroons from "mutineers" of a slave ship who, shortly before reaching Jamaica, attacked the white occupiers and were able to flee.

These examples should suffice to show that oral histories, too, do not simply mirror historical reality. This type of assessment of oral traditions as pure unvarnished truth would misinterpret the process of oral Maroon historiography. In several publications about the "First Time" knowledge of the Maroons of Suriname, Richard Price (1983b, 1990) has reported on the genesis, development, and selective transmission of the history of societies that have been mentally "conserved" by specialists. Special care has been taken to conceal historical knowledge of the early formation of Maroon communities as well as of the wars with the whites (the so-called First Time) from outsiders, thus granting local historians respect and power within their community. Their common store of knowledge may be viewed as a collective memory. Naturally, this would be only partly true, since the historical perspectives and interpretations of the specialists tend to clash with one another. For this reason alone, they fall short of constituting a homogenous view of First-Time history. Moreover, the knowledge stored in the heads of Maroon historians is fragmentary because neither the society as a whole nor individual members have access to the entire store of knowledge. Even the historical knowledge of a specialist does not represent a static entity. Instead, it is subject to regressive processes of forgetting and dynamic development by research and reinterpretation (cf. Price 1983b:25ff.).

All of the enumerated characteristics of historical transmission by Maroons weigh heavily in ethnohistorical research projects, since First-Time knowledge has been disseminated only selectively and conditionally to scholars outside their inner circle. In doing so, the Maroons, aware of their precarious social position, take into consideration mainly their political interests. The living descendants of the first freedom fighters expect foreign social scientists to intercede with solidarity on behalf of their concerns in return for cooperation in communicative historical research. An additional pressure thereby comes to bear to project current experience into the past. Under one methodological point of view, this poses a double challenge to historical research. First, it is imperative to delve beyond the manner in which colonial sources stigmatized the

Maroons as "rebel beings" to make evident the representative participation of their social history in the African-American experience and mode of action as a whole. Second, historians must consider the long period of covert social and cultural achievements of the freedom fighters and their successors on a par with their strategic (military) successes.

"Creativity and Resistance" vs. "Seeds of Change." In the summer of 1992, two events organized by the Smithsonian Institution in Washington, D.C. recalled the 500 years since Columbus. By selecting the theme "Creativity and Resistance: Maroon Cultures in the Americas," the organizers of the annual "Festival of American Folklife" consciously or unconsciously drew a sharp contrast to the Quincentenary Exhibition "Seeds of Change." Its focus on resistance of the Africans (and the First Nations) directly thematized the historical struggle for power, whereas the concept of the simultaneous exhibition for "Seeds of Change" shortchanged the human dimension of the 500-year epoch, and allowed other factors—so-called seeds of change—to exonerate the Europeans from their historical culpability. Genocide of the First Nations and oppression and exploitation of enslaved Africans, although briefly touched on, appear as inevitable negative consequences of a basically positive development. The resistance of the First Nations and the enslaved Africans is marginalized by the dominant focus on European innovations within the frame of an evolutionist paradigm.

In the introduction to the "Seeds of Change" exhibit catalogue, Viola (1992:14f.) writes: "'Seed' is used in a generic sense to illustrate the changes that resulted when plants, animals, diseases, and people were exchanged between the Old and New Worlds as a result of Columbus's voyages of discovery. Although literally hundreds of examples could have been chosen to represent the Columbian exchange, the scholars working on the project selected five: sugar, maize, disease, the horse, and the potato—every seed of change, whether accidental or intentional, had both positive and negative consequences."

These harmonizing tendencies in the "Seeds of Change" exhibition were challenged by the program of the "Folklife Festival," with its focus on Maroon struggles. As a counterbalance to the solemn activities for the so-called Columbus Year, the organizers invited several descendants of the first African freedom fighters in the western hemisphere to Washington. The cultural and historical representatives of various Maroon communities recalled the experience of the enslaved Africans that commenced with European expansion in the Americas. Over the course of two weeks they were able to discuss historical perspectives, cul-

500 years after Columbus: First meeting of Maroon chiefs in Washington, D.C., 1992

tural manifestations, and political concerns both among themselves and with others.

Members of the Saramaka and Ndjuka Maroons of Suriname met for the first time with Aluku from French Guiana, Moore Town and Accompong Maroons from Jamaica, Palenqueros from Colombia, Costa Chica Cimarrónes from Mexico, and Seminole Maroons from Texas. During the full-day conference of the Maroon chiefs and heads of state, the significance of the historical moment was palpable: Five hundred years after the onset of their ancestors' quest for liberation, the descendants of the original rebels were gathering to come to an understanding of the commonalities and differences of their historical experiences. There was no interest in discussing discursive practices and concepts like "voyages of discovery," "cultural contacts outside of Europe," "intercultural exchange," "social evolution of indigenous groups" or "European innovations in the New World," all of which serve to minimize the more significant issues of domination. The comments of the Maroons contextualized their historical practices of resistance within the circumstances created by the Europeans. Genocide, enslavement, and colonial as well as neo-colonial exploitation and violent oppression were ongoing points of reference in the historical narratives, political speeches, freedom songs, dances, and other presentations of the Maroons. The events that were open to the public confronted visitors with evidence of the deep schism between blacks and whites.

Their stories do not simply deplore the enormous victimization of their ancestors. They go beyond accusation of whites by thematizing first and foremost their own cultural, social, and strategic practices of self-assertion. They thereby transcend the role of victim into which African-Americans have been cast, sometimes even with benevolent intensions. In opening up an intensive dialogue between Maroons and other African-Americans, the immense symbolic effect of historical successes of the freedom fighters is evident, far beyond the purely military sphere. For ethnohistorical research, the example of the "Folklife Festival" shows a possible path for cooperative enterprises. If an emancipatory approach to research is taken seriously—in particular the postulate to rewrite history in a manner that takes the experience of all actors into account—the hierarchical arrangement of ethnological text production must also be called into question. In this book I show a decided partiality for the historical and current concerns of the Maroons of Jamaica. In doing so, I reject the notion that cultural resistance in the African diaspora can be neatly categorized and thereby diminished.

Bitter and Sweet—
Whip for the Blacks
and Sugar for the Whites

Plantation, St. James

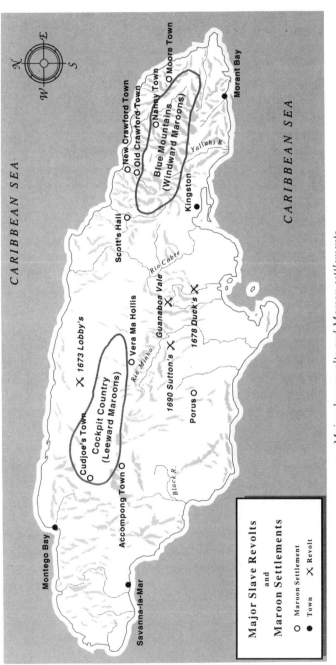

Major slave revolts and Maroon settlements

he historical basis for the presence of Africa in the Americas is slavery. In order to understand black resistance, we need to look back to the structures of oppression, the point of attack for the various subversive practices and strategies of the enslaved. I should like first to examine some characteristics of this system of exploitation to establish the context of black resistance and in particular the Maroon struggle for emancipation. Because the recent literature on slavery is so extensive (see, for example, Binder 1993; Mintz 1986; Meillassoux 1991; Palmié 1995), my brief remarks can only offer a general sketch of this multifaceted topic.[5]

To obtain the "white gold" of the "New World," namely sugar, a large number of cheap laborers was required. The colonizers simply imported a new working class to fill this need: Africans, who became the most important commodity on the plantations[6] once they had been degraded to slaves. Williams (1983:9) formulates this process in straightforward terms: Blacks were stolen from Africa to work the lands stolen from the Indians in America.

The accumulation of capital resulting from slave trade triggered or at least stimulated the Industrial Revolution. Slaves transformed the Caribbean islands into the most valuable colonies of imperialism. Their physical labor constituted one of the most important bases of mercantile overseas trade through the end of the 18th century. In Marxist economic theory, the slave was considered the classic example of extreme capitalist exploitation. "This forced laborer is a peerless producer of surplus value, since he need not be paid anything and even the brief time he uses to satisfy his own need for nourishment serves to maintain his ability to work" (Bitterli 1976:148).

In his classic work *Capitalism and Slavery*, Eric Williams, the former Prime Minister of Trinidad and Tobago, demonstrated the dependence of the British economy on slavery and the extent to which the British and plantation economies were interwoven. Plantation owners and slave traders were not only prominent members of English society, but also dominated the British legislation by buying parliamentary seats and votes (Williams 1983:85ff.).

Banks, heavy industry, insurance companies, and other such enter-

A respected British business

prises were financed with the proceeds from slavery. One conspicuous example is the legendary insurance company Lloyds. In its early years, Lloyds was nothing but a coffee house and meeting place of maritime insurers to which runaway slaves were to be returned, according to announcements in London newspapers of the time. British cities such as Liverpool, Bristol, and Glasgow pulled in such strong profits from the enslavement and abuse of Africans that it would be fair to claim that their houses were cemented with the blood of slaves (Williams 1983:62ff. and 85ff.). The following section will show how the bloody demise of imported slaves required a permanent need for supplies of black labor from Africa.

"Blood, Sweat, and Tears":
Black People as Disposable Commodities

For the Africans, the horrors started long before their arrival in the "New World." After the shock of capture, they were faced with unimaginable conditions on board the slave ships. Right from their initial contact with white men began their forced contributions to the prosperity of people who sipped their tea with the finest gentlemanly etiquette while reading a copy of the London Times. Along with the sugar in their tea, they were also consuming the blood, sweat, and tears of the slaves, essentially oblivious to the "taste" of any causal connection between their sweet treat and the inhuman living conditions that prevailed on the "Middle Passage" from Africa to the "New World." On average, one fifth of the slaves died on this trip; sometimes the fatalities well exceeded fifty percent. Slaves were stowed in the cargo areas of the ships by the hundreds like freight, incapable even of movement. In the event of an outbreak of dysentery or some other epidemic, the healthy, ill, and dead lay chained together in excrement. Hunger, thirst, and brutal treatment by the crew were part and parcel of the daily routine (Loth 1981:100ff.).

Because of the unrelenting erosion of the available work force on the plantations, there was a continual need to "replenish human resources." In this sense, the conditions of the Middle Passage were not a temporary aberration, but rather an expression of the "white" attitude of commodifying black people. Their enslavement and shipping process were therefore, in a gruesome sense, a fitting orientation to the life awaiting these unfortunate souls in the colonies. This new life would be brief, however, since slaves were seen not as precious commodities, but as articles to uti-

Many Africans died en route

lize and discard (see Patterson 1973:80).

In this sense, they were on an even lower par than the livestock on the plantations, which were not as easy to replace. Owners of livestock treated their animals with the prudence appropriate to long-term use. By contrast, when a slave was used up, which is to say dead, the slave was merely replaced by another one. "Two-legged animals," as the literature of the time often called Africans, were therefore the "object" of quantitative, quick, ruthless exploitation; four-legged animals were handled qualitatively (more indulgently).[7]

Various authors have explored in depth the question of which factors most significantly shaped the view of the whites toward the people they enslaved. Marxist scholars (for example, Williams 1983:19f.) emphasized the primary significance of the maximum economic exploitation of the slaves, which was only legitimized by a theory of white superiority, whereas other authors emphasize the inherent economic logic of all rationalizations of domination (see Bourdieu 1972). The discussion seems superfluous, however, if we choose not to reduce the totality of slave exploitation to a one-dimensional, purely economic level. More convincing is an assessment of "white attitudes" that establishes an unholy

26

alliance of greed and racism that stood in a reciprocally reinforcing relationship of justification and rationalization (see Lewis 1983:6f.).

Human beings were sacrificed without a second thought if production could be accelerated. Their life expectancy was considered irrelevant owing to the surplus of labor.[8] Issues of supplying food and other basic necessities were decided solely by their effect on profitability. Exact cost-benefit analysis established that it was more efficient to work slaves to death in a short period of time through unrelenting hard labor than to extend their lives by providing breaks from labor and sufficient nourishment (Loth 1981:133).

Eighteen to twenty hours of labor on a daily basis were not unusual. A constant "means of production" was the whip, which served to keep utterly exhausted slaves away and "avenge" every slackening of effort at the workplace (Halcrow 1982:74). The crack of the whip served as reveille at 4 a.m. and determined the tempo of the day's rhythm for the slaves. Before they were squeezed like lemons in these brutal ways, they first had to withstand a demanding period of acclimatization and inurement called "seasoning." Only two-thirds to three-quarters of the Africans brought to Jamaica survived this phase. Aside from the physical rigor of these first weeks and months, a major contributing factor to the high death rate was psychic stress. Incessant oppression and degradation could destroy the will to live of the newcomers, who were derisively called "Salt Water Negroes" (Patterson 1973:98f.).

In view of the shocking dictatorship and sociocultural deracination that confronted them in their new environment, many shed their fear of death. They began instead to view death as a welcome release from daily torture and hoped that their soon-to-be-liberated soul could return to Africa (see Berner 1984:80). Evidence for this outlook were not only the numerous suicides, but also the high frequency of slave abortions. The experiences of enslaved women made them see all too clearly the fate awaiting their unborn children. Their maternal drive was further diminished by the prospect of separation from their offspring. The sale of slaves did not aim to keep families together, especially since European masters took a cynical view of their slaves and lumped all dark-skinned people together as objects incapable of familial relations.

This view did not keep whites, however, from sexually abusing the "female objects." Here, too, the racist degradation of black people to mere objects[9] served to justify and rationalize the physical exploitation of women by rape and other sexual practices that were often quite sadistic. "Rape functioned not only as a private means of lust but also as an insti-

Husband and wife separated

tutionalized patriarchal means of power and humiliation by trying to make women realize their status as objects" (Kossek 1993:283; see also Patterson 1973:42).

Let us bring our graphic description of the atrocities of the Europeans and the sufferings of the Africans to an end with a fitting summary by Patterson (1973:9): "...Jamaica developed into what it would remain for the rest of the period of slavery: a monstrous distortion of human society."

The Concept of Black Inferiority and Suppression of African Culture

Only in recent times have Jamaica and other Caribbean nations undertaken sociohistorical inquiries into the experience of racial oppression, which inflicted deep psychological wounds that continue to fester even today.[10] Questions of cultural identity are now of principal significance in the sociological discourse of the Caribbean (see for instance the publications of Nettleford 1972 and 1978).

Since the 1960s, when Rastafari philosophy spread beyond its Jamaican foundations, it has provoked a radical reevaluation of the meaning of African culture for the living descendants of enslaved people. This philosophy has had a profound and growing influence on the ways of thinking and quest for a cultural identity of the western hemisphere's black populations. In recent years, Rastafari philosophy has developed a following in Africa as well (see Zindi 1985:20).

In order to evaluate the eminent symbolic significance of historical resistance to slavery for these new scholarly, philosophical, and cultural movements, we need to reconstruct the mechanisms and strategies by which African cultures were repressed. The numerous small-scale everyday forms of resistance on the plantations as well as the great slave rebellions and especially the armed combat of the Maroons all serve to demonstrate that these reactions to oppression were not individual, isolated eruptions of a pyschological breakdown, but expressions of a perpetual rejection of the concept of black inferiority.

Branding of slaves

The contradictory nature of white attitudes toward "their" black slaves, whom they viewed as mere objects, is reflected in white reactions to black resistance.[11] For acts of slave rebellion, the offenders were punished as human beings and often hanged, but for the loss of property incurred by the death of a slave, the owners were compensated with a fixed sum of money. Thus, seen from another perspective, slaves were always in a position to manipulate their status in the white system through resistance (Gaspar 1984:45). Their degradation to objects was so tentative that as soon as they violated the system, their status advanced from mere objects to human beings fully responsible for their deeds.

The oppressed blacks found ever new ways of challenging the status quo. In so doing, they drove the authorities to actions that constantly undermined the very system these authorities were struggling to preserve. By having to protect the ruling order against the purposeful attacks of individuals with brutal means of social control, the authorities themselves refuted the notion of the subhuman character of the Africans. Since this assumption was a vital component of slavery, there were repercussions for both sides when it ceased functioning. Both slaveholders and slaves clearly recognized the precariousness of this social order, in which they lived more in collision than in harmony. For the rulers, this situation meant a constant fear of rebellion; those in bondage had to maintain their human will to resist to prove that their degradation was untenable. In this sense, they could reinterpret every form of oppression and punishment as a defeat for the system constructed by their oppressors, since only *human* misconduct can be sanctioned. Objects, after all, are incapable of theft, indolence, or active resistance.

However, where the basic social order of the plantation world of pro-

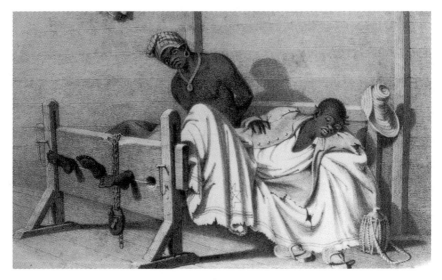

Bed stocks for intoxication

prietors and property was crumbling under the weight of resistance of the "rebellious property" (Martin 1985), the plantocracy took recourse to the ideology of black cultural inferiority to justify their claim to domination. This legitimation was rooted in the European conviction of (its own) racial superiority. Much of the literature of the 17th, 18th, and 19th centuries painted a negative stereotype of the "African personality" as lazy, irresponsible, mendacious, sexually aggressive, intellectually inferior, and biologically backward. "To read that literature is to enter the mindless labyrinth of the white racist psyche" (Lewis 1983:7).

The idiomatic disparagement of Africa as "The Dark Continent" was thus a direct outgrowth of European political, social, and economic interests reaching back to the 17th century (Crahan/Knight 1979b:2). Once the Africans had been declared devoid of history and culture and were reduced to barbarians and savages, they could be forced into servitude. Certainly, discordant discrepancies between word and deed were the result of the simultaneous denial of the mere existence of African cultures and the tremendous European efforts to suppress all practical expressions of those cultures. In any case, the Europeans elevated their own way of life to an absolute norm, while African society was condemned as inferior and prehuman (Bitterli 1976:84f.)

All of this goes to show that racist attitudes can serve as a basis and justification for excessive economic exploitation. Enslavement was thus the most extreme, and profit-oriented manifestation of the European feeling of superiority and claim to rule, which live on ignominiously in the ideology of "developing nations" and categorization of "Third World countries."

Among the most popular themes of European propaganda were the freely invented stories of African cannibalism to fuel the argument that Africans were a low form of animal life that God had condemned to be beasts of burden for the white man. These arguments culminated in a hypocritical pretext that transporting blacks to the Caribbean would improve their lot in life (Hart 1980:107).

As far as the Roman Catholic Church was concerned, the assumption of the animal or subhuman character of the blacks was officially denied and blacks were "attested" to be human, but the institution of slavery itself was considered to be divinely sanctioned (Hart 1980:121). The Christian churches used the religious sphere to bolster the idea of black inferiority, citing African paganism, superstitions, and devil worship. Others sought an artistic or a linguistic basis for their bigotry, or even claimed that Africans had a "primitive physical nature." Churches, governments, and public opinion, which were otherwise so sharply divided in the warring countries of Europe, were united on one point: the inferiority of the "black race" and its cultures. It was therefore considered necessary in all colonies to suppress systematically all African cultural symbols, artistic and religious expressions, sociopolitical relations, and languages (Beckford/Witter 1985:18). This similarity of repressive measures is arguably the most important reason for the similar forms black resistance took wherever slavery was in existence.[12]

The history of Jamaica shows that hardly a week went by without black people rebelling against their enslavement. Despite the tyrannical social context in which they were forced to live, their faith in their own freedom remained intact (Erskine 1981:23). This sociohistorical fact should not obscure the reality that all their resistance failed to bring down the system of oppression for centuries.[13] However, trying to replace the myth of slave complaisance, which has long since been refuted by scholars, by idealizing all enslaved Africans as heroes in the freedom struggle would be simply turning the coin and concocting a new myth in its place. Although a great majority opted for one form or another of resistance and insubordination, only a small minority cast their lot with the Maroons, who pledged armed combat.

Those who remained behind on the plantations viewed the Maroons as more than mere symbols of African heroism. For the enslaved, these plantation runaways represented the only real prospect of escaping the system of deliberate cultural and psychological genocide (see Dallas 1803:47). Flight and a free life as a Maroon became an ideal that was the dream of many, but the reality of very few.

Africans who had just arrived, their cultural bonds as yet unsevered and their self-confidence not yet undermined by unceasing indoctrination, were those most likely to risk flight and "guerrilla war."[14] The longer the brutal "acclimatization to a new life" as slaves lasted, the stronger was the break in the continuity of self-determined forms of human interaction and cultural reproduction. The plantation represented an institution that determined their existence all the way to their death. Deprived of all rights, their daily life was largely out of their control, not unlike life in prison or a concentration camp (Beckford/Witter 1985:18).

It would therefore be misguided to interpret the apparent obedience of the slaves as an expression of loyalty to the plantocracy; instead, this conduct reflected the "success" of a system of social subjugation and control. No area of black life on the plantations was unaffected by this system. The use of African languages, even of individual words, was forbidden, marriage and partnerships between slaves were prohibited and, if need be, thwarted (see Greenwood/Hamber 1980:36).[15] Children were separated from their mothers soon after birth and sold.

African culture as a whole was a victim of suppression, which drove individuals to many different types of reactions to the social reality. Strategies of repression developed into mechanisms to the extent that they forced upon the people they had defeated forms of assimilation that entered ever deeper into the psyches of the enslaved. Of course it must be kept in mind that the superficial expressions of this apparent "internalization" also functioned as a conscious deception of the slaveholders and as part of a cunning role-play by the enslaved constituted forms of resistance, which I will treat in greater depth in the third chapter.

The appeasement policy of the Christian churches also played a decisive role in this process. It consisted in convincing the slaves of the virtues inherent in hard work, which, it was claimed, would be rewarded in the afterlife. According to a study by the Jamaican professor of theology Noel Lee Erskine (1981:70ff.), this policy was continued even after slavery had formally ended and became part of the parochial school curriculum. Its content was designed for the purpose of keeping black people subordinate and socially inferior to the rulers. This satisfied the wish of colonial authorities to retain the essential economic and societal order of slavery. Along with independence movements in the Caribbean and the rise of black nationalism, subtle retentions of older structures came under fire. Rastafari in particular attacked the Eurocratic attitudes of most Christian churches. Through the powerful medium of reggae music, many performers articulated their sharp criticism of religious colonization to young audiences. One well-known example is "Get up, stand up" by Bob Marley and Peter Tosh (on the 1973 album *Burnin'*). The audience is told to stand up and fight for its rights, and

You can fool some of the people some of the time

not to believe it when the preacher promises heaven after death. The church is accused of trying to fool the people, but the singer claims that it only works some of the time.

During the period of slavery, the established churches had a self-serving interest in the continued existence of a dichotomy of white and free versus black and enslaved, which prevailed in all of the colonies. Their attitude toward the ruling system was one of acceptance and can justifiably be called symbiotic. The biblical mission to wipe out paganism through conversion to Christianity was often cited as a defense for this accordance with secular goals[16] (see Erskine 1981:21). This was, however, a mere concealment more for outward economic interests in enrichment by slave trade than for the "salvation" and fate of Africans (Augier/Gordon/Hall/Reckord 1986:74f.). The fact that men of the cloth engaged in slave trade and forms of production using slave labor was evidence of this. Jesuits, Dominicans, and Franciscans were quite involved in sugar production. It is therefore not surprising that in the English harbor city of Bristol, the church bells tolled in celebration when Parliament rejected Wilberforce's bill to abolish the slave trade (Williams 1983:42f.).

Williams decried the arrogance of missionaries who affected exemplary, "humane" treatment of their slaves but were in fact no different from other slaveowners in their abuse of black people as beasts of burden. One drastic example was the Bishop of Exeter, who collected 12,700 pounds sterling as compensation for his 655 slaves when slavery was abolished. Williams summed up this duplicitous conduct with the cynical statement: "Many missionaries found it profitable to drive out Beelzebub by Beelzebub" (Williams 1983:43).

Over a long period of time, a range of social forces united in their advocacy of the systemic subjugation and exploitation of Africans. In Great Britain, Queen Elizabeth I dispatched the pirate John Hawkins on her own ship, the SS Jesus of Lubeck, to Africa with orders to transport Africans to the Caribbean. Parliament voted down the abolishment of slavery even in the 18th century, and public opinion began to doubt the legitimacy of slavery only after 1783, long after slavery had ceased to be profitable.[17]

The resistance of the blacks was directed at the unanimous alliance of monarchy, government, church, and public opinion of the colonial powers, all united in their abuse of the blacks' dignity and denial of their rights. Resistance drew its strength from the memory of Africa and its culture. For the Africans on the plantations, both the rebellious enslaved and the Maroons, death meant a definitive redemption from the domination of the whites. At the moment of death, their liberated souls would surely find their way back to the land of their ancestors. In this view, dying would bring about the reunion with their original community for which they had been longing (Erskine 1981:20).

Looking back to Africa as a source of inspiration for a dynamic cultural renewal, as required by the colonial situation, was strongest among those who had the least contact with the plantocracy, namely the Maroons who lived in freedom. They were not only a thorn in the flesh of the white authorities, but also living proof of the immense will of the blacks to challenge the concept of their inferiority and the suppression of their culture. In Jamaica, their war of independence lasted over eight decades. For the plantation slaves, it signified a potential alternative to brutal manipulation by whites.

A Matter of Life and Death:
Construction of a System of Domination and the Psychology of Terror

Agents of the plantocratic system of rule, who institutionalized relations and behavior toward people with a different skin color as described in the preceding pages, naturally saw no reason to be selective in their choice of means to enforce their claim to dominate. With the same matter-of-factness with which they called Africans wild animals, barbarians, or, at best, inferior human beings, they quartered slaves or burned them alive. In other instances, if they claimed to see some chance for "rehabilitation," alleged infractions against the ruling "order" were arbitrarily punished with floggings of up to 500 lashes.

Even back on the African continent it had proven futile to employ judicial and theological arguments to enforce a legitimate political and religious claim to western rule (Bitterli 1976:84). This case was doubly difficult to make for the newly-established "social order" of the plantation system in the Americas. White paternalism, in its most extreme form of the societal structure of master-slave, therefore, needed the shield of effective coercion from the courts and the military (see introduction by E. Franklin Frazier to Rubin 1960b:vif).

Only by resorting to military and executive power or by threatening to employ it could the "social order" of the Caribbean be held intact. The political instruments of the exercise of power were ultimately grounded in a psychology of terror (Lewis 1983:5), which was firmly anchored in the "slave codes" of Jamaica. These codes were enacted in a loose sequence; their contents were in large part confusing, vague, and to some extent contradictory. They reflected the principal intention of the legislators to guarantee the greatest possible efficiency of the plantocracy. They had not been designed with an eye to giving the legal system of values a character of homogeneity or even satisfying basic judicial criteria. A crucial characteristic of a plantocratic society made this situation possible, namely that lawmakers and plantation owners were one and the same. The very men who ruled the land and made its laws also ran the plantations and owned slaves (Patterson 1973:70f.).

In the absence of higher state control, they could essentially formulate their own system of law and function as legislators, judges, and (necessarily victorious) party to the action (see Augier/Gordon/Hall/Reckord 1986:85f.; also Loth 1981:135). Their personal stake in a severe set of laws becomes evident even after a cursory glance at these laws. All legal regu-

Flagellation of female slave

lations had two goals: to insure a comprehensive protection of the status quo, and to legitimate all measures designed for the utmost exploitation of black laborers.

The first of these goals was attained by having the most grisly punishments carried out in public. There were no legal limits to the fantasy of the judges in their choice of sanctions. For numerous "offenses," they could require capital punishment or any other sentence that seemed appropriate to them, as per a Jamaican law of 1696 (Gardner 1971:77f., and Greenwood/Hamber 1980:31ff.). Court proceedings indicate that in addition to the usual floggings, there were all kinds of unthinkable bodily mutilations, castrations and amputations of various other body parts, nose-slittings, and tortures that could not be survived, such as being set aflame or torn apart on a wheel[18] (Lewis 1983:195; see also Hart 1980:99f.).

To attain the second of these goals, namely to exact the greatest possible toil from the slaves, the overseer had to function as an agency of execution for the plantation owner or his authorized representative.[19] Frequently the "management" of the plantation lay in his hands. Since his economic calculations assumed a constant supply of slaves from Africa, the typical consequence was the physical ruination of the slaves. Absentee plantation owners delegated their authority over the life and death of their slaves to their attorneys, bookkeepers, or overseers[20] (Patterson 1973:43ff.).

The extensive power of the plantocracy was ensured by a political structure that gave Jamaica a substantial degree of autonomy. A governor representing the Crown headed the government. This governor wielded considerable authority, especially over the church and the military. His power hinged not only on his personal effectiveness and diplomatic abilities, but also on the good will of the planters and slaveholders. Working with him was the Council, appointed by the British government on the strength of his recommendation. The Council was Jamaica's legislative equivalent of the British House of Lords. The Assembly of Jamaica functioned as a legislative body, modelled on the British House of Commons. The Assembly stood under the sway of the plantocracy and enjoyed considerable freedom from the Governor and the Council.[21]

For nine tenths of the residents of Jamaica, namely the black population, the political and judicial governmental structures were essentially meaningless. Their "Massa" was justice—or should we say injustice—personified. Since they were utterly devoid of personal and civil rights, they could not even appear in court as witnesses. Essentially, their human rights were limited to the criminal code of offense. They had duties, but not privileges.

Throughout the American and Caribbean colonies, it was this form of institutionalized and individual brutality, coupled with arduous labor under extreme conditions and physical as well as emotional cruelty, that motivated their flight from the plantations (see Schwartz 1983:206). "Pulling foot" was a risk that often failed and was then typically punished with the loss of a foot. For those who nonetheless opted to flee and managed to escape their persecutors, this difficult decision was the beginning phase of their life as Maroons.[22]

"Bush, Bush no Have no Whip": Sociocultural Bases and Forms of Resistance

Aerial photo of the area of Nanny Town, 1968

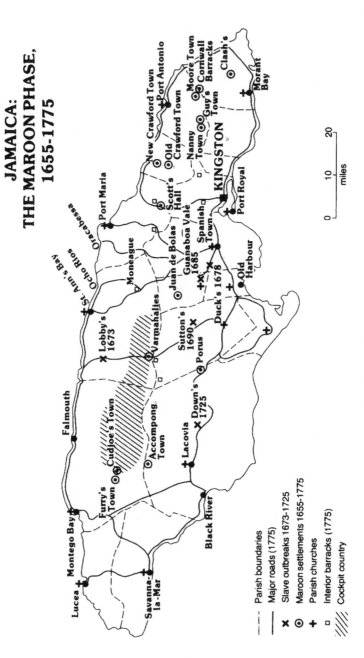

JAMAICA: THE MAROON PHASE, 1655-1775

Montego Bay
Lucea
Savanna-la-Mar
Black River
Falmouth
Furry's Town
Cudjoe's Town
Accompong Town
Lacovia
Down's 1725
Porus
Sutton's 1690
Varmahalies
Lobby's 1673
St. Ann's Bay
Ochos Rios
Oracabessa
Port Maria
Moneague
Juan de Bolas 1685
Guanaboa Vale
Duck's 1678
Old Harbour
Spanish Town
Scott's Hall
New Crawford Town
Old Crawford Town
Port Antonio
Moore Town
Cornwall Barracks
Clash's
Morant Bay
Nanny Town
Guy's Town
KINGSTON
Port Royal

Parish boundaries
Major roads (1775)
✗ Slave outbreaks 1673-1725
⊙ Maroon settlements 1655-1775
✚ Parish churches
▫ Interior barracks (1775)
///// Cockpit country

0   10   20
miles

The Maroon Phase, 1655–1775

"**B**ush, bush no have no whip" is a richly symbolic metaphor I am adopting from a conversation I had with an elderly Maroon woman from Moore Town. "Bush, bush" means the free life as Maroons beyond the range of the whip. Just as the crack of the whip continues to symbolize slavery, the Maroons have always been a symbol for hard-won freedom and independence. Their society became the antithesis of the European reign of terror.

However, a history of oppression, even when it adopts a critical stance that embraces the perspective of the victims, can only reveal one aspect of historical experience. If it treats solely the pressure from above, examining the attitudes and strategies of repression, it runs the risk of degrading the oppressed to passive victims and reducing their history by its better, active half. Repression is only one side of a coin whose other side bears the imprint of the history of resistance to oppression. Only the latter aspect does justice to the active role of Africans in the conflict with "Europe." This also reflects the way Jamaicans today gather strength from the resistance of their ancestors to cope with present-day problems. They locate the essence of their history not in the system of slavery, but in the rebellion against it[23] (see Craton 1982:11f.).

Jamaica holds a unique record in the collective slave revolts within the context of Caribbean history. Even if some colonies stand out as strongholds of armed struggle in regard to frequency and intensity of powerful revolts against slavery (besides Jamaica, particularly Brazil and Suriname), there is still great consistency in the region as a whole in the sociocultural bases and forms resistance took. Africans of diverse social background, with different languages and cultures, developed similar patterns of behavior and reactions when faced with similar circumstances of enslavement in the overseas colonies; the common experience of suffering and oppression thus created a common experience of resistance (see Lewis 1983:14).

Their individual and cultural fight for survival forged a unity against the danger of internalizing alien norms under the influence of brute force. Before they could actively confront the system of injustice, the enslaved Africans first needed to come to terms with their own identities. The plantocracy used every means at its disposal to extinguish all memories of Africa and replace them forcibly with pseudo-European culture. It required creative cultural acts on the part of the enslaved to immunize themselves against such tactics.

As a foundation for the perpetual readiness for resistance, Africa had far more than a purely symbolic function. As a reservoir of ideas and experience, it was both root and source of the dynamic development of a new identity and an African-Caribbean culture needed to cope collectively with a common "fate." Fundamental to a psychic survival on the part of blacks was the fact that their ongoing ties to Africa kept their self-confidence and self-esteem sturdy enough to help them avoid adopting the stigma of their inferiority. This was the only way they could enable themselves to fulfill the basic conditions for resistance by creating and defending their own cultural, socioeconomic, religious, and political manifestations. Only the existence of a relatively stable yet dynamic African-Caribbean culture ensured, as Lewis (1983:224) has explained, the insitutional basis without which no rebellion could ever have succeeded.

This is particularly true of the Maroons, who continue to defend their "state-within-a-state" position even today.[24] In recent years, the significance of the Maroons for the transformation of African cultures in the diaspora has been accorded proper recognition on a societal and a scholarly level. A reevaluation of resistance as a whole resulted, which grants the Maroons their status as "rebellious elite," but also takes into account everyday acts of resistance. This reevaluation is also increasingly acknowledged by the government. Accordingly, the resistance of the Maroons and the enslaved (and in some countries also the First Nations) has been restyled to an "official mythology" of the modern Caribbean nations[25] (Craton 1982:17).

We can recognize a tendency in this development to renounce a centuries-old practice of de-Africanizing primarily black societies. One important impulse to this paradigmatic shift has come from the influence of new sociocultural and scholarly currents that see a positive solution of the identity crisis of diaspora societies in paying closer attention to African roots.[26]

With these introductory considerations I have attempted to lay out the framework for the issues to be treated in this chapter. These include the crucial significance of African cultures in constituting resistance, the techniques and mechanisms of survival, which moved along a spectrum of possible types of behavior from subordination to guerrilla warfare, and the conditions under which the Maroon communities arose and how they consolidated.

"A Civilization Refuses to Die": The Key Role of African Cultures in the Fight for Survival

"The 'middle passage' of transported African slaves was accompanied by a 'middle passage' of ideologies" (Lewis 1983:27). Not just the bodies and the work capability of Africans were "shipped" to the colonies across the Atlantic, but also their philosophies, ideologies, and knowledge of civilization. Cultural perseverance, clinging to what they knew and simply refusing to forget were the mightiest weapons of the enslaved in the fight to retain their own identities. Only determined adherence to cultural resistance promised an effective impediment to European dominance. The effort of the blacks to assert alternative social norms even under the given circumstances of massive force demonstrated the essential incompatibility of African and European cultures (see Ward 1985:43; also Genovese 1981:xix).

Wherever and whenever possible they continued practicing and at the same time developing basically African traditions in political, social, and economic organization as well as in the areas of religion, music, and dance, regardless of prohibition and control. Much of this was hidden from the white masters by going underground (Hall 1985:59). But even when this avenue of social self-realization and means of expression was buried by periods of total control, it nonetheless remained viable. Prohibiting the use of drums, for example, or ordering that all percussion instruments be burned did not achieve the desired goal of extinguishing this form of communicative expression. The drumbeats instead withdrew into the psyche and habitus of the captives and lived on as "mute" codification in various forms of communication and movements[27] (Kremser 1986:154f.; see also Kubik 1981:45f.).

It also follows, however, that no African culture could survive as a cohesive unit, since the new residents of the Caribbean did not simply come from Africa, but from many different African regions. This diversity was clearly mirrored in their self-image. These days, the pan-African idea is widespread (especially in Jamaica), but during the time of slavery Africans viewed themselves as Ibo, Ashanti, or Mandingo, according to their particular social ancestry[28] (see Halcrow 1982:2).

43

Insurrection on a slave ship

Employing a strategy of "divide and rule," the plantocracy consciously promoted ethnic tensions and rivalries. To achieve a minimum of unity, which was the cornerstone of any collective resistance, the enslaved had to form a conglomerate of their African heritages from the various cultural experiences on the Caribbean islands. This conglomerate would not only express the influence of the "Indian" native population, but also expose the imprint of the European claim to domination in the sociocultural sphere.

For the resultant "syncretic product," we now use the expression African-Caribbean culture.[29] This expression implies respect for the creativity of people who drew on the source of what was familiar to them to produce a dynamic culture while living under almost unendurable conditions. Since one of their major tasks was to cope with everyday experi-

44

ences, this culture had to construct an integral dynamic and could not simply reproduce an African culture (Thomas-Hope 1980:6).

The image of Africa lived on because the African roots in the fundamental areas of society and culture, which are the backbone of every community, could not be torn out. Their continued existence is especially evident in the example of the predominance of religions of African origin in the lives of black people in the Caribbean (Crahan/Knight 1979b:16). Their social role was long marginalized by a colonial and academic tradition of explaining African religions as abstruse cults, which at best held an exotic charm. This Eurocentric position holds that the Africans in the Caribbean were quick to become acculturated to Europe by imitating European religions, languages, social customs, and modes of living and dress in preference to African forms (for example, Tannenbaum 1960:63). Such a view would have us believe that African surviving cultural fragments are of negligible significance and continue to exist into the present only as folklore and folk practices in now-"civilized" societies (for example, the introduction by E. Franklin Frazier to Rubin 1960b:viif.).

Without wishing to delve further into this now-refuted argumentation that was sustained by political and/or missionary interests, we must bear in mind that the important task is not to seek out Africanisms or so-called African fragments, but to understand Africa for what it always was: the roots of development in the diaspora (Abrahams 1983:54).

African-Caribbean religious practices such as voodoo in Haiti and obeah or myalism in Jamaica evolved from these roots. They were of overwhelming importance for the black population. Most religious rituals, which were organized in secret, were incomprehensible to the whites and therefore not subject to outside control. These rituals offered a powerful potential for resistance; they also functioned as an internal social control, holding conflict to a minimum. In Jamaica, obeah and myal were not separate aspects of communal life, but an integral part of the broader social context.[30] They were thus able to channel protests in a manner that strengthened the community and eased tensions (Crahan/Knight 1979a:x; also Erskine 1981:32f.).

In this climate of cultural resistance, the African traditions were shaped by "Caribbean" experience. Naturally this experience reflected the contradictions inherent in the way of life between the Maroons and the enslaved, who were severely hampered in their ability to organize and act. However, even marronage could not generate a reconstruction of African society.

The free guerrilla warriors were constituted as a society of resistance—

a circumstance that necessarily affected every facet of their lives. New solutions had to be found for the new geographic, demographic, and political conditions in which they found themselves. Still and all, war always transforms people and their social institutions. The effect of killing and being killed extended far beyond the physical process of dying and invariably had a far-reaching impact on the philosophical and religious outlooks of the victims (see Bastide 1983:199f.).

Nearly every rebellion involved African religious practices. Obeah-men were usually themselves leaders of most uprisings or at least active-ly involved in their organization. In their role as specialists in ritual, they enjoyed the complete confidence of their followers. They also knew how to encourage self-confidence in the rebels by using spiritual rituals in accordance with African traditions, such as consecrating amulets that would render those who wore them invincible in battle (see Craton 1982:99).

In addition to the bond of common religious experience and the per-suasive powers and strength of the leaders, who were usually born in Africa, the degree of ethnic solidarity among the rebels was of great sig-nificance. However, homogeneous ethnic composition of the insurrec-tionists, while basically a positive factor in this common undertaking, could also turn out to be its undoing. Often, slaves who were excluded or loyal to the plantocracy could "avenge" themselves by treachery or expected to improve their lot and gain material advantages in doing so.[31]

Few conspiracies had the desired outcome. Most exacted a high toll in blood for the poorly armed rebels and were crushed by the militia and regular troops after just a few hours or at most a few days, if not already been nipped in the bud even before the actual outbreak of a revolt. However, they proved symptomatic for the manner in which people who remained "African" in their culture and loyalties sought a way out of their slavery (Schuler 1970:381ff.).

Slaves who had been raised in Africa revolted far more often than those born in the Caribbean (often called "Creoles"). They had nothing to lose but their chains. For those who had lived as freemen in Africa as well as for the former African household servants, life as a slave in the Caribbean was a shocking prospect. There was no comparison between "household slavery" in Africa and the outrageous violation of humanity by industrial slavery (Patterson 1983:282).

As long as they had not internalized the doctrine of white superiority and black inferiority in the course of continual brainwashing, they fell back upon their cultural heritage and revolted as captured Africans.

Neither slave uprisings nor marronage should therefore be interpreted as a purely economic resistance of an exploited class to a particular form of unfree labor, but as the resistance of a whole African civilization that refused to die[32] (Bastide 1983:200).

Between Collaboration and Rebellion: Expressions of Resistance

Colonial literature of the time painted a stereotypical picture of the "lazy, lying, childlike, and dull-witted Negro," who was loyal, indeed slavishly loyal, to his master. It presupposed that all Africans had a single personality type.[33] The widely-used term for this personality type in Jamaica was "Quashee." The equivalent term in other colonies was "Sambo." Such "character studies" went unchallenged for a long time in scholarly writings, and this set of characterizations was contrasted with the few exceptions of heroic rebels. The expression "Quashee syndrome" aptly sums up this categorization. Exceptions only proved the rule.

These alleged personality traits of the enslaved Africans may be interpreted quite differently from the vantage point of day-to-day resistance. "Laziness" could be viewed as an act of deliberate refusal to work or at least restriction of work to a bare minimum. "Lying," by the same token, would be a purposeful deception performed with rational trickery and narrative strategies; "dull-wittedness" would signify playing dumb as an act of civil disobedience. The slaves did indeed adopt many types of

Racial stereotypes from anti-abolitionist cartoons

"misbehavior" to register subtle opposition to the standard of living thrust upon them. Individual initiatives in the form of day-to-day resistance were highly effective in alleviating the difficult circumstances in which they lived and were an integral component of the everyday lives of the slaves (Schuler 1970:377ff.).

Interpreting individual forms of obstruction of the system as day-to-day resistance is more convincing than the conclusion reached by Patterson (1983:275), who views them merely as acts of servile recalcitrance. However, this type of interpretation runs the risk of misperceiving forms of assimilation or even extensive collaboration with the regime as resistance.

From our emerging comprehension of the inherent logic behind the actual historical practices of the enslaved we might draw potentially momentous implications for the ongoing debate concerning the historical bases of African-Caribbean societies. Reappraisal of the past takes place against the backdrop of urgent reevaluation of cultural identity, a risky enterprise that has assigned itself the task of self-inquiry of a sometimes painful nature in the search for the appropriate strategies to cast off centuries of subjugation (Nettleford 1972:9).

In this enterprise, diluting the concept of resistance would be as undesirable as an exclusive fixation on acts of rebellion or marronage. The former approach would probably fail to provide suitable answers to current dilemmas, for which only the adoption of determined attitudes toward the historical clash of cultures appears adequate for a reevaluation of the post-colonial conditions. The second approach would fail to encompass the historical experience of the vast majority. Very few can claim descent from rebels or Maroons. Moreover, most Maroons, whose communities continue today, view the incorporation of their history into the national development as expropriation and reject this approach (as the Maroon Colonel Cawley stated in a conversation of September 28, 1985 in Accompong Town).

Collaboration with the plantocracy—as stated earlier, most uprisings were informed against by slaves—and accommodation to avoid conflicts and resultant punishment are just as much a part of the historical reality of the Caribbean as the heroic struggle of the Maroons and agitators on the plantations. Between these two extremes of acquiescence and resilience lies a whole spectrum of modes of actions and reactions, as they were regularly caused by oppression. Even if these are not comparable to the unconditional freedom fight of the Maroons, they were still manifestations of rebellion and insubordination.

Their particular value in reworking the historical experience of slavery and the related problems of identity lies in the fact that, for one thing, they point to a perpetual continuity in the rejection of white rule, and for another, they demonstrate the resilience of African culture. Culture in its broadest sense, comprising all expressions of the experiences of a society, was the essence of all resistance, or, in the words of Lewis (1983:175), the vehicle of the ideology of resistance.

It would be futile to attempt to draw a sharp distinction between the various categories of resistance, because the boundaries between civil disobedience and forms of assimilation are too fluid. Dividing such "sets of actual practices" is highly problematic. Furthermore, the value of such an undertaking would be questionable anyway for those who do not view the types of behavior the enslaved Africans chose as static and permanent. A given individual was likely to favor different options as circumstances changed or as that individual's attitude toward those circumstances evolved. The same person could appear loyal and docile in certain situations, but resort to malingering, sabotage, or rebellion in others. We are operating on the basic assumption that this behavior was not merely a reaction to the situation at hand, but can be traced back to calculation and conscious weighing of options and their consequences (Craton 1982:14).

This praxeological standpoint, which embraces the notion of true alternatives and gainsays the idea that decisions were made reflexively, must reject the use of simple dichotomies. Binary oppositions such as non-violent vs. violent resistance, accommodation vs. rebellion, passive vs. active confrontation, or individual vs. collective opposition fail to do justice to dynamic modes of action and reaction to oppression.[34] Instead, each type of behavior has its experiential and thus historical meaning in the spectrum of resistance (Craton 1982:14).

We must include suicides (occasionally even mass suicides) of the "Indian" Caribbean natives and of the Africans aboard the slave ships and later on the plantations, as well as numerous forms of protest. Dissatisfaction and rebellion against slavery were vented in song, dance, satire, and verbal witticisms. By mocking the white masters through mimicry, the actors could play out aggressions together with the community without risking the usual minimum sentence of thirty-nine lashes with the whip (see Barrett 1979:51).

These activities strengthened the solidarity of the black community and incited a will to rebel. At the same time, these communicative experiences prepared the ground for conspiracies, even if they contained encoded rather than explicit calls to action. Vandalism or "working slow" could be heralded in a manner that was clear to the audience by symbolic contents in storytelling, by parodies of actual situations in dance, or with mimicked entertainment (see Augier/Gordon/Hall/Reckord 1986:84).

Cultural forms of expression were thus intertwined with psychological warfare. Therein lie the roots of mento, calypso, and reggae, which, just like their forerunners, function as means of expression for the oppressed to comment cynically and critically on the social situation and provide a medium to clamor for change (Beckford/Witter 1985:18).

For this form of cultural resistance, which, recalling African forms of communication, marks the beginning of an independent African-Caribbean culture, there is almost no source material from that period. Most sources of the time distorted the observed cultural expressions of the blacks into histrionics, at best. These "descriptions" in the chronicles of leading planters and "historians" are little more than racist effusions. It is now considered quite important to research the roots of today's cultural forms of expression and reevaluate them in regard to their underlying ideology of resistance (see, for instance, Barrett 1979).

This undertaking is easier when regarding forms of non-cooperation and resistance that the Europeans bewailed in numerous literary sources. Among these forms were "slow-goings,"[35] simulation of illness, feigned incomprehension of the "Massa's" orders, intentional misunderstanding, carrying out orders incorrectly,[36] temporary absence from the plantation (*petit marronage*), carelessness in handling the property of the planters, and explicit acts of sabotage including arson[37] (see Hall 1985:46 and Lewis 1983:175).

All of these forms of action were designed by the enslaved to inflict material harm on the plantocracy, by lowering its profits or by vandalizing it. There were also forms of resistance directed against human life without actually constituting acts of open rebellion. Frequently these were self-destructive, entailing self-mutilation, abortion, murdering one's own children at birth, or suicide (Greenwood/Hamber 1980:43). The methods that were employed, such as reopening old wounds, leaving hookworms in their feet (which made them unable to work), and the widespread practice of eating dirt are ample evidence of how oppressive the conditions of living and working were perceived to be, and how strong their will was to remove themselves from these conditions (see Patterson 1973:261).

Occasionally the well-being and life of the white masters and their

50

assistants (overseers or agents) were also imperiled, especially if brutalized slaves expected to improve their situation by dispensing of their masters and if they could engage an obeah man or woman to carry out their plan. The usual working method of the ritual plant specialists involved the use of poison. It left no trace and was easy to mistake for the symptoms of cholera or some other tropical malady. For this reason it is impossible to ascertain the frequency of deliberate murder. It is known, however, that fear of poisoning ran high among the whites, resulting in the saying: "Be good to your cook" (Vestdijk 1941:116).

The blacks resisted slavery and the plantation system wherever they could or had to. The highly imaginative forms this resistance took leads us to conclude with Gaspar (1984:48) that slaves were a very "troublesome property."

Of course, the forms of resistance we have examined thus far did not pose an acute threat to the system; instead, they served to wear down the system over the long term. They could not in themselves lead to freedom and independence. However, they proved possible to incorporate and involved a much smaller risk than organized uprisings. Uprisings required an extraordinary willingness to accept risk on the part of all involved, given the severe punishments that might await them. They needed brave, well-organized leaders. The negative condition was that there be no "leaks" among their own ranks (see Genovese 1981:1 and Schuler 1970:385).

Despite the meager prospect of success, rebellions were no rarity during the entire period of American plantation slavery. Jamaica is a special case, which held the record for collective revolts in the Caribbean islands. Two primary reasons were the strong concentration of Africans who were born free in societies with prominent military traditions and the favorable ecological prerequisites for guerrilla warfare in the rain forests of the island's interior.

Essential to the success of an uprising was an alliance with the Maroons, or at the very least solid relations with them. The Maroons themselves had mostly emerged from slave revolts and had consolidated as largely independent black communities in the backlands since the mid-17th century. They existed as a provocative example of an achievable route to freedom. As long as their ranks were open to runaways and rebels, the Maroons represented the only permanent means of escaping the terror of the whip.[38]

Autonomy and Self-Determination:
The Genesis of Maroon Communities

Assessing the various strategies and practices of black resistance in the diaspora as a continuum of actions speaks against the usefulness of establishing rigid categories. Even the armed combat of the Maroons cannot be isolated as a radical alternative to the "mere civil disobedience" of the enslaved. Most Maroon communities were in fact founded by runaway slaves and continually recruited new members from the plantations.

Wherever there was slavery, there were also runaways. Whenever runaways joined forces and took charge of the organization of their own lives, a new, largely autonomous community came into being. Even then, however, they maintained contact with their former companions in misfortune. The bonds were in some cases familial; others involved trading goods and information (Craton 1982:61ff.).

From the perspective of the enslaved, the social order of the Maroons, based on a system of justice they themselves created, certainly embodied the antithesis of the system of injustice imposed upon them. Up until the peace treaties with the colonial rulers, which was to alter the relations between free and unfree blacks fundamentally, the Maroons were a lofty ideal. Genovese (1981:57) metaphorically proclaimed that their very existence triggered earthquakes in the slave barracks. Certainly their military activities always had the potential to culminate in a slave insurrection throughout the island and eventually to bring about the downfall of the local plantation societal order, as the history of the Haitian revolution demonstrates (see Fouchard 1981; also James 1963).

In every plantation colony, a Maroon group formed sooner or later. Many of them enjoyed only a brief existence. In Suriname and Jamaica there are still major Maroon communities that can look back on a long, continuous history. In the British West Indies, only the Maroons of Jamaica survived the entire time of British colonialism from 1655 to 1962.

Small groups of emancipated or fugitive slaves of the Spanish had already established themselves in the inaccessible rainforests by the time the English invaded Jamaica. In their *palenques* (self-sufficient settlements) they led a relatively carefree existence as smallholders and hunters. They had paved the way for this existence as "cowboys" and shepherds of the Spanish, who left behind no plantations when they were driven from the island (by the British in 1660). While roaming with the herds and hunting for their masters, they could acquire the knowledge of the topographical situation and the ecological conditions of Jamaica. All this was to seal the reputation of the island's first Maroons as specialists in the "natural sciences" and as "children of the forest," a renown they have retained to the present day. Blending into the jungle was only one of the abilities ascribed to them. This ability should not be interpreted simply as a hero myth, but as a parable of the rebel survival tactics and later as "guerrilla" tactics.

In the confrontation between the Spanish and the superior English occupying power (from 1655 to 1660), some of these first free Jamaican blacks fought on the side of the Spanish, fearing that the English would enslave them once again. When the Spanish finally fled to Cuba in 1660, some Maroons entered into peace negotiations with the victorious colonial power. Juan Lubolo[39] was the first Maroon leader to reach an agreement with the colonial government, represented by Governor Lyttleton, which assured the residents of his palenque thirty acres of land as well as all freedoms and privileges of English subjects (Hart 1985:5f.; see also Craton 1982:70f.).

Most likely this consent brought about Lubolo's undoing, as yet unknown to him when he agreed to lead the black regiment of the militia at the rank of Colonel in return for land and freedom. Other Maroon communities interpreted Lubolo's close alliance with the British as a threat to their existence and finally as treachery. Someone who knew their territory, the forest, as well as they themselves and suddenly stepped into the service of the opposite side constituted a danger that could not be underestimated. Only a few months after the treaty, Lubolo died in an ambush, at the hand of Juan de Serras, the leader of the Vermahaly Maroons (Craton 1982:71).

The colonial government could not reach any lasting peace with the rebels of Los Vermahalies. They carried out military attacks against the British settlements from their palenques with a "hit and run" technique and continuously killed hunters and other whites who had dared to advance too far into the interior. Juan de Serras and his followers thus succeeded in preventing an expansion of the plantations throughout the entire island. They also designed strategies and combat techniques that were used throughout the first 85 years of black armed resistance against the British colonization (Schafer 1973:25f.).

All efforts of the white government proved fruitless. Not even the location of the Vermahalies, who greatly augmented their numbers by adding runaways, could be pinpointed. From a plantocratic perspective, the problem doubled when a second large Maroon group settled the impassable mountain regions in the hinterland of Montego Bay and Falmouth.

Colonial distortion of the peacemaking process

This area was known as the Cockpit Country. A slave uprising on the plantation of one Major Selby in 1673 began a trend that was soon followed up by four noteworthy rebellions lasting until 1690 with successful mass escape. The most dramatic escalation occurred with the last of these in Clarendon. All five hundred slaves owned by Sutton participated in this rebellion (Dallas 1803:26). Many men, women, and children escaped together to the mountains, a circumstance that can scarcely be overestimated in the formative phase of the Maroon communities. Both genders worked together to establish a social order that today still constitutes a dynamic Caribbean yet essentially African basis of communal life in rural Jamaica.

Together with the rebels of earlier revolts, the freedom fighters formed a strong, homogeneous social union. Calling themselves the Leeward Maroons, this group was to rule over broad sections of western Jamaica. Particularly under the aegis of their most famous leader, Kojo, a self-ruled polity came into being with pronounced African characteristics. Kojo was the son of a leader in the bloody uprising on Sutton's plantation. In his endeavor to bring together a viable and powerful union of Maroons under his central leadership, a fortuitous circumstance worked to his advantage, namely that the participants in these revolts were almost exclusively so-called Kromantis. Their preponderance insured a high degree of cultural commonality (Craton 1982:77).

Since the original rebel leaders were also Kromantis, Kojo could build on an existing idea of political organization and ethnic solidarity. Additionally, these first organizers of armed combat, who were primary forces in unifying the Maroons, happened to have contributed substantially to the establishment of a common cultural basis. With the creation of Kromanti culture, lingering differences in ethnicity could be reconciled (Schafer 1973:45).

Who were those Kromantis, whose name appears in various orthographic guises, including Coromantines, Coromantees, and Koromantynes? The term *Kromantis* uses African pronunciation and current Maroon spelling (see Bilby 1992). Their name features mostly in Jamaican historical writings in connection with rebellions, resistance, and marronage. The name did not derive from any African ethnic designation, but goes back etymologically to the Fanti settlement Kromantine on the Gold Coast, where the English had established their first fortress in 1631 for slave trade. The British called all Africans who were transported from this place to the Caribbean Coromantees. Subsequently the familiar notion was extended to include all enslaved who had been loaded as human cargo at any of the trading posts of the Gold Coast (Hart 1985:9f.).

One consequence of this historical and cultural expropriation and deracination is the paucity of information today about the true identity and ethnic heritage of the Maroons of Jamaica.[40] Of the several major theories that have been advanced, one has the most compelling facts on its side. It assumes that although most Kromantis descended from West African ethnic groups and nations of the Ashanti, Fanti, and Akim, the lineage of a small minority can also be derived from Ga and Andagme. A comparison of the personal names common among the Maroons with those of the obligatory naming system of the Akan or Ga lends credence to this theory. Kojo, Kwako, Kofi, Kwao, and other common Maroon names have their counterparts in the custom of naming the Akan according to days of the week. One component of an Akan personal name is the name of the day on which the child is born[41] (see Hart 1985:10f.).

Although the Akan reputation for rebelliousness and uncompromising attitudes preceded their arrival in the Caribbean, Jamaican planters preferred buying them, unlike their "colleagues" from the eastern Caribbean islands. Slave traders therefore often falsely hawked their product as "Kromantine export," which potential buyers automatically associated with physical strength and high productivity. It would seem that the prospect of higher profits won out over the fear of the martial war traditions of the Ashanti and other Akan groups[42] (Halcrow 1982:27).

Many of them were at the age at which they had already been initiated into the warrior class and thus had completed a lengthy, strenuous military training. However, some may have already been Maroons in

*View of the village of Kromantine (in Ghana), still in existence
roughly 400 years after its name became a common denominator
of identity for the Jamaican Maroons*

Africa after having been expelled from their community because of violations of the social order (Genovese 1981:19). The Jamaican planters soon felt the effects of the great pride and spirit of resistance of the Akan and Ga.

Virtually all slave uprisings of the 17th and 18th centuries were carried out by Kromantis, most of whom came from the empire of the Ashantis, which was at the height of its expansion and power.[43] At first glance it might appear surprising that rebel groups were not constituted strictly according to their original ethnic identity, but instead were willing to accept the identity of Kromantis assigned to them by their oppressors. Earlier writers tended to see this circumstance as an indication of cultural breakdown in the aftermath of deracination from an accustomed social environment; these writers assumed that the sense of belonging to a collective had disintegrated. More recent research allows for an altogether different interpretation of the self-identification of black people whose original bonds and affiliations had been forcibly ruptured.

In the formative phase of Maroon communities, there is clear evidence of flexibility of ethnic identification and distinction from other groups. Under the living conditions Africans encountered in the plantation colonies and earlier on the slave ships, they found themselves forced to redefine their ethnic identity and group affiliation. By broadening the foundation of their ethnicity to find a uniting common denominator, they were drawn together (Kopytoff 1976:34).

To surmount cultural barriers, it was essential to move away from identifying with a particular lineage, village, or chieftaincy in Africa in favor of an expanded reference group, whose boundaries could be redefined by ancestry from a larger region or by the use of a similar language. Additionally, there was always the option of creating new bonds, for instance when a group of people had shared the experience of enduring Middle Passage or belonged to the same plantation.

When the Leeward Maroons and other rebel groups assumed a Kromanti identity, they did not merely sacrifice old ties, but consciously and collectively acquired new ethnic and cultural structures of solidarity. Some Kromantis might have been bitter enemies in Africa as a result of tribal conflicts and may have engaged in war in their former identity as Ashanti or Fanti, but in Jamaica their roughly similar sociocultural backgrounds served as the foundation of societal formation and ethnicity among the Maroons. Even the common experience of enslavement could be symbolically expressed by seeing oneself as Kromanti. Old loyalties to the village, group, or chieftain were replaced by the newly created ethnic identity, which should be seen as a uniting principle rather than a fixed attribute (Kopytoff 1976:350).

Thus the Leeward Maroons succeeded in transcending ethnic rivalries and merged into a more or less homogeneous entity by constituting themselves as a reference group that allowed people with different cultural heritages to identify with them. Not in all Maroon groups did the conditions to form a unity turn out as favorably as was the case with Kojo's followers who could build on common cultural and historical experiences. Wherever these experiences revealed more differences than similarities, other solutions had to be devised to make peaceful coexistence possible, as was most likely the case with the Windward Maroons, the second largest Maroon community in Jamaica.

The genesis of the Windward Maroons began with the "Spanish" Maroons of Juan Lubolo and especially Juan de Serras, who went by the name Vermahalies. For a long time they were reluctant to accept too many outsiders from other rebel groups that had fled British slaveholders. Their descendants established the famous guerrilla village of Nanny Town and built the nucleus of the Windward Maroons. Following the example of African and possibly "Indian" First Nation societies, they formed a loose confederation under the leadership of various chiefs in the early eighteenth century. This had the advantage of taking into account potential differences of various natures. In the event of a crisis, this form of political organization allowed for a rapid and cooperative response (see Zips 1998a:205 and Craton 1982:75).

Contemporary sources support this interpretation of the genesis of the Windward Maroons,[44] as does the heterogeneous composition of their society. Besides the "Spanish" Maroons, two additional rebel groups laid claim to the Blue Mountains rain forests. One group was composed of survivors of the slave uprising on the plantation of Madame Grey in Guanaboa Vale, in which several white people died. Here, too, the rebels belonged primarily to the Kromanti population. It is reported that the other group, which came from Madagascar, was shipwrecked before reaching the coast and came to safety on land (Patterson 1973:268).

It is not entirely clear whether the "fragmentation" of the Windward Maroons into at least six settlements (Nanny Town and the neighboring villages of Guy's Town and Cornwall Barracks as well as Charles Town, Crawford Town, and Scott's Hall) actually proceeded according to ethnic differentiation. It is equally possible that this division into several autonomous groups was a tactical response to ecological and strategic considerations for which the divisional principle of Akan chieftaincy might have functioned as an organizational model (see Zips 1998a:205). The ecological situation in the settlement area of Nanny Town, with its many mountains and dense forests, was unsuited to sustain a large number of people. Had the entire group opted to live together, the immediate area would have inevitably been depleted of wildlife,[45] and the soil, which was not very fertile in the first place, would have been worn out (Schafer 1973:78).

This division into several villages also offered strategic protection, since the villages served as places of refuge in the event of surprise attacks by the military and the militia. When Nanny Town was raided in 1734, its residents retreated to Guy's Town, where the last direct descendants of the Spanish-speaking Maroons lived. They were able to take in the expellees and provide them with food from stockpiles hidden from the British, who would have destroyed them, until a New Nanny Town was established (Craton 1982:89).

We therefore see that the "organizational weakness" or "lack of cohesion" that has been alleged in most literature on this topic is just as likely to have served as a highly effective political and social division that was appropriate to the particular existential conditions. Furthermore, this division took ethnic and linguistic diversity into account. Bonds between the individual groups could be maintained and bolstered by communal religious and recreational activities. In times of crisis, they provided reliable foundations of military cooperation (Schafer 1973:77ff.).

The internal organization of both major Maroon communities worked to secure a harmonious relationship between all members to meet the need for solidarity. Leeward and Windward Maroons chose different paths to attain the social goal, at least in the formative phase. The Leeward Maroons declared their Kromanti ethnicity and in doing so created a reference group that was sufficiently broad to give people with similar languages, cultural traditions, and historical experiences the opportunity to identify with this group.

The Windward Maroons opted for a quite different variant. They organized in village communities that interacted, but were essentially independent of one another. They laid claim to fierce loyalty of their members as primary reference groups. Presumably they originated along ethnic and cultural lines.[46] Through an agreement to confederate, albeit loosely, and to use common norms and means of communication, they were able to create the foundations for further development as a society (see Kopytoff 1976:33ff.).

This "political" course was essential, since they could not endanger their own existence by rivalries and discord. Therefore, a more general identification with the reference group "Maroons" was needed as well in order to achieve the necessary harmony between different units, although initially this identification was considerably weaker than within an individual's own community. This blending process of essentially heterogeneous political, socioeconomic, cultural, and religious traits characterized the path to a new Maroon identity and culture. The resultant blend was African in character and molded by Jamaican experiences.

• • • • • • • • • •

EXCURSUS:
The Alliance of the Early Maroons
with the Arawak First Nation

Just 160 years after the Arawaks had provided Columbus and his crew with provisions after they ran ashore, they were repaid for their efforts with complete annihilation[47] (Schafer 1973:8). By this point, however, they had already had an influence on the culture of the black people arriving from Africa, however. These Africans were to succeed them as the enslaved of the white occupiers, who themselves borrowed elements from Jamaica's native population.

Arawaks lived in the Blue Mountains until the 17th century and mounted opposition to the Spanish colonizers.[48] Some Maroons, especially those from Scott's Hall, believe that their early ancestors fought a war together with the "Indians." It can no longer be proven conclusively whether there was ever so close an alliance. In the context of our investigation, it seems important to mention at least the possible forms of Indian influence on Maroon cultures (see Kopytoff 1976:37f. as well as Schafer 1973:8).

In all likelihood, the first Maroons received guidance from the First Nations in acculturating to ecological conditions that were to some degree new for them. The original inhabitants of the island were in a position to provide valuable information about obtaining water, choosing land suitable for agriculture, using plants for medicinal purposes, and finding the best hunting grounds, and could supply general topographical information about the island (Craton 1982:61f.).

Although their influence in some particular areas of material culture such as methods of cultivation, architecture, hammock weaving, and toolmaking is undeniable, there is some uncertainty as to whether the Maroons also adopted "Indian" forms of social interaction or religion (Crahan/Knight 1979b). In other colonies, such as Mexico, Colombia, and Suriname, there is clear evidence of cooperation between the two groups. There, the Maroons and Indians established trade relations and joined together in military actions in which they fought side by side. They also intermarried and had social connections. There can be little doubt that in these countries the Indian influence was substantial (Price 1983a:15).

Relations between the Maroons and First Nations were by no means always harmonious. In addition to the many forms of alliance there were abundant historical examples of hostility, subjugation, and war. One contributing factor was surely the Maroon habit of capturing Indian women, whose influence on the sociocultural aspect of the black rebel groups has been unjustly neglected. These women brought to their new surroundings not only Indian technologies such as pottery and weaving, but also the religion, belief systems, and ways of thinking of their people (see Price 1983a:12ff.).

There are many unanswered questions that allow ample room for speculation. The current state of research does not provide an accurate substantiation of the actual historical relationships between Maroons and Arawak, what type of contact the native inhabitants had with the free black communities, and whether their relations were a true alliance or laden with conflict. Comparable situations of encounters between First Nations and Maroons in other plantation colonies that led to various types of influence on the emerging African-Caribbean or African-American cultures by the original inhabitants lead us to assume at least the likelihood of a similar state of affairs for Jamaica.

•   •   •   •   •   •   •   •   •   •   •

The Jamaican coat of arms with Arawaks

61

"Pull Foot": The Flight to Freedom

Starting with the introduction of slavery in the transatlantic colonies, there were free black people who had emancipated themselves by fleeing their oppressors. As long as they were too small in number to establish settlements that could be defended when necessary, they led a nomadic life or were taken in by First Nations such as the Miskito in Honduras and Nicaragua (Price 1983a:15).

In their earliest days, they were only on the defense and attempted to avoid all contact with the plantocracy. Their primary strategy consisted in constructing an ingenious system of defense. Toward this end, they retreated to the most remote areas and began to live together in fortified villages called *palenques* (Perez de la Riva 1983:49).[49]

In Jamaica it was mainly the newly-arrived Africans who seized the first available opportunity to flee. After months spent crossing the Atlantic under unimaginable conditions, an extreme measure of brutality descended upon them, designed to crush their spirit of independence and inure them for their future work as essentially two-legged mules.

Slave chains

This period of "seasoning" was when many "pulled foot" and joined with others whose attempt to escape slavery had not ended with the loss of a foot (a common punishment) in pursuit of new social and military alliances (see Patterson 1973:100, 262).

A slave law of 1696 (Acts of the Assembly of Jamaica, 1691–1737) differentiated in detail between runaways, who had been away from the plantation fewer than twelve months, and rebels, who were gone for a longer period. Rebels were sanctioned with capital punishment or deportation, whereas runaways faced "only" brutal flogging. However, even the harshest laws could not prevent the establishment of Maroon societies. The existence of established free settlements accelerated the number of bloody revolts, which brought the Maroons new, well-armed recruits. At the height of the first Maroon war in 1730, it was not uncommon for the white manors to go up in flames (Schafer 1973:29; see also Dunn 1972:261f.).

The steady influx of runaways created a connecting link between Maroons and black culture on the plantations. Moreover, since newly-arrived Africans invariably brought their cultural traditions along with them, any isolationist development of the internal organization of the Maroons was avoided. However, tensions inevitably resulted, which endangered social cohesion. The manner in which the Maroons reacted to these tensions and depending on which system of integration of new members they selected determined the direction of their way to a new identity.

"The Way to a New Identity": Transformation and Structuring of Maroon Ethnicity and Cohesion

The development of Maroon societies should not be seen as a single, self-contained act, but instead as a dynamic process that demanded a high degree of flexibility of the internal social organization during the permanent state of war. Windward and Leeward Maroons used differing methods to transcend their inner rivalries in order to become more effectual together. However, the methods employed did not ensure the viability and durability of these social constructions, which were subject to constant grueling tests of their ability to cope with existing ethnic differences.

Even if individual groups were reconstituted ideally according to their African ethnicity, the rudimentary conditions essential to carry on their various cultures were no longer the same. The experience of enslavement, flight, and marronage had fundamentally altered their identities. Even if they kept alive all kinds of ties to Africa, in part by means of mythology, and made them the starting point of the structure of their social organization, their new identity had to take into account the existence of a hostile environment. Although their flight had enabled them to elude the direct control of the plantocracy, the actual situation of marronage—life as Maroons—determined their self-organization in virtually all social arenas. It was crucial to develop communal norms and means of communication that would allow various languages, cultures, and customs to fuse into one collective culture that would function as a bearer of an indepen-

63

dent Maroon identity. Synthesizing various African heritages, behavioral patterns, legal and political ideas, and social structures resulted in a meaningful co-existence of people who had found their way into one another's lives coincidentally by having lived through a common experience. The resultant culture, which was actively shaped by the Maroons, did not become a mere aggregation of elements, but evolved from group interactions (see Kopytoff 1976:34ff.).

Africans had tried to cope with the dissolution of their old ties and to fashion a "family of the displaced" from their trans-Atlantic passage in slave ships. The circumstances under which Maroons came together required them to accelerate this social process. By assuming a group identity, they formed a basis to develop Maroon ethnicity and a strong social unity.

Political unification was aided immeasurably by Maroons who were born in freedom and raised within a Maroon society. Kojo, who was born in the mountains, is said to have been fluent in the Kromanti language and well versed in and respectful of the cultural traditions of his ancestors, yet as a leader he reportedly saw himself first as a Maroon and only second as a Kromanti. Ties to the new primary reference group of the Maroons came at the cost of African ethnic identity or at least an ethnic identity derived from their country of origin.[50]

Much of the African heritage was forfeited in this process. If, however, the diversity of "tribal" cultures had been maintained, it would have impeded the establishment of a common culture and a new identity. A measure of social cohesion and cultural consensus did manage to develop a political unification, even if the process was not always smoothly "democratic." However, the resultant solidarity created the requisite conditions for successful resistance against the colonial power. Seen in a positive light, the loss of African traditions led to the creation of a new African-Jamaican culture. The maintenance of so many ethnic differences would have fueled rivalries and hostilities and would have blocked the path to unity. As it happened, however, the painstakingly constructed Maroon identity became the primary means of encouraging affiliation, and served to surmount cultural and ethnic differences from Africa (Kopytoff 1976:46f.).

The Integration of New Runaways:
A Threat to Political Unity and Cultural Continuity

With their flexible sense of ethnic identity, the blending of various African heritages to a common reservoir of cultural experience and the creation of a unique culture befitting the singular circumstances, the Maroons had broadened the framework of their ethnicity so far that they could integrate both individual runaways and entire rebel groups. This ability to integrate others easily was crucial, since the constant state of war and the resultant poor living conditions caused the death rate in their communities to exceed the birth rate (see Patterson 1983:279f.).

They were constantly seeking to recruit new members so as not to reduce their combat strength or suffer losses of productivity in their self-sufficient system of subsistence. As important as an influx of plantation fugitives was in maintaining the strength of Maroon communities, it also threatened their political unity. Various steps were taken to facilitate the incorporation of newcomers and to minimize potential threats to harmony within the community.

Most Maroon communities had a two-step admissions process. First, all aspirants had to undergo an initiation rite, which obligated them to swear holy allegiance in blood. The violation of this oath would result in the harsh sanction of capital punishment accomplished by supernatural intervention or the hand of another Maroon. Initiates were thus permanently bound to the community and became an integral part of it, although initially on a lower social level than the older members.

They remained in this subordinate position during the complete second phase of their initiation, known as probation. Before they were fully integrated, novices would need to learn everything essential about the new community. After this political, cultural, and psychological socialization, they learned to interpret and master the forms of communication and conduct from within the framework of the Maroons. Only then were they in a position to act in accordance with community norms. By specifying a period of study and observing a strict division of roles as teacher and pupil, novices would not be in a position to undermine the existing culture and social organization. Unity and cultural continuity could be retained even with the frequent initiation of "foreign" adults into the society[51] (Kopytoff 1976:44).

Additional strategies further safeguarded and stabilized Maroon identity. Kojo proscribed the everyday use of African languages and ordered communication to "Jamaica talk," a syncretic language that adopted many African grammatical forms but whose lexical vocabulary was mostly English even at that time[52] (Craton 1982:77f.).

Nonetheless, the incorporation of new members continued to be the Achilles heel of Maroon communities, especially when large rebel groups with highly developed solidarity and leadership structures or even competing Maroon communities were to be taken in.[53] There were instances of treachery when runaways left the Maroons after finding themselves unable to adapt to that society. If they were captured while attempting to live in town without being recognized and subjected to torture to force them to reveal the locations of the Maroon settlements and other secrets, their "confessions" endangered the existence of the insurrectionists.

Besides the military threat by the colonial troops, who were superior both in number and in equipment, the danger of a possible outbreak of ethnic conflicts or rivalries between new Maroons and Maroons born in freedom raised troubling doubts about their physical survival. When they finally ratified a peace treaty with the British, they were able to dispense with both the military threat and potential conflicts with new Maroons. This treaty obligated the Maroons to stop taking in runaways, and so they evolved into closed societies with the exclusive power to make decisions concerning their further social development (Kopytoff 1976:46).

They had thus succeeded in putting a stop to the potentially divisive influence of other cultures, averting the danger of treachery, and insuring peaceful coexistence. In addition, the former freedom fighters created a new source of income for themselves by capturing and returning fugitive slaves for financial compensation. Had the Maroons suddenly been transformed from the epitomes of black resistance fighters to traitors and collaborators with the slaveowning regime? This question can be answered with a counter-question: Shouldn't the Maroons themselves have felt abandoned, when after 85 years of armed combat they were still only a small minority, which was often fought and betrayed even by fellow blacks?

Only a moral judgment could address these two questions, and passing moral judgment from a chronological distance of 250 years is simply out of the question. However, if we seek to understand rather than to pass judgment, an intense scrutiny of the period of war and its implications for the lives of the Maroons is essential. The following chapter will turn to this topic, and will also elucidate the Maroons' relationship to the black people on the plantations and the transformation caused by the peace treaty of 1738–1739, which became the foundation of further societal development.

A War with Unequal Weapons: Maroons Versus the English Colonial Power

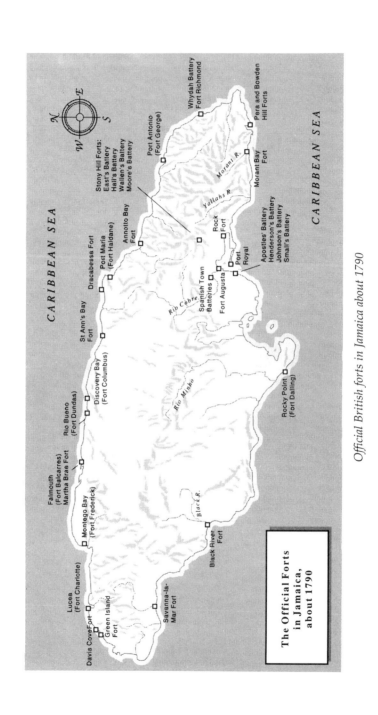

The Official Forts
in Jamaica,
about 1790

CARIBBEAN SEA

CARIBBEAN SEA

Lucea
(Fort Charlotte)
Davis CoveFort
Green Island
Fort
Savanna-la-
Mar Fort

Falmouth
(Fort Balcarres)
Martha Brae Fort
Montego Bay
(Fort Frederick)

Rio Bueno
(Fort Dundas)

Discovery Bay
(Fort Columbus)

St Ann's Bay
Fort

Dracabessa Fort

Port Maria
(Fort Haldane)

Annotto Bay
Fort

Stony Hill Forts:
East's Battery
Hall's Battery
Wallen's Battery
Moore's Battery

Port Antonio
(Fort George)

Whydah Battery
Fort Richmond

Pera and Bowden
Hill Forts

Morant Bay
Fort

Morant R.

Yallahs R.

Rock
Fort

Apostles' Battery
Henderson's Battery
Johnson's Battery
Small's Battery

Port
Royal

Fort Augusta

Spanish Town
Batteries

Rio Cobre R.

Rio Minho

Black R.

Black River
Fort

Rocky Point
(Fort Dalling)

Official British forts in Jamaica about 1790

Much has been written about the guerrilla-type warfare of the Maroons. Whereas the contemporary pro-slavery literature denounced the Maroons as cowardly murderers and animalistic cannibals (see, for instance, Vestdijk 1941:327), modern historiography hails them as heroes of the war of resistance—with good reason, since one can hardly overestimate the impressive strategic achievement of the Maroons. The Maroons, who numbered only a few hundred men and women, defied Great Britain, the "superpower" of the era.[54]

However, this modern assessment, which credits the historical accomplishments of the Maroons, entails a potential pitfall as well. Narrowing the focus to martial conflicts can skew our understanding of the black rebels and lead us to see them as nothing but war machines. It seems better advised to shift the analytical emphasis to cultural resistance, which, in my view, underlies military resistance.

In the following remarks, a historical recital of the facts of the war will be dispensed with in favor of structural considerations that explain the military tactics and attitudes of both opponents in the war in light of each of their cultural and sociohistorical backgrounds. This approach is also justified because several outstanding historical works are already available that provide an exact chronology of the war on the basis of documented source material (see among others Hart 1985, Kopytoff 1973, Campbell 1990, and Craton 1982).[55]

Unfortunately, the available sources are so tainted by a colonial bias that even the most conscientious critical reading of the sources cannot always clear a path to a comprehensive historical depiction, which needs to give due consideration to the perspectives of the Maroons. Given this impossibility, the only choices are silence or speculation. But because silence has the undesirable potential to solidify the colonial falsifications, distortions, and outright lies, speculative considerations are called for in cases where historical, comparative data and well-known comparative sociocultural structures and cultural-ecological facts make a particular "free" interpretation of a set of evidence or course of an event more plausible than one based solely on the written sources (see Zips 1998a:191ff.; also Wernhart 1986a:58, 61).

The attack of the rebels on Montpelier old works

Plausible assumptions reached by structural comparison for which there is no definitive proof can still help to revise a previous understanding of a particular scenario whose validity may have seemed improbable. This chapter will present detailed examples of this kind of plausible assumption, but brief mention of them should be made here. Referring to the report of the commanding English officers Captain Stoddart and Colonel Brooks, the historian Charles Leslie (1739:310ff.) hailed the "conquest" of Nanny Town as a crushing defeat for the Maroons. Stoddart and Brooks received lavish rewards (300 pounds sterling for Stoddart, 600 pounds for Brooks) for their reports (Hart 1985:79). If the Maroons had truly been decimated, it seems impossible only a short time later, political representatives of the colonial power would entertain the idea of signing a peace treaty (Hart 1985:85), which could solely be interpreted as a defeat given the sheer preponderance of the British in war technology and manpower. The idea that the Maroons could have rallied their strength so quickly after an allegedly severe defeat seems as thoroughly unlikely as the victory claimed for the English troops after a surprise attack.[56]

By interpreting the event in the light of the system of defense of the Maroons, a more plausible scenario of the actual events emerges, which is corroborated by both the oral tradition of Maroons living today and a comparison of the rebel tactics in similar situations. Nonetheless, this interpretation does remain speculative: "but often the ethnologist has only the option of hazarding an explanation or dispensing with one altogether" (Bargatzky 1986:140).

Further examples would include the description of Kojo as a deformed cripple (Dallas 1803:54) and his supposedly servile attitude at the signing of the peace accord (Dallas 1803:55f.). Both of these examples are obvious distortions of reality to suit colonial interests, but were accepted at face value by numerous writers (for instance, Patterson 1983:261). White historians in particular have tended to give credence to the easily accessible depictions of white oppressors or reports of early travelers rather than inquiring into the other perspective of the silent majority of the black populace. This is just as true of studies of the daily reality of slaves as it is of reports on the Maroons.[57] "One measure of the degree of caution required in evaluating extant writings is the fact that several sensational cases of manipulation have been exposed" (Martin 1985:143).

Over the past two decades, historians and sociologists from the countries in question have therefore repeatedly attempted to remedy this problem of previous historiography. Using clearly emancipatory scholarly approaches, they set about shaping a new view of history that accorded adequate recognition to the active, formative role of the oppressed in the fight for their emancipation. It is no coincidence that this scholarly development came about simultaneously with the formal political independence of Jamaica (and other Caribbean nations). As the national consciousness grew stronger, the need arose for a way of framing the genesis of their own society and their political and cultural traditions other than the one that historiography driven by colonialism had formulated.

Nanny, the legendary "chieftainess" of the Windward Maroons, and her male counterpart, Kojo of the Leeward Maroons, were proclaimed Jamaican national heroes, which symbolized the successful reevaluation of the military conflict between Maroons and the slaveholder society (Zips 1998a:191ff.). However, the relationship of the social elite to the Maroons remained ambivalent. Political leaders in the Caribbean find it difficult even today to give adequate appreciation to the African roots of their society, especially since they were educated in the west and they considered their main reference groups Euro-American elites.

In this situation, it was up to new sociocultural trends[58] and dedicated scholars to become pioneers of a transformed, reworked historical out-look. The goal of most studies has been, and still is, the rehabilitation of the slaves as historical subjects who had made their own history and had certainly not contented themselves with the role of willing victim that had so often been ascribed to them (Martin 1985:18f.). Most authors who adopted an emancipatory point of view saw marronage as the most unconditional and radical of many possible forms of resistance. They accorded the Maroons themselves the outstanding position of paragons or "embodiments" of black resistance fighters.

The remarks in this chapter accord with such a perspective by concentrating on the particular traits, organization, and knowledge of the Maroons that resulted in their military superiority over the English troops. Many aspects have been neglected, such as the highly significant interaction of Maroons with their natural environment under the adverse conditions of war. Usually historians were content simply to note how well the Maroons adapted to their natural environment (see, for example, Lewis 1983:230). This type of assessment, which is based on the notion of a nature-culture dichotomy, would be meaningless to the Maroons, who saw themselves as a part of nature.

Explanations of Maroon survival that employ the concept of "optimal adaptation" to the tropical rainforest suggest reflexive and instinctive, essentially passive forms of reactions of people whose actions in the fight for survival actually reveal calculated and strategic achievements. A related danger is posed by those who would conjure up romanticizing notions of primitivity, which are unfortunately as long-lived as they are racist. Such theories presuppose that no articulate culture would be required to form a free society under the historical conditions of seventeenth and eighteenth century Jamaica.

Accommodationist considerations also ignore the complexity of the concrete circumstances of Maroons facing continuous persecution. It simply was not enough to find solutions to the particular challenges that the rain forest biome posed to its inhabitants if they had to assert themselves simultaneously in a military conflict. Their difficulty lay in the fact that they had not only to learn to survive in an "undisturbed" natural environment, but also to seek effective means of repulsing the attacks of an aggressive human "environment."

This situation often resulted in a conflict of goals, because steps that benefitted their economic subsistence could also have devastating consequences for military defense. One example is large-scale slash-and-burn farming, which might have been the most efficient method of self-sufficiency but was irreconcilable with the necessity of a functioning defense system. Forest fires would have made it easy to spot the settlements and arable lands.

Working from an analytical concept focused on the notion of stabilization that is perpetually restored by accommodation appears anything but plausible in light of the almost permanent state of crisis in Maroon communities. It makes more sense to emphasize their active and exploratory actions, since they laid the groundwork for the development of sophisticated fighting techniques and creative survival skills. They were based on comprehensive cognitive and experiential processes that helped them acquire the ecological knowledge they could apply in a two-pronged strategy to safeguard their subsistence economy and as a weapon against the white aggressors. The Maroons utilized their environment far more effectively than did their opponents in achieving their dual goals of sustenance and battle.

Despite the presumably high "skill" of the free blacks in shaping their interactions with the environment not only for economic subsistence, but also in the battle against the slaveholders, their chances of survival remained highly uncertain. One misinterpretation of environmental conditions or the appropriate defense measures could result in the complete eradication of their society. Bearing this in mind, the fact that almost all Maroon communities entered into peace treaties with their enemies, even if these treaties obligated them to serve henceforth as accomplices in preventing revolts and capturing runaway slaves, appears in another light.

Numerous authors (for instance, Campbell 1990; Hart 1985:128) have shown little or no understanding of the rebels' willingness to compromise after eighty-five years of fighting. In chapter after chapter of their books, heroic revolutionaries are turned into traitors to their sisters and brothers on the plantations. But the decision to seek peace seems more logical if we acknowledge that the cost of battle extended far beyond the military sphere. When the men waged war, women faced the daunting task of feeding economically unproductive warriors. The latter portion of this chapter deals with the conditions of these treaties and their significance for the Maroons. First, however, the discussion will turn to the military and political strategies of the English colonial power.

The pertinent chronological framework spans the conquest of Jamaica by the English in 1655 and the peace treaties in 1739. The culmination of the first Maroon war from 1720 on will be the focal point of these remarks. The closing section of the chapter will briefly discuss the flare-up of war between the colonial power and the Maroons of Trelawny

Town in 1795 that came to be known as the second Maroon war. An excursus about the guerrilla war that Maroons in Suriname waged against the military regime of Desi Bouterse from 1986 to 1992 reinforces the notion that the living rebels descendants continued to merit the awe-inspiring title of "tallawah"—"full of fight" as had their ancestors centuries before them.

"So We Made Soldiers out of the Trees": Ecological Knowledge as the Potent Weapon of the Freedom Fighters

Up to the present day, occupiers of any foreign territory make the painful discovery that their technological superiority falls short of the absolute efficiency they had anticipated. Effective means to enforce a claim to rule are not bound to any time or place, but rather are "situational," that is, dependent on the concrete conditions in which they are applied. American intruders in Vietnam as well as Soviets in Afghanistan, to name two examples from recent history, committed the same anticipatory blunder as the English troops of the seventeenth and eighteenth centuries in Jamaica. They obviously failed to gauge the significance of their supposedly inferior opponents' superior ecological understanding.

Runaways had already explored their natural environment while they labored on the plantations. When their masters sent them on a hunt, or had them build roads, or put them to work in the fields, they sought to expand the knowledge they had brought with them from Africa in the areas of botany, geology, zoology, herbal medicine, and the production of staples and other foods with new insights about the specific ecological conditions of the Caribbean islands. They would then exploit these insights to alleviate the stressful conditions of their lives. Whatever knowledge they had managed to gather on plantations, more often than not covertly, they could amplify by means of detailed observations and exchange of information with other fugitives or Maroons once they lived in freedom (see Martin 1985:246).[59]

Even today, the farmers of the island's interior continue to shape their lives with this knowledge, as was evident to me each time I visited Cockpit Country, the former territory of the Leeward Maroons. My Jamaican friends and hosts never ceased to amaze me with their extensive and practical knowledge of natural science during our countless "jungle walks" through the tropical rainforest.

During those walks, we drank water from plants that store rainwater and even keep it cool. These plants are called wild pine because of their resemblance to the non-edible part of a pineapple. Pine leaves are used to transport water over long distances. Folded together in the proper manner, a pine leaf remains impermeable. Its sturdy stem functions as a handle. One pine leaf holds roughly the amount of water a person needs to drink in the course of a day. "Jungle walks" are never undertaken for frivolous pursuits, such as entertainment or giving guided tours to foreign visitors. They always have a particular economic objective. My companions used every available opportunity to improve their livelihood, which is based on agriculture, by obtaining and utilizing natural products.

Maroons once collected wild honey as barter for black people on the plantation in exchange for information about white plans for attack and their advancement of troops. From "five finger wiss," vines that resembled lianas, strings are peeled out to use in making furniture. They are sold to carpenters in town. These strings had a function for the Maroons as well. When stretched over pitfalls, they secured the camouflaging foliage. Pointed stakes were rammed into the bottom of the traps to impale unwary animals or people. In times of peace, this technique was used exclusively for hunting, especially the hunting of boars. In times of war, however, it served as an important component of the defense system to protect the rebel villages. It was peculiarly suited to this task because of the devastating pyschological effect on attacking soldiers. Seeing their comrades succumbing to a slow death on these stakes must have shocked them deeply (see Martin 1985:231ff. and Marshall 1976:29).

My informants generally knew the historical function of particular information or abilities, either through books, school, or oral traditions in their circles of family or friends. Once they learned of my intention to write a scholarly study of the Maroon resistance fight, they shared their knowledge of this subject with me on numerous occasions. If they were in the process of some related activity, they would draw parallels to the battles for liberation, introducing the topic with a phrase like "It is said that the Maroons were. . . " or "The Maroons used this for. . . " In this way I learned through a kind of visual presentation that, for example, bat-filled stalactite caves were an excellent refuge in times of peril since they provide not only pools of water, but also berries and other fruits that the bats bring into the caves[60] (Hill, conversation of August 7, 1985).

Bathing in a mountain stream or waterfall requires not the use of soap, which would be detrimental to the environment, but the leaves of a certain plant that give the body a fresh lemon aroma. This plant is used to

mask body odor. If the Maroons heard that enemy troops were advancing in the interior of the island, they sent out spies to gather precise information on the size, constitution, and weaponry of the opposing units. To get as close as possible to the Englishmen, they hid in shrubs or on trees that emitted their own odor. The spies could thus camouflage the scent of their bodies and fool even Indian scouts or the dogs of the Cuban slavehunters who were recruited to fight the Maroons as mercenaries and had been brought to Jamaica for that express purpose.

This specialized botanical knowledge was also an essential basis for the optimal use of camouflage, one of the most important techniques of the Maroons. The goal of camouflage was to render partisans virtually invisible. They developed a method to disguise themselves with a garment fashioned from plants found in the natural environment of the location for the military action. "Bushing up" was the term for clothing the warriors in leaves, branches, and blossoms to make them impossible to spot. Not until the camouflage was so complete that the soldiers had "become" bushes or trees were they useful for ambush or "spy missions." Motionless Maroon warriors lay in wait for their enemies, disguised as muskwood trees, whose aromatic bark could even fool bloodhounds, or as bushes from which all pollen and thorns had been painstakingly removed so as to avoid sneezing or itching. They then covered over their faces, hands, and machetes with clay or blueberries.

The Maroon warriors were thus able to wait inconspicuously near the path of the foreign troops gathering the necessary information to decide on their further plan of action or to carry out an immediate surprise attack. When they set up an ambush, it must have appeared to the English "red coats" as though a whole forest were rushing in on them. The Jamaican author Vic Reid (1983:156f.) has his protagonist, the story-teller Kwame Oduduwa, describe this type of surprise attack in Reid's anthropological novel *Nanny Town*[61]:

> But all they saw were trees, some real, some walking. Often one would fire off his musket at nothing more harmful than a fustic, before he was cut down by an avocado-pear covered from head to knee in john-crow vines out of which flushed the combolo that finished him. . . The Englishmen were not cowards! But how can you fight a banana stalk? Do you put a bayonet through an okra tree? Do you chop your sailor's cutlass through pumpkin vines? What do you do, when running through the high grass, the earth rolls under you and you fall on the point of a wamperer held by a pineapple? And this was how we fought them, for we were few. We made the forests join our armies—O, so we could battle the Red Hostiles when they came in their numbers.

At the October 16, 1985 Maroon Festival ("Nanny Day") in Moore Town, an elderly Maroon donned the traditional camouflage to symbol-ize his alliance with his embattled forebears. Even in full daylight, on an open festival square in Moore Town, the camouflaged man had to stick his hands out of the plant attire to make his presence known from under the opaque foliage. If this image is mentally transferred to the Jamaican thick forest, the realism of the impression of the camouflage conveyed in the novel with literary license is evident.

After hours or days spent marching through the extremely challenging terrain of the rainforest, the last impression in the life of many a British

Wayne Rowe with a sword his forefathers gathered from a British soldier

soldier was being attacked by a banana stalk or falling onto a machete ("combolo" or "wamperer") held up by a pineapple. Every plant of the region could be hiding a "guerrillero." Effective defense against this type of attack was scarcely possible. How were they to attack trees and plants—by pushing their bayonets through an okra tree? And what if the okra tree next to it was actually the Maroon warrior. . . ?

The distinctive military accomplishment of the Maroons was to refine their traditional African methods of waging war and supplement them with strategic innovations or "loans" from Indian military techniques in such a way that their interaction with their natural environment rendered them virtually invincible (see Lewis 1983:230). The Maroons would only be in a position to offer effective long-term resistance if they had exclusive or primary knowledge of the essential ecological links.

When no Arawaks were left in Jamaica, only the Maroons claimed the tropical rainforest as their biome. Unlike their opponent, who penetrated this unfamiliar environment only to fight them, the Maroons were not disadvantaged by climate conditions, hunger, thirst, or lack of decent spaces to rest and sleep. Their intimate knowledge of nature, combined with an emotional connection to the land "that held the bones of their ancestors," were decisive factors in their successful battles. They regarded the territory of the forests and mountains as their innate property and as the foundation of their existence.

Their keen observations of nature combined with extensive experience in dealing with this terrain gave them a crucial edge in the military conflict. The English viewed the foreign natural environment—the terrain of their enemy—as hostile and threatening, but the black freedom fighters knew how to turn their territory to their advantage. Assuming the role of the hunted, they lured their hunters into dangerous regions, then disappeared unseen. Exhaustion, injuries caused by the difficult terrain, snake bites, and disease sometimes forced the red coats to return to their garrisons without even making contact with the enemy—"lame, and for some time unfit for service" (Dallas 1803:41).

Today's Maroons comment on this decisive advantage over their opponents with the words: "They were children in the forest, but we are children of the forest" (Dawg in a conversation of September 11, 1984). These words also explain the strength of the

Maroon warrior

Maroons in countries such as Brazil, Suriname, Cuba, Haiti, and especially Jamaica (Zips 1987b:114ff.), which had expansive areas to which the Maroons could retreat but which were generally inaccessible to the colonial troops of those countries.[62]

Jamaican Maroons had nearly ideal regions to wage "guerrilla" warfare in the Blue Mountains, a mountain chain on the eastern section of the island whose highest peak reaches almost 2,300 meters, and the Cockpit County in the west, a pitted karst topography with deep hollows (known as Cockpits in Jamaica) and limestone conical hillocks. Both areas were covered with a dense evergreen rainforest that is partly intact even today.[63] In the warm and humid climate with its relatively frequent sustained rainfall, the limestones are weather-worn to deep sinkholes that made passage extremely cumbersome especially for the European soldiers' untrained legs (see Dallas 1803:137ff. as well as Edwards 1983:234). Speaking from my own experience several centuries after the Maroon wars, I can still report the difficulties of the rugged terrain for those unacquainted with it.

On the deep ground it is difficult to secure a foothold. Constantly sinking in also saps a walker's strength. To make any headway while conserving energy, a quick gait is required, which in turns necessitates excellent physical conditioning and a good overview of the local terrain. If unaware of the impediments along the way—be they hidden rocks in the underbrush, pitfalls, inconspicuous roots, or plants that cause inflammations accompanied by unbearable itching on contact, just to name of few of the "greenhorn traps"—even today a pleasure stroller can be headed for agony.

If we add to the equation the fact that the Englishmen of three centuries ago went without native guides, had to carry heavy weapons and hiking equipment, and were parched with thirst, the superior position of the Maroons can well be imagined. The aid of an important ally must also be mentioned here: the anopheles mosquito, carrier of malaria, which felled a large number of white intruders. Their lower resistance to this and other tropical diseases (especially yellow fever) further weakened them (Craton 1982:83). In the first year alone of the British occupation of Jamaica, seven hundred soldiers succumbed to tropical fever within a single week (Patterson 1973:17).

When flying over the island by airplane, it is easy to recognize its "pockmarked" topography. The hilly landscape full of craters is separated by mountain valleys that enabled black communities to establish settlements. They chose valleys with natural water supplies, which were flanked on all sides by "cockpits" with heights of 300 to 600 meters. On these hills they posted guards for protection against enemy attacks (Dallas 1803:50; see also Hart 1985:113). These guards employed a system of communication that was tantamount to yet another form of camouflage to maintain contact with one another and with spies that had been sent out. The first rebels had developed, or rather reintroduced from their treasure trove of African experience, this procedure to transmit messages covertly.

For this purpose they used animal voices, which required not only extended observations and training, but also specialized zoological knowledge. The human voice comes from the larynx, whereas bird sounds are produced by a different mechanism.[64] The voice of birds originates in the syrinx (located under the larynx), and its tones are produced either by breathing out over vibrating membranes or by warbling at the onset of a breath—the exact mechanism is not known (Burton 1985:120).

We infer from this description how much practice was required just to imitate bird voices. In addition, the pretend (human) bird needed to know precisely during which season, in what region, and in which vegetation that bird would sing a particular song. Incubating, mating, or hunting songs can only be heard during the appropriate season or time of day. If the enemy troops had a specialist, for example an Indian, in their ranks, an error of the bird imitator, such as a mating song out of the mating season, could be quite obvious. And if this task were not difficult enough already, the bird voices needed to transmit human thoughts in the form of messages. This process required a recipient who could decipher the animal sounds and filter out its encoded information (Hill and Broggs, conversation of September 19, 1985).

For longer distances, two "speaking instruments," the abeng horn and the drums served the same purpose. They, too, were incomprehensible to the English, but were recognized as Maroon communication (see Hart 1985:116). Two aspects of ecological warfare, both defensive strategies, also deserve mention in this briefest of overviews: the art of making fire without being discovered, and of utilizing natural hiding places such as caves.

In contrast to the English, whose fire emitted unintended smoke signals and revealed their whereabouts, the Maroons knew how to produce smokeless fire. "Choosing the right type of wood that did not make much smoke and making a particular type of fire were their secret to success. They ignited the end of wood, which was split lengthwise like our logs, and layered it so tightly that no flame was visible, but warmth could always be felt" (Drake, quoted from Martin 1985:233f.).[65]

Discovering and exploring caves belonged to the same complex of security measures. In times of danger, they were used as places of refuge, to care for the wounded, or as safe havens for children and the elderly. In certain circumstances, the rebels incorporated conveniently located cave hideouts into their plans for attack, whereby they would let the enemy pass by them and then attack from the rear (Hart 1985:96). These caves needed to have access to a second exit so that they did not become a trap if discovered by the enemy despite painstaking camouflage with rocks and plants. The best caves were those whose entrance was obscured by waterfalls. These caves were called "back-o-water" in Jamaica.

An entire book could be devoted to the elaborate ecological knowledge of the Maroons. In connection with the military aspect of the Maroon resistance, this set of examples should at least suffice to fuel the argument, put forth at the beginning of this chapter, that the relationship of the Maroons to their environment cannot be described and explained as accommodation. Instead, their interactions with their natural environment were grounded in deliberate action and purposeful behavior that was designed to make the most of nature in the resistance struggle. Instead of arguing with an adaptive vicious circle that those who survived must have also accommodated themselves to their circumstances, I have attempted to credit the active and explorative behavorial components of the Maroons (see Bargatzky 1986:175f.). Kwame Oduduwa, the protagonist of Vic Reid's novel, expresses a similar sentiment: "They were too many for us, so we turned the forest trees into soldiers. We armed and drilled the rocks and gullies and waterfalls and made them fight for us. We taught ourselves the ambush" (Reid 1983:147).

Hit and Run—The Art of Laying an Ambush: Guerrilla Combat Techniques

Nearly every treatise on the Maroon wars comments extensively on the military strategies of the black rebels (see, for example, Dallas 1803:39ff., 255f.). They dwell on every detail of numerous ambushes and surprise attacks on the slaveholders, with an inescapable acerbic undertone that conveys the impotent rage of their white authors.

Edwards (1983:233f.; first published in 1796) did not even bother to mask his helpless fury when commenting on the plantation raids and the surprise attacks by the Maroons on the colonial regiments, which he deemed cowardly:

> By this dastardly method of conducting the war, they did infinite mischief to the whites, without much exposing their own persons to danger, for they always cautiously avoided fighting except with a number so disproportionally inferior to themselves, as to afford them a pretty sure expectation of victory. They knew every secret avenue of the country; so that they could either conceal themselves from pursuit, or shift their ravages from place to place, as circumstances required. Such were the many disadvantages under which the English had to deal with those desultory foes; who were not reducible by any regular plan of attack; who possessed no plunder to allure or reward the assailants; nor had anything to lose, except life, and a wild and savage freedom.

Like Edwards, the English soldiers judged these altogether unaccustomed proto-guerrilla tactics to be signs of cowardice and called them

Maroons in ambush on Dromilly Estate, Trelawney

effeminate. When these soldiers were attacked, they accepted the challenge of their (invisible) foe without seeking cover. Of course this phase rarely lasted long, since ". . . the red coats were too conspicuous an object to the Maroon marksmen, who seldom missed their aim. . . . The regular soldiers . . . disdained for a time to have recourse to rocks and trees as a shield against their enemies' fire, accounting it base and unmanly in a soldier thus to shrink from danger" (Stewart 1823:316ff.; quoted in Price 1983a:8).

These descriptions reveal not only a strategic predominance of the Maroons in battles against their enemies, but also their decisive advantages over revolting slaves. Maroons could construct a hierarchical military organization and practice their combat tactics on a continual basis, such as staging maneuvers. Most importantly, they could learn from their mistakes, whereas revolting slaves had to rely on the success of a single attack (Genovese 1981:18).

Both girls and boys received a quasi-military training from a very young age. The boys were instructed not only in defensive strategies, but also in offensive combat techniques and the operation of all available weapons. Their major weapons for camouflaged close combat were machetes, which are treasured even today in an almost personified form as "good friend and protector." Only rarely do farmers leave their homes without their multifunctional instrument, which can be used as an agricultural tool to weed the fields, as a tool to beat wild fruits off trees or clear a path through the forest, and as an effective defense weapon.

Machetes were so highly valued by the Maroons because of their superiority to the firearms, which in "the old days" had to be reloaded after every shot. Maroons could decapitate their opponents with a single blow of their machete (Dallas 1803:46). The "combolo" therefore assumed mythical proportions, feared exceedingly by the colonial troops. We learn the chilling details in an autobiographical narrative by the Cuban cimarrón Esteban Montejo:

> They went crazy when they saw us, and flung themselves on us, but their attack was over in the twinkling of an eye. In a moment we were cutting off heads, really slicing them off. The Spanish were shit scared of machetes, though they didn't mind rifles. I used to raise my machete a long way off and shout: "I'll have your head now, you bastard!" and then my little toy soldier would turn tail and fly. Not having criminal instincts, I used to let him go. In spite of that I had to cut a few heads off. . . . (see Montejo 1968:177)

Other weapons were also employed for surprise ambush attacks. Rifle shots generally initiated the attacks to get the troops they were assaulting to squander their first shot on marksmen who had long since returned to their hiding places. While the hapless troops were reloading, the "machete men" had their optimal time. Fleeing soldiers were the targets of spears or bows (see Hart 1985:63f., 87).

Maroons also used wooden sticks in the shape of guns to fool the whites when they ran low on weapons (Price 1983a:8). This trick exemplified their strategy of employing psychological warfare tactics to dissuade their opponents from fighting back. Their situation of numerical and technological inferiority made them inventive. They tried a variety of means to startle and even shock their adversaries. Screaming loudly, blowing their abeng horns, and beating drums heightened the effect of their sudden emergence from camouflage and induced panic in their enemies (Craton 1982:84).

The more unrestrained the reaction of the latter, and if they ran away as fast as their legs would carry them, their losses would only increase, as happened in the failed attempt of Governor Hunter to reconquer Nanny Town in 1732. Hunter deployed six hundred men for this task, who

Camouflaged abeng-blower

marched toward Nanny Town in two troops. Both troops came up against ambushes several times, then panicked and fled in defeat. Schafer (1973:194ff.) considers this incident a further example of the brilliant organization of Maroon guerrilla warfare, which put the Maroons into a position to win out over regiments with daunting numbers.

This historical event also attests to the strength of the "hit and run" method. After a quick, precise first strike the Maroons withdrew with lightning speed without suffering a counter-strike. If, however, their adversaries made the mistake of pursuing them, they were lured to a place that the Maroons considered suitable for renewed attack. The Maroons were consummate masters in switching roles from hunted to hunter, and controlled this role-play in every way. Sometimes they ran their pursuers ragged and waited until the latter realized the hopelessness of their pursuit and turned back, only to have the Maroons cut off the exhausted red coats' return route at an appropriate place (Dallas 1803:68f.).

Even Dallas (1803:41f.) begrudged the Maroons respect for their "hit and run" method, as is evident in the following passage:

[They] lay covered by the underwood, and behind rocks and the roots of trees, waited in silent ambush for their pursuers, of whose approach they had always information from their out-scouts. [The troops] after a long march, oppressed by fatigue and thirst, advance toward the mouth of the defile. . . fire upon them from one side. If the party surprised return the fire on the spot where they see the smoke of the discharge. . . they received a volley in another direction. Stopped by this, and undecided which party to pursue, they are staggered by the discharge of a third volley from the entrance of the defile. In the meantime, the concealed Maroons, fresh, and thoroughly acquainted with their ground, vanish almost unseen before their enemies have reloaded. The troops, after losing more men, are under necessity of retreating; and return to their posts, frequently without shoes to their feet, lame, and for some time unfit for service.

Dallas's detailed description also demonstrates that the Maroons fought only when they themselves wanted to fight, and could set the scene of a military encounter. Europeans were accustomed to the rigid conventions of the open battlefields of Europe; they were horrified by the guerrilla tactics of the Maroons, who struck with no warning, opened a brief crossfire, and disappeared just as quickly as they had come (Price 1983a:7; see also Hart 1985:109, 171f.).

Their method of melting back into the bushes was also employed for raids on plantations. These attacks had two aims. First and foremost, they aspired to prevent white planters from establishing settlements in the interior of the island. The second aim was economic; these nighttime raids constituted one of the five cornerstones of their economy (see chapter five). The Maroons would not tolerate any white settlements in their proximity and did everything in their power to prevent an "occupation" of their territory. They continually raided remote country houses, possessions, and plantations, killing any settlers whenever the opportunity arose, but primarily their cattle. They abducted slaves and set cane fields on fire.[66] In this way they were able to frighten off others from establishing a country seat, guard against extensive acquisition of land by whites, and maintain their control over large connected areas (Patterson 1973:269; also Edwards 1983:231ff.).

Without assuming any appreciable risks, they inflicted great economic harm on the whites. When the raids reached crisis proportions around 1730, the military expenditures of the plantocracy soared so drastically that white Jamaica experienced a financial crisis in 1731 (Schafer 1973:87ff.).

At the same time, the acceleration of raids on vulnerable plantations was a reaction to a severe threat to the Maroon economy posed by so-called punitive expeditions of the white militia. These expeditions targeted the Maroons' permanent installations, such as villages and cultivated lands, since they could hardly get at the black rebels themselves. The Maroons reacted to the destruction of their provision grounds by the military by altering their survival tactics and resorting more frequently to depredation, which yielded them not only food, but also valuable weapons, ammunition, and new recruits[67] (Schafer 1973:108).

Particularly in the historiography of the Caribbean, the Maroon struggle for emancipation, with its many small and grand triumphs of the weak over the strong, has become legendary. Just as in the stories of Anansi, the West African trickster figure and the current folk hero of Jamaican oral literature, the resistance fighters prevailed time and again in defeating the mighty white aggressors with tricks and cunning. Perhaps this is why the struggle of the Maroons, though now distant in time, still comes to mind these days when a self-appointed Big Brother simply sends GIs to "set things right," as happened in Grenada in 1983 (see Kossek 1993:32f.).

The subject of Maroon resistance seems more relevant than ever today, which is evidenced by an increase in scholarly interest as well as the republication of *Black Albino*, a novel by Namba Roy, a traditional wood-carver of the Maroons of Accompong Town who came from a family of storytellers.[68] This novel had first appeared in print more than twenty-five years earlier. In *Black Albino*, the Maroon leader Tomaso's dramatic call to arms to his warriors reveals a facet of the psychology of guerrilla warfare against the white man ("bakra"):

> The bakra will find to their sorrow that rain in the forest is no food for muskets. Use your bows and arrows, your spears, your blowing darts. Strike silently. Let the bakra in the forest look for the one who struck, and find nothing! Let them find death from the trees under which they pass, behind the rocks, at the cave mouths. It matters not if some escape but first they must know what it is to fear. Let them feel that the hills are our mother, the rocks our father, the trees our brother, the sinkholes, gullies, and even the snakes, our kinsmen. Let them know the night is our friend and the darkness our clothing. (Roy 1986:168)

Covert Operations, Talking Drums, and Fatal Traps: The Defense System of the Maroons

Many of the defense measures of the black rebel groups to safeguard their villages and cultivated lands have already been discussed. No sharp distinction can be drawn between their offensive and defensive operations, as their adept role-switching from hunter to hunted and attacker to defender demonstrates. Most strategies could serve both purposes. Some, including the installation and protection of villages or food depots in hiding places, were conceived exclusively to protect the community and to increase its readiness for defense.

Being constantly informed as to the intentions of the enemies proved especially important for an effective defense system. Most defense actions of the Maroons were based on the principle of prevention and were carried out long before the red coats had even approached the villages or fields. Scouts alone could not possibly oversee the entire area that needed to be patrolled, so there was also a need for the assistance of "secret agents" from the ranks of the enslaved.

Many runaways had left behind friends, former shipmates (from the Middle Passage), or even relatives on the plantations, with whom they were able to establish an intelligence and communication network (Craton 1982:83). Existing contacts were broadened to include other slaves by encouraging trade relations and doing small favors. Particularly on market days, light-skinned Maroons pretended to be house slaves and mingled with the traders. They brought their informants "gifts" such as jerk pork (a piquant Jamaican specialty) or wild honey to trade for information. They also used this opportunity to purchase weapons, ammunition, gunpowder, salt, iron, and clothing. If they were checked by the whites, they justified these purchases by claiming that their masters were sending them on a hunt (Dallas 1803:34f.; Hart 1985:45; Roy 1986:91).

In this way the Maroons were nearly always informed about large concentrations of troops. House slaves, however, could collect even more detailed information about upcoming military operations of the red coats, which they gathered from dinner table conversations of their masters. Passing along this knowledge can itself be interpreted as a form of resistance. When necessary, information obtained in this way could be passed along quickly by using "speaking" musical instruments. With an abeng horn or a "talking drum," acoustic communication over long distances was possible when the messages were broadcast over several stations from one Maroon to the next (Craton 1982:100).

It is uncertain whether the Maroons were able to communicate complex information with their talking drums.[69] They could definitely transmit warnings of approaching dangers with the horn and drum signal system (see Martin 1985:187ff.). In most cases they knew about any advancement of troops and had time to take suitable countermeasures.

Numerous additional safeguards protected the defense complex of the free black community groups from unpleasant surprises. Along the path to the Maroon refuges, which often led through well-guarded gorges and

*Stone found at Nanny Town, inscribed
"Decem 17 1734/This town was took/
By Coll. Brook/And after kept/
By Capt. Cooke/Till July 1735"*

narrow ravines, the afore-mentioned hidden pitfalls were also in place. Spring shooters were probably Indian inventions. They released arrows or spears when lianas or branches were displaced and belonged to the arsenal of weapons of the "South American" cimarrónes[70] (Martin 1985:231f.).

Even if the red coats surmounted all obstacles and reached the "ante portas" of the Maroon villages still fit for action, the battle was hardly won. From the first-hand report of Philip Thicknesse, a participant in the expedition to conclude the peace treaty with the Windward Maroons, we get a picture of the sheer determination of the rebels to defend their villages. The only passable access led over a narrow path, protected on both sides by trenches. In front of each trench, crossed branches served as rifle supports. At each station two men could take turns shooting to give one time to reload; for attacking soldiers, this was a virtually insurmountable obstacle, since the narrow space required moving in single file (Thicknesse 1790:75f.).

In spite of all safeguards, Nanny Town was occupied at least once for a prolonged period, from 1734 to 1736. After Colonel Brooks and Captain Stoddart had captured the village, the English even erected a garrison on this spot to prevent resettlement of the rebel village. It is unclear whether the victory over Nanny Town was actually as glorious as the military and plantocracy claimed. It may have been more of a Pyrrhic victory, as the Maroon oral tradition relates the event.

The first published report was by Charles Leslie (1739:310ff.), according to which Captain Stoddart carried out a successful surprise attack that cost the rebels hundreds of victims, even though, in Leslie's own description, Nanny Town was situated in such a way that only a few men were required to defend it against the onslaught of thousands.

There is of course no such thing as an absolutely flawless defense system—everything can fail at some point—but could the close-meshed security net of the Maroon villages really be penetrated as the description tells us? Without wishing to create a myth of Maroon infallibility, we can still entertain substantial doubts concerning his depictions of the events in the light of several clear absurdities. We have to wonder why, a mere three years later, the colonial power was so intent on entering into a peace treaty with the allegedly crushed adversary. Was it truly possible for two groups of several hundred troops carrying heavy guns (most likely swivel guns) to approach the rebel village without being noticed by the sentries?

When evaluating triumphant reports like these, we must take into account the need of the military and the colonial administration to report successes in the otherwise fruitless fight against the Maroons. The oral tradition of the Maroons seems more plausible, which reports that the rebels knew of the approach of the enemy troops and chose to sacrifice the village as bait for an ambush[71] (see Craton 1982:83). The oral version shows a defensive strategy that was employed once the enemy knew the setup of the village and it had therefore lost its value as a retreat, as was true of Nanny Town. Only two years before the capture by Colonel Brooks, the village is likely to have been occupied already for a brief time, under the leadership of Christopher Allen and Thomas Peters.[72]

Dallas (1803:78) had obviously acknowledged this tactic when he wrote: "It is not clear that the Maroons were always to be considered as defeated when they retired and left the ground of action to their enemy: for surprise and ambush were the chief principles of their warfare."

After the loss of Nanny Town, which was never again settled even after it was ceded by the English, the Maroons retreated to a site nearby. The existence of this site indicates that there were various divisions comparable to the divisional setup of Akan chieftaincy, which in times of crisis became a vitally important component of the system of defense. Guy's Town was obviously capable of taking in the refugees from Nanny Town and providing them with food (Hart 1985:64f.).

Although it cannot be proven that Nanny Town was deliberately used for an ambush, this possibility serves to indicate the complex variants of Maroon defense.[73] For 85 years the colonial power in Jamaica could not crush the defense of the freedom fighters. We will later examine the methods the British plantocracy tried and why they ultimately failed, and why the white masters of the plantations were forced to make peace with the black masters of the forests and mountains.

•   •   •   •   •   •   •   •   •   •

EXCURSUS:
Maroon War in Suriname (1986–1992)

In Suriname, several Maroon communities have been able to hold their own to the present day. With the possible exception of Haiti, they were the largest Maroon population in the western hemisphere. Like the Maroons of Jamaica, they could not be forced to their knees and in the 1760s they signed peace treaties with the Dutch. On this legal basis they continue to exist as vital societies, which in many respects have remained "states within a state" (Price 1983a:293).

The Saramaka, the largest Maroon Nation today, with approximately 20,000 members, call the time of the conflicts of their ancestors against the Dutch colonial power and plantocracy "First Time." In his book of the same name, *First-Time* (1983b:12), Price made an almost prophetic claim that the memories of the time of war more than 200 years earlier signify far more than an expression of nostalgic pride. "Rather First-Time ideology lives in the minds of twentieth-century Saramaka men because it is relevant to their own life experience—it helps them make sense, on a daily basis, of the wider world in which they live."

In contrast to the situation in Jamaica, the Maroons of Suriname never earned recognition from their "own" countrymen or from "their" government. In this multiethnic nation, which has only been formally independent since 1975, they are not considered freedom fighters, but rather country bumpkins. They are like aliens in their own land, doing menial jobs that others would not deign to do for the lowest wages.

From today's perspective, Price's (1983b:12) emotional analysis reads like a warning that obviously did not reach the right audience or was simply disregarded:

> For all those respected Saramaka historians or ritual specialists, for all those renowned wood-carvers or dancers who are forced by economic necessity (and lack of Western schooling) to clean out toilet bowls in the French missile-launching base at Kouvou, First Time ideology cannot but remain a powerful relevant force. And for all Saramakas, the recent construction of the great hydroelectric pro-

ject (that flooded fully half of the lands their ancestors had fought and died for, and that caused the forced resettlement of thousands of their people) represented an expectable continuation of the kind of behavior that their First-Time ancestors routinely suffered at the hands of the bakaas. Continuities of oppression from original enslavement and torture to modern political paternalism and economic exploitation have been more than sufficient to keep First-Time ideology a living force.

In a situation that Price's text characterized both forcefully and aptly, all it took was the proverbial spark to explode the anger of the Maroons over their ongoing humiliation. When Ronnie Brunswijk, the highest-ranked Ndjuka Maroon in the Suriname military, was demoted from sergeant to foot soldier, then deserted the army and returned to Moengotapoe, his native village, Desi Bouterse, who had come to power in a bloody coup in 1980, obviously seized the opportunity to demonstrate his strength. He deployed troops to Moengotapoe to arrest his former bodyguard, which led to provocations against the Maroons, who regarded Brunswijk as their military leader. After they were assured of some support from the Suriname opposition, which had emigrated to Holland, they opted for confrontation with the National Army (DeKort/Zwarthoed [Workgroup Indigenous Peoples] 1986).

The rebel group, which numbered no more than fifty men at the beginning of the military conflict in July 1986, was soon reinforced by fighters from other Maroon settlements whose communities had been victimized by massacres of the military on civilians. After that, western newspapers reported sporadically on the conflicts in the country's interior, and were obviously somewhat baffled by these events. One of the first targets of the Maroons was a refinery of the Suriname Aluminum Company (Suralco), a subsidiary company of the Aluminum Company of America; the group responsible for this inundated half of the territory of the Saramaka Maroons in 1960 in collaboration with the Suriname government of the time to construct a gigantic hydroelectric project (see Price 1983a:296).

Parallels to the First Time are inescapable. Just like the slaveholders three hundred years earlier, the Suriname government called the black rebels bandits who had to be liquidated, in the words of Minister of Foreign Affairs Henk Herrenberg in an interview for Trans World Radio of November 19, 1986 (see also interviews with Desi Bouterse for Latin of November 23, 1986 and for United Nations Television of October 3, 1986).

The tactics of the Maroons were also largely unaltered. With raids of the "hit and run" type they secured extensive control over the interior rain-forest region of Suriname, especially on the Marowijne River along the border of French Guiana.

On April 8, 1987, the rebel leader Brunswijk, together with the former President Chin-a-Sen (who had been relieved of his office), even pro-claimed an independent state with the name "Free Suriname," which would comprise approximately 40,000 square kilometers, about one-fourth of the whole territory of Suriname (O Estado de Sao Paulo of April 8, 1987).

All of this should not mislead us into believing that nothing had changed since the days of the First Time. The Maroons were no longer in a position to provide sufficient protection to their embattled civilian pop-ulace. Thousands of Maroons fled to a refugee camp at the airport of St. Laurent du Maroni in French Guiana, which also had to accommodate many refugees of the First Nations. These refugees had gotten caught between the fronts and were afflicted as sufferers of the conflict from both the army and the Maroons and were in need of food and provisions (Van Bladel 1987:9f.).

The political situation of the Maroons had also changed radically. They had long since ceased to be independent freedom fighters striving to real-ize their goals on their own. No longer could they create the proper mil-itary aura with wooden guns and machetes. Dependent on modern mili-tary apparatus, they were in a sense at the mercy of superpower politics. Some European nations (France and the Netherlands) as well as the United States used the military opposition of Brunswijk's so-called jungle commando to destabilize the dangerous military dictatorship under First Lieutenant Desi Bouterse. They supported the (Maroon) guerrilla fighters to exert pressure on the military leaders to hold democratic elections.

Brunswijk, who certainly did not enjoy the support of all Maroon com-munities of Suriname, showed no interest in running for political office. His goal was to restore autonomy in the territory where they had lived for centuries and to put an end to perpetual governmental encroach-ments and discrimination (see Zips 1987a:7ff.).

Desi Bouterse capitulated to international pressure toward the end of 1987 and permitted democratic elections, but even afterwards continued to function as the real power behind President Ramsewak Shankar in Bouterse's capacity as commander-in-chief of the army. For this reason alone the democratic government was also unable to ratify a peace treaty with Brunswijk's Maroons. Meanwhile, the rebellion paralyzed the country's important bauxite and aluminum industry and brought logging to a virtual halt. Without consulting the government, army chief Bouterse arrested the guerrilla leader Brunswijk in March 1990 in Paramaribo, the capital, where Brunswijk had gone to expose the cocaine trade of the military. Brunswijk had previously seized an airplane loaded with a ton of cocaine, which had made an emergency landing in an area under Maroon control.

When the Minister of Justice intervened, Brunswijk was freed, which further escalated the already substantial tensions between the civil government and the army. On Christmas Eve, 1990, the military organized another coup. Desi Bouterse engineered this coup from behind the scenes, and Lieutenant Iwan Granoogst was used as a front (Hetzel 1990). Over the next few months, however, until the May 1991 election, the military dictatorship under Bouterse was also unsuccessful in crushing the Maroon guerrilla revolt comprising about two hundred men, especially since an Indian rebel group called the Tucaya Amazonas had formed (in 1989), along with several smaller armed opposition groups.

As a result of its total international isolation, the country's economy came to a *de facto* standstill. The announcement of new elections was inevitable. An interim agreement between Bouterse and rebel leader Brunswijk was intended to facilitate the transition to a democratically legitimate form of government and the future settlement of the conflict. After the election victory of the democratic front and the unmistakable threat of the Dutch parliament with military intervention in the event of a new coup by Desi Bouterse, the path to a peace treaty in Suriname was clear.

On August 9, 1992, after six years of guerrilla warfare, the time had arrived. The newly-elected government under President Ronald Venetiaan reached an agreement on reconciliation and national development with Ronnie Brunswijk's "jungle commando," the Tucayan Amazonas led by Thomas Sabajo, and two smaller rebel groups. A delegation of the Organization of American States was in attendance for the ratification of the treaty at the parliament in Paramaribo. In exchange for an express agreement not to pursue an investigation of human rights violations on the part of the former military dictatorship, representatives of the guerrilla troops got a say in a commission to develop the interior of the country. The First Nation insurgents were promised land rights to their territory as well as hunting and logging rights in surrounding areas for their subsistence economy.

It would be an exaggeration to claim a new historical victory for the

Maroons—Brunswijk's rebels do not represent a Suriname Maroon community, after all—but the symbolic effect of the peace treaty should not be underestimated. Once again, Maroons have affirmed their identity as freedom fighters and their claim to autonomy. In any case, their armed resistance confirms the conviction that political manipulation and economic exploitation have kept First-Time ideology alive (Price 1983b:18). Even in the third century after the successful wars of independence, the historical consciousness of the Maroons remains vital: "To be a Maroon means to be a fighter; nobody can change that" (Roy "Nigerian" Harris in a conversation of October 2, 1985).

• • • • • • • • • •

"With Drums and Cannons against Invisible Enemies": The Military Inferiority of the Colonial Troops in the Jungle War

Hundreds of pages of the *Journals of Assembly* [74] from the years 1728 to 1739, full of reports, studies, and plans devoted solely to failed attempts to defeat the Maroons, attest to the psychic, physical, and strategic unpreparedness of the English troops and the Jamaican militiamen sent by the white residents[75] for guerrilla warfare (Gardner 1971:116).

It took the commanders a long time simply to recognize their inferiority, as is evident from numerous reports to the legislative assembly celebrating non-existent victories. Full of confidence in their own strength, they misinterpreted the strategy of the Maroons not to place themselves in open battle in military formation as a sign of defeat and surrender. However, as we have often seen, the Maroons had usually just retreated in order to raid the unsuspecting drum-rolling British troops at a suitable spot.

A certain Colonel Hayes (quoted in Hart 1985:46) wrote a report about his expedition against the Maroons on March 9, 1731—a mere two months after his arrival in Jamaica: "The Affair of the Rebellious Blacks a Trifle—They have been defeated and the Town burnt—Never more than 30 of them seen together." Hart notes sarcastically that Colonel Hayes did not live long enough to find out how colossal his error was. He succumbed to fever and diarrhea on March 20 of the same year.

His fate was not unusual. A typical battalion survived only two years of service in the West Indies. Yellow fever, malaria, and dysentery made the British soldiers fearful of the islands, which is why being drafted into service in the Caribbean was tantamount to being transferred to a penal company, a circumstance that was of crucial significance for the selection as well as the morale of the soldiers (Augier/Gordon/Hall/Reckord 1986:97f.).

To offset their disadvantages in bush fighting, they relied on the aid of others. General Hunter's report (quoted in Hart 1985:33) to the "Lords of Trade and Plantations" of July 17, 1729 revealed this dependency: "The Militia consisting of hired Servants who are not to be depended upon and the Country thin peopled tho' full of Slaves, you'll think it strange but it is true, my chief Dependence, in case of an Attempt, was upon the trusty Slaves for whom I had prepared Arms. . . "

Recruited slaves, called "Black Shot," did indeed prove invaluable in the war against the Maroons (Bilby 1984:15). Brought into action primarily to carry equipment, they had to transport cannons, rifles, and gunpowder into the mountains while chained together. But if they were armed (when the troops lacked sufficient numbers of [white] soldiers), their white commanders lived in fear of possible reprisals from the ranks of the oppressed. They were keenly aware that each slave was a potential foe who could seize the rare opportunity to "massa-cre" a white man in a vicarious strike against his own "massa" (Martin 1985:35f.).

Black Shot desertions were no rarity (see Hart 1985:54ff., 77), but they were more the exception than the rule. Using these men thus remained the most effective means to enforce a scorched-earth policy. They were best able to ferret out and eventually destroy the settlements and fields of the Maroons. From the perspective of the Maroons, they posed a grave danger. The deserters, who on occasion reinforced the ranks of the Maroons with weapons and ammunition, did little to alter this state of affairs. On the contrary; they were living proof that desertion and insubordination were fundamentally possible reactions, even if only a small minority would act on them.

As long as the black riflemen and carriers only accompanied the expeditions against the Maroons after their successful raids on plantations, the latter generally had a sufficient head start to get to safety or to set up a carefully planned ambush. Once the Assembly had realized the ineffectiveness of the "flying parties," from which the black rebels could easily escape, it had barracks built, which were surrounded by palisades. In each fortress was stationed a strong garrison with White and Black Shots and slave baggage carriers, supplemented by packs of dogs donated by the churchwardens of the respective parishes: ". . . it being foreseen that these animals would prove extremely serviceable, not only in guarding against surprises in the night, but in tracking the enemy" (Edwards 1983:235).

The major targets of these troops were the provision gardens, villages, and hideouts of the Maroons. All cultivated lands and hunting villages, which could be tracked down with the help of dogs and slaves, were destroyed, usually by setting them on fire. This scorched-earth policy made matters especially difficult for the freedom fighters (Greenwood/Hamber 1980:49; see also Craton 1982:217).

The installation of the garrisons put severe pressure on the Maroons. To compensate for the diminishing food supply, they had to undertake even more raids on the plantations, which not only became increasingly dangerous, but also lessened their ability to defend their settlements. It is therefore hardly surprising that Edwards (1983:235) considers this situation the decisive step in forcing the Maroons to sign a peace treaty.

Before matters had reached that stage, however, two further moves on the part of the colonial rulers worsened the situation of the freedom fighters: when the government hired Miskito (Mosquito) Indians[76] (from the coastal region between Nicaragua and Honduras) in 1738, and when it began "importing" Spanish slavehunters ("rancheadores" or "chasseurs") from Cuba in 1739 along with their dreaded bloodhounds.

The Indian "mercenaries," who were outstanding trackers, proved to be the troops best suited to detect the haunts and villages of the Maroons. ". . . and when they had once hit upon a track, they were sure to discover the haunt to which it led" (Edwards 1983:235; see also Dallas 1803:38).

However, it was the arrival of the Spanish chasseurs with their legendary "hounds of hell" that finally impelled the Maroons to seek peace (Craton 1982:220). A majority of their traditional techniques of guerrilla warfare would have become far more difficult to employ with the animals that had been trained in slavehunting. It was nearly impossible to trick the bloodhounds, no matter how ingeniously one's body scent had been camouflaged by particular plants (see Robinson 1969:120ff.).

All of these measures, along with new strategies, led to a substantial rise in the military combat effectiveness of the colonial troops and to a shift of balance to the detriment of the Maroons. Despite their indisputable military superiority in the rainforest, their situation was precarious. In contrast to their opponents, they did not have generous military aid from a mother country at their disposal, which would have helped to balance out their losses.

Of course, the plantocracy had an even more vital interest in bringing about peace. A single slave uprising ignited by Maroons could fan a "revolutionary wildfire" at any time, which would have threatened not only their possessions with flame. Before we turn to the cause and consequences of the peace treaties, we must examine two strategies of domination that averted both an overthrow of the plantocracy through an island-wide uprising and a greater increase of Maroons through new runaways.

"Death or Any Other Punishment": The Politics of Intimidation by Mutilation and Torture

A social order with slavery as its foundation cannot survive without a regime of calculated brutality. The front between the two major classes, slaveowners and slaves, is irreconcilable. The plantocracy was never satisfied simply to punish a runaway or insurgent. Sanctions always had to fulfill two functions: to keep the party in question from repeating his or her "bad behavior" (specific prevention), and to deter the general public from committing the same "bad behavior" (general prevention). Any means of achieving these goals was "sanctified."

Special and general preventive measures were marked by cruelty. Punishments were not only atrocious, but highly sadistic. It is not easy to find the appropriate words to describe this system of injustice. Terms like bestial, barbaric, horrifying, etc. seem too hackneyed, in part because of their overuse in sensationalist and voyeuristic contexts. Nonetheless, we cannot altogether avoid an examination of colonial criminal law because of its effects on the resistance of the black populace.

On almost all Caribbean islands, the various colonial powers were able to prevent the spread of aggressive forms of resistance of open rebellion to the majority of the oppressed. Toward this end, "slave codes" were issued, which granted judges (who were often themselves slaveholders) complete liberty in punishing slaves. A law passed in 1696 limited the latitude of the judge in choosing sanctions against slaves for most transgressions of the law with the vague formulation "death or any other punishment." Thus, if the judge did not opt for immediate hanging, he could impose any punishment that struck him as suitable in a given set of circumstances (Gardner 1971:177f.).

The white rulers also made extensive use of this "law." They inflicted virtually every imaginable body mutilation or torture (see Hart 1980:99ff.). Stigmatizing the "perpetrator" was a crucial goal in choosing

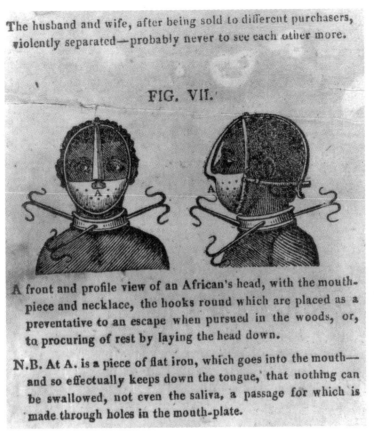

The husband and wife, after being sold to different purchasers, violently separated—probably never to see each other more.

FIG. VII.

A front and profile view of an African's head, with the mouth-piece and necklace, the hooks round which are placed as a preventative to an escape when pursued in the woods, or, to procuring of rest by laying the head down.

N.B. At A. is a piece of flat iron, which goes into the mouth—and so effectually keeps down the tongue, that nothing can be swallowed, not even the saliva, a passage for which is made through holes in the mouth-plate.

African's head with mouthpiece and necklace

a particular punishment. Severed ears, branding, and other mutilations made convicts stand out from the masses of slaves. They were easily identifiable and carried around clear indicators of their offenses (Martin 1985:78ff.).

A broadly defined criminal code served as a judicial basis to prevent "minor offenses." Making full use of the whip served to restore "order" when there were work slowdowns, unauthorized speaking, and similar alleged offenses. Almost all other infractions of the law were subject to free interpretation by the judge, who was empowered to impose a sentence of "death or any other punishment." Obviously, actions that posed a threat to the system, such as flight, rebellion, and marronage, were pun-

101

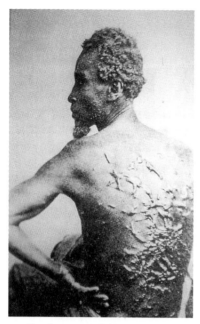

Death or any other punishment

ished with especially harsh deterrents.

In an ordinance of the authorities of Cartagena (in Colombia) there is explicit reference to the effect of general preventive deterrence. According to this ordinance, every runaway captured after more than a month of absence would have his genitals cut off in public and displayed at the city pillory to discourage other slaves from fleeing (Escalante 1983:75).

Amputations were also a favorite means of thwarting runaways' renewed attempts at flight. Many a dream of freedom came to an end with a severed knee or Achilles tendon or the loss of an entire foot (Price 1983a and 1983b:12ff.). Less brutal by comparison were the obligatory iron chains used to restain a prisoner's freedom of movement when placed around the feet[77] (Debien 1983:118).

Punishments for rebellion and marronage were even harsher. Anyone suspected of leading a slave revolt was executed after enduring unimaginable torture. Typical methods of execution were progressive mutilation, slow burnings, breaking on the wheel, drawing and quartering, and starvation in mounted cages.[78] The executioners left the butchered bodies lying on public squares to decompose. Generally they beheaded the corpses and returned the severed heads to the "home" plantations of the rebels. Poles with impaled heads were displayed as visible threats for all friends and acquaintances of the victims. One additional fact compounded the deterrence effect of these gruesome measures: the widely-held African belief that the longed-for return to the spirit world of their ancestors in Africa was barred to souls of dismembered bodies (Craton 1982:100).

Many insurgent slaves, especially captured Maroons, used even their hour of death to land a last minor victory against the hated regime. Numerous eyewitness reports were surprised to note that the tortured people showed no pain or even begged their tormenters for mercy. After the rebellion of Bybrook,[79] the overseer of this plantation gave the following account of the sadistic execution of a rebel: "His leggs and arms was first broken in peeces with stakes after which he was fasten'd upon his back to the ground—a fire was made first to his feete and burn'd uppe by degrees; I heard him speake severall words when the fire consum'd all his lower parts as far as his Navill. The fire was upon his breast (he was burning neere 3 houres) before he dy'd" (Joseph Bryan to Matthew Bryan, July 12, 1677, quoted in Dunn 1972:260).

This degree of self-control in the face of incomparable tortures must have appeared superhuman to the slaveholders, as the obviously hyperbolic description of the overseer of Bybrook demonstrates. The obstinate fighting spirit of a rebel involved in the 1760 Tacky's Revolt and condemned to death by burning also became famous. With his legs already reduced to ashes in the raging fire, he was able to free one hand from his shackles, whereupon he grabbed a burning log and hurled it into his executioner's face (Craton 1982:136f.).

For the plantocrats, the execution of a slave did entail a material loss. They therefore opposed the infliction of death sentences until a 1717 law guaranteed them monetary compensation for the destruction of their "human property" (Hart 1985:88). The high number of compensation claims for executed slaves with reference to this law are an indicator of the frequency of the revolts (Gaspar 1984:52).

Despite all of these repression and control measures, slave uprisings remained constant, as did acts of individual revolt and flight (Schafer 1973:41), which has led some historians (for instance, Martin 1985:79) to conclude that no concept or method of oppression was particularly effective in the final analysis. This interpretation appears untenable; the very survival of the system of slavery until well into the nineteenth century suggests the exact opposite. Although rebellion and marronage were certainly frequent reactions, but generally remained exceptions in relation to the other forms of resistance and reaction from the black population majority. Many were scared off from open battle against their enslavers by the ubiquitous torture, death, and mass executions. This, then, was the deplorable success of a regime of calculated brutality (Hart 1985:282; see also Genovese 1981:34).

It took extraordinary courage and great presence of mind to assume these risks and decide to revolt. Every slave had witnessed countless companions in misfortune suffer hideous torment or die. When slaves fled or revolted, they were well aware of both their small chance of suc-

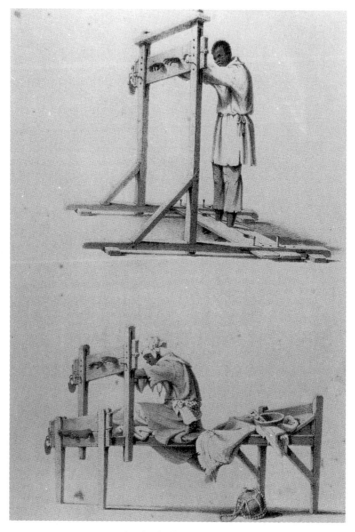

Stocks for hands and feet

cess and the probable outcome of their act. The fact that relatively many still opted to do so indicates the unbearable nature of plantation "life."[80] They found it preferable to face possible death by flogging or slow burning than to continue living in bondage and humiliation.

Nonetheless, the ongoing pressure of continual terror and incalculable arbitrariness of the rulers weighed heavily on the majority. Their policies of intimidation were rooted less in an institutionalized, totalitarian, and centralized system of dictatorship than in the authority of individuals to mete out sentences of "death or any other punishment."

"Divide and Rule": A Time-Honored Policy for Maintaining Slavery

Right from the earliest days of imperialism, all European powers relied on the effectiveness of their policy of "divide and rule." In the precarious situation of slavery on the Caribbean islands, in which a small group of oppressors confronted a far greater group of oppressed, this political principle was the key to maintaining power.

The slave traders had already pitted individual rulers or whole communities against one another in Africa, and the plantocrats in the "New World" extended this strategy of control even further. Systematically separating families, fueling ethnic rivalries, and splitting the slave population into classes were time-tested means of precluding unity among the exploited. Slaveowners deliberately granted a few slaves special privileges to make them help maintain the status quo. For this purpose, a hierarchy was introduced among the enslaved, which developed into a primary means of social control on the plantations (Beckford/Witter 1985:19f.).

Near the top of the hierarchy were black drivers working under a headdriver. In the role assigned to this "slave elite," we recognize elements of the system of indirect rule as later practiced in colonized Africa. As central figures in the exploitation of black labor, the black foremen were vulnerable to the temptation to wield power, but also stood under the pressure to perform and the watchful gaze of the white masters.[81] Their authority was expressed only too often by using the whip, which earned them a higher status in the establishment, but contempt from the other slaves (Augier/Gordon/Hall/Reckord 1986:81f.; Halcrow 1982:79; Patterson 1973:62f.).

In determining differences in status and social strata within the slave society, caution is warranted, since most information stems from the slaveholders and "their" chroniclers. In arriving at class distinctions or even just relative prestige, they necessarily used criteria other than those of the enslaved themselves. Attributes that were highly significant to the black population, such as age, place of birth, family background in Africa, eloquence, physical and artistic abilities, healing powers, and obeah, usually did not even occur to the plantocracy at all (Hall 1985:49). The plan-

105

Interior view of a Jamaican house of correction

tocracy's hierarchy considered two main factors: the slaves' productivity and their proximity to the domestic sphere of their white masters. House slaves, drivers, and specialized workers were ranked higher from a plantocratic perspective. Many of them internalized this classification by adopting external symbols, especially European dress, speech, and manners (Rubin 1960b: 113).

It is unclear whether house slaves and other privileged nonfree blacks really constituted a "slave aristocracy"; the doubts expressed by Patterson (1973:57) are probably justified. The fact that they flaunted their feelings of superiority to so-called field slaves does not reflect their actual standing within the black community. The *cimarrón* Esteban Montejo disdainfully called all drivers toadies and squealers who strutted about like fine gentlemen. The house slaves hardly come off better: they are said to be nothing but messengers of the clergy because they read from the catechism to the field slaves and played the role of devout Christians (Montejo 1968:19, 36).

Although domestic slaves and trained black workers were spared the rigors of field labor on the sugar cane plantations, they had to work under the direct supervision of the "massa" and were at the mercy of his moods. For women this meant the constant threat of sexual persecution. Female house slaves may have suffered even more than others from the general objectification of black people. "Free" from any moral strictures—which were so numerous regarding white women in puritanical England—the white masters raped, humiliated, and abused their female "slave possessions" according to their often sadistic whims (see Patterson 1973:57ff.).

Even so, whenever there was a "conspiracy," some male or female slave loyal to the master—usually from the group of domestics—would turn up to betray the plans for an uprising to him (Greenwood/Hamber 1980:44). The result for the rebels was normally torture and death. The traitors earned recognition and often emancipation as a reward for their deed. Opportunism was not always the motive for denunciation. Personal acts of revenge and ethnic hostilities could be ventilated in this way too, producing devastating consequences. Almost all revolts had been foiled from "within the ranks," namely by black collaborators with the plantocracy (see also Dunn 1972:262). It scarcely mattered that the majority of the black populace saw through the "divide and rule" policy of their enslavers and tried to neutralize it by alliances that transcended ethnic and cultural boundaries.[82] A single leak in the conspiracy sufficed to have an attempted revolt wind up instead as a series of floggings, mass mutilations, and executions, as happened in the uprising of Port Royal in 1685. A slave loyal to his master bought freedom for himself and his wife in exchange for betraying his companions in misfortune (Schafer 1973:37).

These examples show up the heterogeneity in the relations between various strata and sectors of the black community. On the one hand, there were comprehensive and successful efforts to counter the "divide and rule" strategy by forming alliances committed to an ideology of "unite and resist." On the other hand, these alliances "functioned" only rarely with the flawless perfection that alone would guarantee effective resistance. Too fragile was the identification with a common cause, too deep ran the chasms between various group interests, which became more complex, the more diverse individual and collective interests had to be subsumed.

House slaves might cooperate with insurgents on one occasion by passing along information or even poisoning the slaveholders' food, but on the next occasion side with the white oppressors. This very process of conscious, personal decision-making on the part of each individual initiated into the conspiracy made the setup unpredictable for the rebels. For the "divide and rule" strategy to succeed, no insurmountable walls between discrete segments of the "slave population" were needed, which would only have reduced work productivity, but just enough friction to discourage a coalition of the exploited. From the viewpoint of the plantocrats it was a matter of sowing or retaining the amount of mistrust among their slaves to be able to insure the loyalty of a group or of particular individuals in crisis situations. For this purpose they purchased Africans of diverse ethnic backgrounds whose cultures and languages were alien to one another, treated so-called Creoles (slaves born in the Caribbean) better than new arrivals (who were mocked by other blacks, who labelled them "salt water negroes" and "guiney birds") and split up the slave communities into groupings by work assignment, which also determined their level of privilege (Halcrow 1982:4, 82; also Patterson 1973:145ff.).

Not every rivalry and rupture between blacks in Jamaica resulted from cunning calculations of the plantocracy. The system of terror known as slavery developed its own dynamics that fostered discord in the daily fight for survival. Efforts to achieve solidarity in the struggle for liberation often went awry because of the treachery of a single individual who attained his freedom by insuring the death of others (see Hart 1985:14f.).

A second path of emancipation was open to collaborators. They could serve in the military as Black Shot in the fight against Maroons to earn their release with special merit. Some, however, seized the first available opportunity to free themselves and cast their lot with the rebels without relying on acts of mercy from strangers. Some Maroon oral traditions continue to express their great bitterness that even among their ranks were traitors who fled back from the rebel villages to the plantations after a period of time and then led government troops (Schafer 1973:86f., 110).

Despite a very high rate of desertion, black troops became the most dangerous weapon against the Maroons. They proved equal to the demands of guerrilla warfare and more familiar with the ecological conditions of the battle zone. As they were used increasingly in this capacity, a new threat to the survival of the Maroon communities grew. As experienced trackers, who were far more adept in the jungle war than their white counterparts and could anticipate a "hit and run" attack, they became highly valued partners in combat for the colonial governments (see Buckley 1979).

In Jamaica, the legislative assembly had recognized the value of the black recruits and suggested that these recruits comprise at least three quarters of all troops. To maximize both their motivation and their loyalty, they were to be paid in advance, acquire the right of depredation after rebel settlements were seized, and receive additional rewards such as hats, uniforms, medals, and other status symbols. The greatest impetus to fight on the side of the slaveholders against the black "separatists," however, was the prospect of freedom (Jones 1981:262ff.). It is certainly an irony that two groups with similar historical experiences and congruent ideals fought against rather than with one another for their freedom. "Divide and rule" in the special "Caribbean" sense meant getting blacks to fight blacks.

It is no wonder that the antagonism of the Maroons toward those who had not chosen their way of life and struggle continually increased. It became more and more difficult to differentiate friend from foe of the same skin color. Anyone could be a traitor. Hardly any outlook takes a greater toll on reciprocal relations than does mistrust. Although the freedom fighters were perpetually aware of the necessity of maintaining a good relationship with the enslaved, they had no choice but to react with increasing isolation as their contacts became less reliable (see Genovese 1981:78).

During the long conflict between the colonial power and the Maroons in Jamaica, many interactions and communications between free and nonfree blacks had developed.[83] Even the division between the two groups was far from absolute, since slaves could become Maroons by fleeing. Such close relationships existed that occasionally Maroons temporarily lived on the plantations to gather intelligence information, to trade weapons and rum for food, or to maintain social and/or familial connections.[84] The opposite situation also occurred, in which slaves spent time in rebel villages (Jones 1981:70).

Many risked life and limb to cooperate with Maroons in a great variety of ways; others cut off ears, arms, or heads of murdered rebels to use as proof in claiming their reward. In the eyes of the Maroons, the slaves were just as likely to be potential enemies on the side of their military adversary as potential allies, on whom the acquisition of intelligence information and resupply of arms and ammunition greatly depended. The ambivalence of this relationship was even more evident since Maroons for the most part were nothing but ex-slaves who had made a successful getaway (Patterson 1983:279f.).

Which consequences arose from these historically grounded and necessary, but dangerous relationships between black people in the slave barracks and those in the rebel villages? Although it was never of matter of two completely mutually exclusive societies in which each was out to

deny admission to the other, the hatred Maroons felt toward black traitors and Black Shot in the service of opposing armies resulted in a cultural split and the detachment of the Maroons from all other African-
Jamaicans. Moreover, those who had liberated themselves assumed an
increasingly dismissive attitude toward their former companions in suffering, which fostered suspicion and a feeling of antagonism. The free
blacks began to distance themselves from their "sisters and brothers" on
the plantations, whom they accused not only of valuing a life in slavery
over a life in freedom, but also of supporting their deadly enemy. Instead
of combining forces against the slaveholders, at least some of them had
sold out to the very power that was responsible for their own oppression
(Bilby 1984:15).

Isolationism that had developed from the Maroons' feeling of superiority over the "Bell-Quashies," as they called the slaves because of their
servile obedience when hearing the call of the slave bell, grew stronger
over the years. This isolationism is still evident today. The rupture
between Jamaicans in the mountains and forests and those on the plantations along the coast was brought about and always exacerbated by the
white rulers, but other factors were involved, including the effort of the
black population to counteract with a "unite and resist" policy to the
"divide and rule" principle of the rulers, and to the deliberate separatism
of the Maroons to protect their ethnic and social integration. A key to
coexistence was needed that would fulfill the need for a dual identity as
well as make possible further relations and communications between the
two groups.

Bilby (1984:10ff.) demonstrates how this division is still perceived and
accepted by using an orally transmitted genesis myth of the Windward
Maroons. Social relations between the two groups are reflected on a
metaphorical level in the oral tradition of the two sisters—as apical ancestors of Maroons and slaves. According to this mythological explanation
of the dual ethnogenesis, the "mother" of the Maroons, Grandy Nanny,
opted for battle, while her sister feared bloodshed and allowed herself to
be enslaved. Fanti Rose, usually identified with Nanny, began the mythological genealogy of the Maroon nation; Shanti Rose,[85] one of several
names for Nanny's sister, became the mother of the slave nation, which
the Maroons pejoratively refer to as "niega."

Similar to the way in which oral traditions in matrilinear societies in
West Africa where Akan is spoken characterize the relationship between
lineages or clans, the Jamaican "Two Sister Pikni" genesis myth defines
the historical and cultural alienation that came about among the Africans

who had crossed the Atlantic in common bondage (see Bilby/Steady 1981:454ff.). After sharing Middle Passage, the lives of the two "sisters" diverged when they chose different paths. Nanny became not only the cultural icon of the (Windward) Maroons, but also their metaphorical mother. All Maroons saw themselves as her "yoyo," which in Kromanti ritual language means "descendants" or "children." As "pikni (children) of one belly," they felt part of one single family although they lacked any actual genealogical ties (Bilby 1984:11f.; see also Mathurin 1975:36).

The primary purpose of the genealogical metaphor imbedded in the "historical myth" of the "Two Sister Pikni" was a sociocultural differentiation of Maroons and slaves, but it also provided a symbolic means of mending the split between the two "families" of black Jamaicans by extending the kinship ties of Nanny and her sister to their "children" as well[86] (Bilby 1984:11). This equipped the children with the ability to be more flexible in structuring their relationships to one another. Even the dreaded "Black Shot" were in this sense boorish sons of the sister of their mother, but their mere existence did not cause any insurmountable rift between the two groups. Just as "real" families are able to form alliances or to cooperate among themselves to reach specific goals, in spite of a potential split into two camps, the "Two Sister Pikni" interacted at all times for all sorts of reasons. Even after ratifying the peace treaties, Maroons occasionally broke with their obligation to hunt new runaways and took some into their ranks despite the treaty conditions (Jones 1981:70).

Bilby (1984:22) sees in the oral tradition of the two sisters "the European's ultimate failure to bring about a definitive rupture between peoples of African descent in the Americas. For even as this myth preserves the memory of a painful past separation, it celebrates the fact that, several centuries after this parting occurred, Maroons and their neighbors. . . continue to be capable of using shared cultural traditions to bridge the gulf between them." The emphasis here is on *definitive* rupture, because most earlier relationships between free and nonfree African-Jamaicans were broken off in the aftermath of the peace treaties.[87]

The policy of "divide and rule" had driven a wedge between slaves and Maroons that forced the latter to view their "mythical relatives" on the plantations as potential enemies. Disillusioned by their unreliability and driven into a corner by adversarial actions, Maroons reacted with isolationism and separatism. The ratification of the peace treaties must be considered the climax of this development, since it closed the ranks of the Maroons to enslaved "African brothers and sisters" and set the tone for subsequent societal development. After enduring eighty-five years of war without armed support by most of the black population, Maroons declared themselves ready to capture all future runaways and return them to their white oppressors for payment. Seemingly out of the blue, the rebels had become slavehunters. On the surface, this development could be seen as an overnight switch from heroic revolutionaries to corrupt counterrevolutionaries, but actually it was the culmination of a long-term process of change in the relationships between free and enslaved African-Jamaicans.

Jamaica was no exception in this regard. Numerous treaties of a similar nature in other colonies documented the willingness of other Maroon communities to switch their primary allegiance (Price 1983a:3f.). "By this compact they achieved a necessary breathing space and a definition of their communities without which they would have remained amorphous and unfixed. Even the change of sides for which the maroons are often condemned was far from an object surrender. By hunting runaways rather than acting as a focus for slave resistance maroons preserved their communities from further dilution and reduced the threat of competition for the backlands" (Craton 1982:65). Moreover, the almost total exclusion of outside influences by newly-integrated fleeing slaves guaranteed an undisturbed development of Maroon ethnicity and culture (Kopytoff 1976:46).

The peace treaties were no mere outgrowth of the "divide and rule" strategy, but also reflected the desire of the Maroons to achieve a stable existence while retaining their own hard-won identity. Two hundred fifty years after the fact, we are hardly in a position to condemn the Maroons for counterrevolutionary abandonment of the enslaved. Had they not themselves been left in the lurch by the black majority on the plantations during the battles that stretched over generations? War in the jungle pitting machetes, lances, and camouflage against rifles and cannons may strike a modern observer as romantic, but the rebels of the eighteenth century could not indulge in sentimentality. Their existence hung by a thread. The peace treaties signalled a triumph over those who pictured black people as mere beasts of burden.

"After 85 Years, the Rifles of War fell Silent": The Peace Treaty Between the Maroons and the Colonial Power, 1738–1739

There was no definitive loser in the bitterly fought military conflict. However, considering the Maroons' apparently hopeless situation at the outset, the Maroons seem to have won at least a moral victory. They had worn down the slaveholders with their constant attacks on the latter's most sensitive spot—their wallet. The slaveholders suffered great military as well as economic losses. In the 1830s, the colonial power went to great lengths to respond to the challenge to the regime in an appropriate manner.

When even these reprisals did not bring about the desired results and the drums of the Maroons inspired more and more of the enslaved to attempt flight, the white masters feared for the continuation of their rule (see Patterson 1973:270). Maroon resistance always carried the potential of escalating to a slave revolt throughout the island (Schuler 1970:377; see Hart 1985:71). Picturing the ruin of the entire colony, the slaveholders only sought relief from the unending anxiety of Maroon raids, the rigors of military service, and the financial burden of maintaining a standing army (Edwards 1983:236f.). After all attempts to eradicate the free black communities had failed, only peace negotiations with the black rebels would avert the threat to the system.

The Maroons also had a literally vital interest in putting an end to the inevitable limbo the war had brought to its communities. Far too much of their labor was consumed by unproductive defense measures; this labor was urgently required to obtain food and other necessities (Martin 1985:254). Nonetheless, the freedom fighters once again began an offensive in 1738 as a response to the last desperate attempt on the part of the colonial power to defeat them militarily with the aid of slavehunters, bloodhounds, and Miskito Indians from Central America. With this offensive, they reinforced their aura of invincibility, and succeeded in affirming their right to (co)existence. No longer would they have to plead for freedom or land, but instead could place counterdemands for a promised halt to military actions.

Succumbing to pressure from the white population, which was no longer willing to wage war, Governor Edward Trelawney reluctantly agreed to move ahead with a peace treaty. Governor Trelawney commissioned Colonel John Guthrie[88] either to destroy Kojo's main settlement or to seek peace. As could be expected, only the second option was feasible

Treaty between the English and the Maroons

(see Hart 1985:96ff.), since the Maroons were not cowed by colonial power and were determined to defend themselves. They refused to be coerced into unfavorable treaty conditions or persuaded by ultimata. After rugged negotiations punctuated by military actions over the course of ten days, colonial officers Colonel Guthrie and Lieutenant Francis Sadler received a mandate from the Governor and the Council to sign the treaty. On March 1, 1738 (1739),[89] the former adversaries endorsed a fifteen-provision peace treaty (see Craton 1982:87ff.).

Besides calling a halt to all hostilities and guaranteeing freedom for the Maroons, its major provisions laid out the rights and duties of both parties. The free "separatists" were granted the right to plant 1,500 acres of coffee, cocoa, ginger, tobacco, and cotton on lands belonging to them; to breed cattle, hogs, goats, and any other livestock; to sell their products in the marketplace; to hunt wherever they wished; to call the authorities in the event of white raids; and to inflict any punishment (other than capital punishment) they deemed proper for crimes committed by Maroons within their own communities.

Their primary duties were the following: to serve in the military in order to protect the colony against slave uprisings or other rebellions and to avert attacks by foreign powers; to capture all future runaways for a premium and return them to the colonial authorities; to hand over criminals from their own ranks to colonial courts; to allow access to the major roads of their villages; and to grant two white "diplomats" rights of residence and allow the governor or colonial commander certain rights of nomination in appointing future Maroon commanders (Dallas 1803:58–65).[90]

The parties to these treaties concurred on their content, but applied different criteria to evaluate their significance. Even their accounts of how the treaties were ratified reveal how little their interpretations overlapped. Dallas (1803:56), needing to mitigate the supposed disgrace of not having won the war against the black rebels, portrayed the Maroon commander Kojo as an ugly, deformed, and altogether inhuman cripple who groveled before the idealized figure of Colonel Guthrie at the signing of the treaty:

> [Kojo] threw himself to the ground, embracing Guthrie's legs, kissing his feet, and asking his pardon. He seemed to have lost all his ferocity and to have become humbly penitent and abject. The rest of the Maroons, following the example of their chief, prostrated themselves, and expressed the most unbounded joy at the sincerity shown on the side of the white people.

This account seems more like wishful thinking and deliberate plantocratic propaganda than a plausible scenario of the event. Patterson (1983:276ff.) provides some unconvincing psychological speculations about the "slave personality" of Kojo and others and their alleged technique of expressing their contempt for the slaveholders by redirecting it to themselves. It is far more likely that Dallas's depiction, published more than sixty years after the actual event, strove to preserve the doctrine of white racial superiority and erase the impression of the disgrace of having negotiated with escaped "Negro slaves." Certainly this was a fundamental defeat for slaveholder ideology, the very foundation of which hinged on negating the humanity of the black people. It took some narrative effort on the part of the plantocratic propaganda to salvage whatever it could of the racist rationalization of subordination (see Schafer 1973:127). The war hero Kojo therefore had to crawl on the ground like an animal, kiss the white master's feet, and beg for mercy (Dallas 1803:56). Patterson (1983:276f.) seems to accept all of these inventive renderings at face value, although he himself a few pages earlier (1983:271) quotes an anonymous observer on the scene who attests to the anxiety and respect shown by the white negotiators. To obviate the understandable distrust on the part of the rebels, the whites offered gifts and hostages, and the governor himself undertook the arduous journey to the vicinity of the Maroon villages to ratify the treaty without delay. It is also noteworthy that Colonel Guthrie and Lieutenant Sadler received nearly three times as much payment for negotiating the peace agreement than had been paid out for the capture of Nanny Town[91] (Craton 1982:91).

A few months after the contractual agreement with Kojo, the Windward Maroons under Captain Kwao (Quao) signed a similar accord, although some details seem to have been less favorable to them. The Windward Maroons pledged to return all runaways who had joined up with them during the three years preceding the ratification of the treaty, whereas Kojo's recent recruits had the option of staying with the Maroons (Hart 1985:124).[92] But the conditions had not been one-sidedly dictated to the Windward Maroons either, even though the fact that a large rebel group had already silenced the "rifles of war" certainly created indirect pressure to accept any conditions so as not to run the risk of having to fight against both the colonial power and its new ally, the Leeward Maroons. In Article 6 of the Peace Treaty (quoted in Hart 1985:119), Kojo had indeed pledged "to take, kill, suppress, or destroy . . . all rebels where so ever they be throughout the island, unless they submit to the same terms of accommodation granted to captain Cudjoe, and his successors."

With these peace treaties, the Maroon communities of Jamaica entered into a new affiliation with their former enemy, which gave rise to a complex social, economic, and political network. However, understandings of the reciprocal rights and duties varied greatly and in some aspects were diametrically opposed.

Maroon woman in Moore Town

Historic photograph of a slave market in East Africa (19th century)

500 years after Columbus:
First meeting of the Maroon leaders in Washington D.C., 1992

Enslaved Africans and white colonialists

The letter X represents the stolen African name of the enslaved

Farmhouse in Maroon territory

Cockpit Country: Historical battleground of the Leeward Maroons

The Blue Mountains, a Maroon retreat

Maroon town, formerly Kojo's Town

Abeng player in camouflage

Myal expert Gladdys Foster

Michael Rose:
Reggae as medium of Rastafari

Jamaican rain forest:
The guerrilleros were practically invisible when in camouflage

Celebration of independence near Kindah, a historic meeting place

On the morning of the celebration, the Maroons roast a hog

Dance under the Kindah tree

The hog is prepared in the traditional manner to honor the ancestors

Female dancers communicate with the ancestors

The hog is served

Abeng, the symbol of armed resistance

Procession to Accompong

Nigerian Harris recalling the camouflage

Nyahbinghi drummer:
Death to the black and white oppressors

Rastafari elder of the Nyahbinghi order

Freddie McGregor and Dennis Brown:
Chant Down Babylon

Judy Mowatt:
The voice of today's resistance

"Sacred Charters" or Profane Legal Documents?
Divergent Interpretations of the Treaties

While colonial chroniclers such as Dallas construed submissive gestures of the Maroons as evidence of white racial superiority, the Maroons' own oral tradition presents the conclusion of the treaty in an entirely different light. Descendants of the freedom fighters now living in Accompong and Moore Town insist that the treaties were solemnized in blood. Following an old Kromanti custom, the leaders of both sides are said to have cut into their arms, mixed their blood in a bowl with rum, and drunk it (Colonel Rowe to Beckwith 1969:185; also State Secretary Mann O. Rowe in a filmed interview of January 1989; see Zips 1991b:71f.).

Such is the basis of the Maroon conviction that the treaty rights are inviolable. Any cancellation or modification by judicial derogation would be impossible, since these accords are no simple legal documents on paper, but blood treaties. If these blood treaties were to be annulled, it would not suffice to tear up the paper on which they are written; human bodies would have to be torn up (Martin 1973:176). Maroons consider the mixing and drinking of blood the actual pact, whereas the signatures on the document itself served only as verification. The English legal system, of course, had altogether different views on how treaties are formalized. The colonial negotiators probably saw the exchange of blood as a mere ceremonial act and regarded only the written signatures as legally relevant.

This distinction is crucial because it reveals the opposed foundations of the parties for the future interpretation of the agreements. For the English, the accords were a means to an end, namely to terminate a threat to their rule and assure loyalty and support in exchange for civil rights and freedom. The successful freedom fighters invested these accords with far greater significance:

> For the Maroons the treaties were sacred agreements, carrying the promise of a new life. Consecrated at the Maroons' insistence by a blood pact, the treaties brought about so many changes in the Maroons' existence that they radically transformed their societies, and in time became sacred charters of these new societies. While reinterpreations did occur, any attempt to tamper with the treaties themselves was seen as a direct threat to the Maroons' corporate existence. (Kopytoff 1979:46)

Even if the colonial power entertained hopes of reinterpreting the content of the treaties to their own advantage, they were certainly not in a position to nullify them without slipping into new armed conflict with the Maroons, who were prepared to defend the rights they had finally attained with all means at their disposal. For the Maroon communities, the accords did not represent profane pacts, but fundamental documents that established their new free and peaceful existence. For the Maroons of today, it was not the original freedom fighters in the mid-seventeenth century who count as the First-Time Maroons, but those whose fortitude brought about the treaties, primarily Kojo, Accompong, Nanny, and Kwao. They are revered in the genesis myths as superhuman cultural icons responsible for structuring and preserving the collective Maroon identity still in existence today. An important factor in preserving collective land ownership was their obstinate insistence on the inviolability of the blood treaties as the basis and guarantee of their sovereign political identity. Just as the resistance of the first rebels was impelled by territorial claims, they later viewed the land rights they had acquired as an inalienable facet of their existence. They interpreted attacks on the land of their birth not so much as a threat to their existential foundations, but as an attack on the sacred tradition of their community: "a threat to the bones of their ancestors" (Kopytoff 1979:52, 56ff.).

Once they had achieved political independence, they resisted all efforts of the colonial power and the Jamaican government to convert their communal property into individual or government property with private rights to use, and demanded tax exemptions or at least relief, citing their special sovereign status established through the treaties (Schafer 1973:177). In a conversation of September 1985 in Accompong Town, Colonel Cawley objected to the arrogance of the Jamaican government, which presumed to demand tax contributions from the Maroons. He argued that the Jamaican national state had received independence over 200 years after the Maroons from the same colonial power. Moreover, he went on to say, the Commonwealth member state Jamaica still owes its allegiance to the English Crown, which is represented by the Governor General as the formal Head of State. Thus, Colonel Cawley held that all negotiations should be conducted directly with the (English) ruler and not with its Jamaican subordinates.

But even the colonial ruler had tried to invalidate the special status and rights of the Maroons in 1842, soon after the abolition of slavery. With the Maroons Land Allotment Act (Act. No. 3465, PRO: CO 137/79), it declared null and void all valid laws concerning the Maroons, including the laws ratifying the peace treaties. Henceforth they would be entitled to the same rights and obligations as all other Jamaican subjects and the land rights would revert to the Crown in order to be reapportioned to individual Maroons. While the Jamaican Maroons honored the African tradition of respect for treaty obligations (Genovese 1981:55), the British decision between loyalty to the treaty and breach of contract came down to a question of political opportunism, which reflected a general colonial habit.

After the Maroons had served their time as allies against runaways and insurgents once slavery had ended, Viscount Goderich, Secretary of State for the colonies in London, ruminated: "I am not aware of any sufficient reason for perpetrating the distinctions between those persons and the rest of his Majesty's subjects of free condition. The warfare which first gave birth to these rules, is now of so remote a date, that the time would seem to be ripe for amalgamating all the free people of every class into one body; subject to the same general laws and partaking in the same privileges" (Goderich 1832; quoted in Kopytoff 1979:53). The alleged "right" to repudiate the treaties unilaterally was claimed to be justified by the allegiance of the Maroons to the colonial power.

Noting the unflagging insistence of the black communities on the sacred character of the treaties and their willingness to defend them with force if necessary, the colonial government opted against full disclosure of the new law. Since they were not preparing to enforce its regulations on a compulsory basis, the Maroons Land Allotment Act could simply not become effective, at least by today's legal standards (see Fischer/Köck 1980:117). Once again, the English acceded to the resistance of the Maroons, this time with a legislative trick. Even today, the Maroons still maintain their successful block of land parcelling and conversion to private property. They were equally unwilling to be integrated into the free Jamaican populace and defended their special status as a predominantly independent, sovereign nation. Treating them judicially as if they were ordinary subjects owing allegiance to the Crown was of no use to the colonial government, as long as in practice the Maroon communities under their own political leadership went on living in the same way on their communal land (Kopytoff 1979:47f., 55f.).

Beyond the symbolic tie of the collective Maroon identity to communal land ownership, the land was also of immense economic significance. After the treaties, the Maroons as the first free black communities of the "New World" had become far more integrated into the monetary economy. Women were now free to sell their surpluses at the island's markets, and the men produced various products to sell, earned money as wage laborers on nearby plantations, or collected rewards for hunting runaways. When this last source of income dried up with the abolition of slavery, they became even more dependent on income from sales at the marketplace and exports of cash crops (Schafer 1973:155, Kopytoff 1979:56). Thus it was not only a firm resolve not to betray the heritage of their ancestors that made them continue to insist on the inviolability of the blood treaties, but also concern for the continued existence of the community.

The Maroons resisted all efforts to interpret these blood treaties as "normal" legal documents subject to the usual legal regulations of amendment or invalidation with the argument that these were sacred charters. They maintained that these charters confirm rights and obligations in a manner that resembled constitutions, but were legally irrevocable and therefore permanent owing to their ritual mode of conclusion. They could not be altered or voided even with the consent of contemporary Maroons because they were safeguarded by the apical ancestors Nanny and Kojo; therefore, renouncing their enduring validity would amount to renouncing their very identity.

"The Black Gendarmerie": Maroons as Enforcers of Law and Order after the Treaties

In times of war, free and nonfree blacks had frequently faced one another as military adversaries, which bred hostility in the Maroons toward the enslaved who were loyal to their masters and had sold out as collaborators of the slaveholders. The peace treaties allowed them to turn the tables. Slaves had fought on the side of the colonial militia for payment; now Maroons could themselves serve as mercenaries against slaves who sought freedom. They were henceforth obligated to close their ranks to plantation fugitives and capture them for payment, thus effectively blocking the establishment of new Maroon communities.

This decision was no simple act of revenge. As mentioned earlier, all Maroon communities in the "New World" who were offered peace treaties agreed to similar sets of provisions. The free black communities had long since acquired an identity that emphasized their divergence from the rest of the black population rather than any unifying elements. This very identity was destabilized by the constant admission of new members. An integral component of their survival strategy was confirmation of their sociocultural solidity from within, which necessitated a degree of deliberate detachment of the Maroon communities from the outside world (Schafer 1973:132f.).

With their liberty, rights, and privileges now formally endorsed in treaties, the Maroons looked down on the downtrodden children of Nanny's sister. As a "superior nation" they now felt justified in enforcing the rules to which all non-Maroons were subject (Bilby 1984:10). When the Maroons agreed to serve as a tracking force, as stipulated by the colonial government, the fate of all future freedom fighters was sealed (Gardner 1971:119). The enslaved now bitterly saw any future path to freedom cut off by the "King's Negroes," as they now sarcastically called the Maroons (Patterson 1973:279; Price 1983a:22).

Until slavery was abolished in 1834–1838, roughly a century after the peace treaties, the Maroons sought to retain the status quo. Even if it is difficult not to see an irony of fate in this, we should not ignore the fact that they had attained their primary goal of freedom. The now-widespread notion of "pan-African-Jamaica" and solidarity among all blacks were alien to the social fabric of the early eighteenth century in Jamaica. In the eyes of the black rebels, every non-Maroon was a potential enemy. Apparently they were not plagued by moral scruples when working as paid "police" in hunting down blacks who were in pursuit of the same freedom they had attained for themselves (Jones 1981:66). This new source of income replaced the proceeds from plantation raids of pre-treaty times.

As mercenaries, they participated in crushing almost all subsequent slave revolts (Dallas 1803:10ff.). Even the famous uprising under the leadership of the Kromanti rebel Tacky in 1760, which came to be known as Tacky's Revolt, failed because of Maroon intervention. Tacky himself is said to have been killed and decapitated by Lieutenant Davy of the Scott's Hall Maroons (Jones 1981:67; Craton 1982:136). In addition to the regular mercenary pay, the Maroons received a premium for Tacky's head. In several times of crisis, they proved trustworthy allies of the colonial government who lived up to their treaty obligations,[93] even though they sometimes acted with some flexibility and sanctioned runaway villages outside of their territory (Patterson 1973:264) or even allowed fugitives into their villages (Robinson 1969:10). However, these exceptions did nothing to undo the basic split of the African-Jamaicans into two camps separated from one another by divergent sociocultural development.

By agreeing to the peace treaty, the Maroons had opted for independence under a set of conditions they had no intention of revoking. One of these conditions involved their control of exclusive rights and privileges as free black people. It was altogether consistent with their own interests to work as a black police force to ensure the factual monopoly of freedom and self-government. Only by birth were additional members able to join their "family."[94] For this reason, they are criticized today for having been won over to a counterrevolutionary role in the English policy of "divide and rule" and playing this role all too well, thereby helping to stabilize an oppressive system (Bilby 1984:10f.).

Once again during Jamaica's largest slave revolt in 1832, in which 20,000 slaves participated, the mercenary service of the Maroons turned the scales, thus quelling the slave insurrection and causing emancipation to be postponed for another two years (see Hart 1985:291ff.). Even after emancipation, "blood ties" to the English counted more than the same skin color and place of origin. With the help of the Maroon special commandoes, the peasant revolt of 1865, under the leadership of Paul Bogle (who is now a Jamaican national hero), was crushed. Bogle himself was captured by the Maroons and hanged from the burned-out courthouse[95] (Craton 1982:328).

Clearly the Maroons did not concur ideologically with the colonial aim of stabilizing the system of utter oppression and exploitation. They were nonetheless impelled to cooperate because of their ideological tie to their political identity as established in the peace treaties and made permanent by the blood pact, even to the point of fighting against one another to fulfill the sacred accord, as the second Maroon war of 1795–1796 demonstrated.[96]

"Jamaica's Wounded Knee": The Second Maroon War of 1795–1796

The alliance between the former enemies lasted for over half a century without notable incidents. Their reciprocal trust grew to the point that the colonial administration no longer saw the necessity for the constant presence of two white superintendents in Trelawney Town, the former settlement of Colonel Kojo, which had been named after the English governor Edward Trelawney, ratifier of the treaty. The period of peace ended soon after the appointment of a new acting governor, the Earl of Balcarres, who wanted to prove himself in war as quickly as possible as commander in chief of the forces (Hart 1985:159). As an initial step he

Abolition of slavery in Jamaica

arranged for the engagement of two new agents of the colonial government in Trelawney Town. The Maroons saw this act as a declaration of mistrust that poisoned mutual relations.

Only one final straw was needed to bring the smoldering conflict, which was fueled still further by a dispute over land rights, to the point of eruption. It was not long in coming. Two Maroons from Trelawney Town were indicted in Montego Bay for allegedly killing tame hogs, and the Maroons were sentenced to flogging. The punishment was carried out in public by a slave, which was highly insulting to the Maroons. They interpreted the incident as a breach of treaty and reacted to the particular humiliation of being flogged by a slave by expelling the new superintendent in Trelawney Town, Captain Thomas Craskell, along with his assistant, John Merody. Now Balcarres' opportune moment had arrived. He imposed unacceptable conditions on the Maroons. When these were rejected, he had the pretext he needed to impose martial law. Simultaneously he set a price for every captured or murdered resident of

Flogging a slave

Trelawney Town. This was reason enough for the aging, conciliatory Maroon commander Colonel Montague James to come to Vaughansfield to visit Balcarres with thirty-seven of the best of his retinue, intending to settle the altercation. This effort was unsuccessful. They were placed in chains and brought aboard a warship in Montego Bay. When the other Maroons learned of this incident, they decided to accept the challenge, set their village[97] on fire and retreated to the Cockpit Country rainforest, which was familiar only to them (Hart 1985:159ff.).

Despite a paucity of both manpower and weapons, they managed to hold out against the troops of the red coats led by General Walpole for over six months. According to Dallas (1803:255), they killed many English soldiers, yet sustained very few losses themselves. They also inflicted severe economic damage with plantation raids and the "blockade" of militia soldiers and Black Shot. Obviously their fighting ability had been severely underestimated by Governor Balcarres. Under the leadership of traditional captains, especially Johnson and Parkinson, they could once again prove their prowess at guerrilla fighting. They had maintained their accuracy by hunting, and had not forgotten their old "hit and run" method, as the Eighteenth Light Dragoons learned during one raid that left five times as many dead as wounded (Craton 1982:92ff., 215).

This time, however, all colonial forces were concentrated on a single Maroon community, which traced its heritage to Colonel Kojo. All other free black communities declared themselves neutral and for the time being did not take part in the fighting. The resistance fighters thus remained essentially isolated. They tried to compensate with the strategy of splitting up the front by forming small guerrilla troops. The situation became quite precarious when at least some Maroons from Accompong Town (the village that had been founded by Kojo's brother Accompong)

declared their willingness to go to war as mercenaries against their former comrades in arms.[98] There had been conflicts between the two groups
concerning the right to custody of the peace treaty, which both claimed
for themselves as a symbol and embodiment of their identity (Kopytoff
1979:51; Schafer 1973:167, 194).

General Walpole received crucial information about sources of water,
accessible routes, and rebel retreats from the Accompong Town Maroons,
who at that time already considered themselves more as competitors for
land and hunting grounds than as ethnic and ideological allies of
Trelawney Town (Dallas 1803:243). Once Balcarres had also imported
Spanish slave trackers with their "hounds of hell," there was no point in
the black guerrilleros continuing to fight. They had no choice but to
declare to the overpowering enemy alliance their willingness to cease all
fighting, to surrender, and (almost 57 years after Kojo's accord with the
English) to sign a new, less favorable peace treaty. Once again, the
Maroons remained undefeated, an almost incredible accomplishment
given their isolated position beset from several sides. Colonel Montague
James and General Walpole signed a document that guaranteed the
Maroons specific land rights in Jamaica (Hart 1985:184).

Balcarres, however, had altogether different intentions. Although he
ratified the treaty on December 28, 1795, he set the time and place of
capitulation and surrender of arms for January 1, 1796 in Castle Wemys
on the coast of Falmouth, which meant that the Maroons would not possibly be able to get there in time to meet the deadline. He then seized the
pretext that the trusting resistance fighters had breached the treaty and
demanded their deportation from Jamaica. He was able to address the
decisive committee to the Assembly and convince the Council to banish
the Maroons from Jamaica against their will and in violation of the
arrangements that had been agreed to, thereby making the Maroons victims of his duplicity. Meanwhile the Maroons, relying on the text of the
treaty, laid down their weapons over the coming days and weeks, and
surrendered to Walpole.

When Walpole learned of the intended deception, he wrote a furious
letter to Balcarres:

> My Lord, to be plain with you, it was through my means alone
> that the Maroons were induced to surrender, from a reliance which
> they had on my word—from a conviction impressed upon them by
> me that the white people would never break their faith. All these
> things strongly call upon me, as the instrumental agent in this busi-

ness, to see a due observance of the terms, or, in case of violation, to resign my command; and if that should not be accepted, to declare the facts to the world, and to leave them to judge how far I ought or ought not to be implicated in the guilt and infamy of such a proceeding. (Walpole, quoted in Hart 1985:199f.)

All interventions by Walpole and other white settlers dismayed by Balcarres' deception and breach of contract were futile. The Maroons of Trelawney Town were deported to the harbor city of Halifax, Nova Scotia (in what is now Canada). This involuntary exodus of the largest Maroon community on the island was the Jamaican equivalent of Wounded Knee. Craton (1982:66) remarks sarcastically: "But given the power and tireless duplicity of capitalist colonialism, the survival of any maroons at all was a remarkable and inspiring achievement."

Nothing need be added to Craton's fitting words, but the chapter on the fight for liberation and independence of the first black freedom fighters in the "New World" should not close on such a sour note. The history of the Trelawney Town Maroons went on from there. As could be expected, their remarkable spirit of resistance was not broken even by the long Canadian winter. The Maroons refused to accept Christianity and to do the work assigned to them, ultimately creating so much trouble for the Duke of Kent, the Governor of Halifax, that he ordered them banished to Sierra Leone on the west coast of Africa after four trying years. Soon after their arrival in Sierra Leone, they suppressed a revolt against the Sierra Leone Company. By thus demonstrating their loyalty to the government, they attained positions of responsibility. The old Colonel Montague James was appointed the Co-Administrator of the colony. In Freetown, the capital of Sierra Leone, a Maroon enclave with a relatively autonomous political organization and jurisdiction was established. The return to Africa was certainly no reason to forgo their cultural traditions. Their allegedly most ardent political aim—to return to Jamaica—was something they could not accomplish, even though Schafer (1973:204ff.) reports that some of them did return to Kojo's and their land of birth after the abolition of slavery. According to the information (conversation of January 7, 1988) of Mann O. Rowe, the historian of Accompong Town and safekeeper of the peace treaty, two Maroon chiefs accomplished the "trick" of reenacting the Middle Passage of their forefathers on their own initiative, voluntarily as free people.

"In the Spirit of Freedom": Cultural, Social, and Ideological Characteristics of Maroon Communities

Ghanaian Chief Nana Kwow Ackon VII

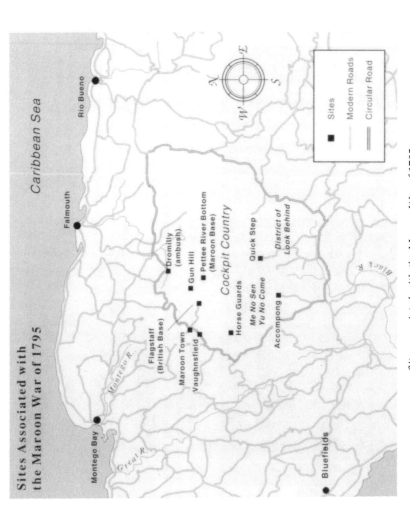

Sites associated with the Maroon War of 1795

Virtually all African-Jamaicans clung to their essential "African-ness" in the diaspora so as not to perish psychologically or meta-physically even before their already premature physical death. Memories of Africa as expressed in music, dance, poetry, storytelling, herbal medicine, religious rituals, and in concepts of nature and the supernatural served as permanent infusions in their will to survive and their pride. They also implied rejection of Europe and thereby created a cultural link between free and non-free black people as mental forms of resistance (Compton 1980:27ff.).

Although the enslaved relied on their feelings and thoughts of Africa as the true refuge of their self-respect and their identity, the lack of free-dom to reorganize socioculturally separated them from the freedom fighters. The dictatorship of the whip prevented them from reshaping their social structure according to their African heritage. They had few options open to "transplant" African sociocultural principles to the "New World." Below the surface of the system of repression, in the inalienable psyche of the oppressed, the "African memory" clung to life in a kind of cultural grammar. Only in this way can numerous commonalities and overlaps in the cultures of the free and nonfree African-Jamaicans be explained. Common roots in Africa assured that there be no insurmount-able hurdles (at least until the time of the peace treaties). Runaways suc-ceeded time and again in closing the gap for themselves by successful socialization with the rebelling black communities.

Even though some enslaved Africans managed to establish the com-monalities necessary to achieve freedom by their integration into a par-ticular Maroon society, this fact should not obscure the fundamental dif-ferences between the cultures of the enslaved and the Maroons. How could it be otherwise, since the culturally and socially formative process of Maroon society took place under military threat, but entirely apart from the control of white colonial rulers? On the basis of a realistic assess-ment of their specific situation, they could lean on the foundations of the various African cultural systems and forms of organization. The resulting "product" had distinct African characteristics, but neither the social, political, legal, religious, nor aesthetic system can be traced back to any particular "tribal" or national heritage (Price 1983a:28f.).

In a nutshell: the cultures of the Maroons differed from those of the blacks on the plantations by their "birth in freedom." Their spiritual mothers and fathers created new forms of organization on the basis of their various African experiences, deliberately relinquishing the possible "adoption" of a specific African culture, even when the majority shared an ethnic heritage.

State Within a State:
Political Bases and Realities of Self-Government

Since the peace treaties of 1738–1739, the Maroon systems of self-government may be characterized as "states within a state." Even Jamaica's Declaration of Independence has had little effect on this system. The Maroon administration insisted on retaining quasi-sovereign autonomy, as had been established in perpetuity by the blood treaties. The fact that the British treaty partner itself granted Jamaica independence without handing over the appointment of a head of state to the "young" state supports this argument[99]; at least formally, a high degree of political continuity remained.

The Maroons have insisted on continuity where their independence and rights of autonomy are concerned. Of course the Jamaican governments have attempted to check or even dismantle altogether the tax exemptions, rights of autonomy, and other judicial privileges. In the end they had little tangible success. Most likely pro and con arguments of international law could be found for consistently retaining the status quo; politically, the "pros" seem to predominate at the moment for the Jamaican government. Over the last years, there has certainly been no lack of overt and tacit declaratory acts on the part of the government to affirm Maroon status. These include regular official visits of state delegates to Maroon independence celebrations and recognizing Maroon cultural heroes as Jamaican national heroes as well as non-collection of land taxes, considerable non-intervention of the executive branch and state jurisdiction in the internal affairs of the self-governed communities and the reports on the autonomous areas of the Maroon administration in the government media. Obviously the possible advantages of a stronger incorporation of the first free black communities into the Jamaican state are in disproportion to the feared disadvantages of a defensive minority whose slogans of freedom and independence could find a fertile breed-ing-ground in the tense social reality of the Caribbean nation.

But what are the pillars of Maroon autonomy? The primary pillar, of course, is the collective will to preserve Maroon independence, which has many cultural manifestations. In addition, two facets of their African heritage predominate. The first is a hierarchical political system that provides for an elected Colonel as head of state with broad quasi-legislative, judicial, administrative, and representative powers, including the nomination of the Council; the second is a system of land distribution based on communal ownership.

All Maroon villages insist on autonomous control of the land agreed to in the treaties to forestall gradual assimilation of their communities. The *de facto* territorial sovereignty over these areas serves to ensure communal land ownership. Jamaica's interest in dissolving the "state within a state" or at least loosening its boundaries founders on the incompatibility of the judicial institution of communal property and European civil law (which also determines the Jamaican legal system in the form of English common law). As long as English-Jamaican law cannot be enforced on Maroon territory and therefore does not apply fully, Maroon autonomy and separate cultural identity are uncontested (Schafer 1973:176f.).

Moreover, the system of distribution, which was similar to the usufruct of land in West Africa, prevents taxation of the communal property, since the English tax law is aimed at assessing private property. Yet another legal dilemma would result from introducing taxation of communal property, since it is impossible to separate taxation of Maroon property from official recognition of communal property by the authorities of the independent state of Jamaica; it would create a potential precedent because of the English case law system. Practical considerations may also have entered into the decision not to limit the autonomy of the Maroons by lifting the tax exemptions as well. The reactions of the Maroons to a compulsory collection of taxes are all too easy to anticipate. The autonomists, who do not welcome the sight of officers in uniform other than as guests at the annual celebrations of independence, would most likely employ force against them if they came to collect the taxes.

As long as their territorial sovereignty endures, the political leadership of the Maroons can continue to disburse allotments of the communal property according to need and ability of an individual or the families to work the plot. If the family size shrinks because members have left the community or died, an appropriate portion of "their" land reverts to the community and is redistributed. If a plot of land has been in the usufruct of a family for generations, it can derive, at least in the social system of Accompong, a kind of prerogative from the cultivation rights of the grandfather or father. This right, however, is forfeited if the family does not need or cannot cultivate a plot of that size. Individuals who seek a bank loan find themselves at a disadvantage. Without a title of land possession in accordance with civil law, the Maroons lack the collateral needed to obtain bank credit (Bill Peddy, conversation of January 9, 1988 in Accompong Town; see also Schafer 1973:176f.).

In any case the allocation of land bolsters the authority of political leadership—especially that of the Colonel, who gets the last word in this situation as in most internal and external affairs of the Maroon communities. Of course, the last word need not come from him alone, but can be suggested to him by influential members of the Council.

The Highest Authority:
The Maroon Colonel as Head of State

Since the days of the First Time, Maroon communities in the diaspora have opted for a system of government based on African traditions of chieftaincy, or kingship as it was then called. Especially before the eighteenth century, absolutist Maroon rulers tended to legitimate their claim to rule with kinship ties and based their authority on royal African lineage. The best known case was King Ganga Zumba, the ruler over the Palmares "Maroon monarchy" in Brazil; others included the Venezuelan Maroon leader el Rey Miguel, Domingo Bioho (also known as Rey Benkos and Rey del Arcabuco ["king of the craggy spot"]) in Colombia, and King Bayano in Panama, all of whom claimed princely descent from their African homeland (Price 1983a:20).

Ganga Zumba was known to have delegated territorial power and key government posts to his relatives. This aspect highlights the strong similarity between the political system of Palmares, which was probably derived from several Central African models (see Kent 1983:187f. as well as Hofbauer 1986), and General Kojo's government,[100] which was most likely influenced by several West African organizational structures, particularly the Akans. Kojo also exercised his leadership with the aid of his brothers Accompong and Johnny (note the resemblance to the Akan name Gyany), who functioned as his right-hand men in the various villages of the Leeward Maroons with the rank of captain.[101] He placed military companies under their loyal command. These companies guaranteed the coordinated deployment of guerrilla units under his supreme command. As in the genealogical system of succession of Palmares, the Leeward Maroon claim to rule in Kojo's day was also ancestral and probably passed from Kojo's father to Kojo and from him to Accompong and Johnny in accordance with possible patrilinear succession, which is by no means certain, if we take the role of Nanny as a possible Queen Mother into consideration (Schafer 1973:61ff. and Zips 1998a; see also point 15 of the peace treaty in Hart 1985:120).

Both King Ganga Zumba and Kojo were elected rulers, although it is unclear whether to attribute a purely declarative or a constitutive character to the elections (see Kent 1983:187 and Dallas 1803:28). Furthermore, these "elections" involved the community as a whole or were "selections" by a council of elders comparable in its function to Akan kingmakers. Yet, it appears even more difficult to gather reliable statements about the political system of the Windward Maroons for the time preceding the peace treaty. It is debatable whether their political system fundamentally differed from that of the Leeward Maroons (as claimed by Craton 1982:77)[102] or whether organizational differences in the cooperation between the individual rebel settlements can be explained instead by the different genesis of the Windward and Leeward Maroons.

Kojo united several rebel groups under his central leadership. As mentioned previously, he is said to have subjugated the Madagascar Maroons competing in his territory and killed their leader in the process. By contrast, the three largest Windward Maroon villages remained under the control of their own independent chiefs. By reciprocal participation in ceremonial and religious occasions, they are said to have confirmed existing structures of solidarity in order to be able to rely upon military willingness to cooperate without needing to construct centralist forms of organization. However, we cannot automatically assume a fundamental difference in political views between the Leeward and Windward Maroons. It is more likely that the individual communities of Windward Maroons were both ethnically and culturally too heterogeneous to unite in a centralist (or "paramount") polity without risking considerable conflict. The history of the formation of one social group goes back to the first "Spanish" Maroons, but the other rebel groups were constituted from the alliance of runaways who had banded together.

Despite the relatively loose interactions between the various social groups to pursue common vital interests, the political structures of each individual community formation examined in isolation seem to have been quite similar to that of the Leeward Maroons. This might indicate the geographic proximity of at least one Maroon village, Guy's Town, to Nanny Town, which were most likely under one rule (see Hart 1985:64f.). It would then be more correct, however, to speak of at least five political units before the peace treaties: the Maroons united by Kojo, and those of Nanny Town, Crawford Town, Charles Town, and Scott's Hall.

The subsequent social history of the Leeward Maroons after the peace treaties shows how the success of a unified political system depended on the personal abilities of the rulers. The death of Kojo also spelled the end of this form of rule, which led to a split between Trelawney Town (formerly called Kojo's Town) and Accompong Town, with well-known negative consequences in the second Maroon war.

Kojo's role as a key political figure and as military commander-in-chief is richly documented; Nanny's is not. Since the political stance of Nanny can only be partially reconstructed, uncertainty surrounds the system of government of the Windward Maroons. As mythological supreme cultural heroine, called Queen Sovereign Mother Nanny, our Goddess and Our Heroine, by Maroon Captain Willoughby (in an undated pamphlet), modern oral traditions assign her a higher position outside the narrowly-defined political system. According to the frequently cited statements of the Maroon deserter Cupid (for instance, Schafer 1973:114 and Hart 1985:86), who fled to the English, Nanny co-ruled with her husband in civil matters, and a man named Adou took over the military sphere. Nanny's fundamental significance for the Windward Maroons may serve as an example of how a transcendentally legitimated authority can constrain the social force of military and political rulers and even supplant it (see also Kopytoff 1973:83ff., who assumes a dual political leadership structure for the Windward Maroons).[103]

We now move from historical observations that rely heavily on conjectures and unreliable sources to the current internal organization of the Maroons. The following still applies: The political power of the Colonel is comprehensive, but depends heavily on the personal aptitudes and effectiveness of the elected official. Additionally, it is limited by the institutionalized power of the Council in "legislation," administration, and jurisdiction as well as by the social power of particular individuals who base their right to political influence on cultural-historical and philosophical knowledge or transcendental abilities. Every Colonel is probably well advised to provide the desired bottle of rum to "mediators between this world and the other" if he is interested in inspiring the ascendants to heal the sick with libations in the old town (Colonel Cawley in an interview of January 13, 1988). By preserving cultural tra-

*Colonel Rowe marching in the procession from Kindah
during the annual celebrations in Accompong, 1994*

ditions and showing respect for the members of societies who partake in these rituals, he can encourage social harmony and retain the favor of his voters.

In Accompong, the post of Colonel is subject to reelection every five years. There is no limit to the number of times a successful candidate can be reelected.[104] The Colonel has the right to appoint the members of Council. The Council is in charge of staffing particular offices. The decisions of Privy Council in which the Colonel has the final say carry normative power (Thomas Rowe, interview of January 12, 1988). In the management of administrative matters, the Council, which assists the Colonel in his capacity as the highest administrative authority, is similar to a Cabinet Council, since the individual office holders are also responsible for particular areas of internal administration, such as the department of health and the cultural division. In attending to the matters of their assigned domain, they follow the directives of the Colonel and are always subject to his control. "You have different offices of agriculture, you have community development, social aspects of it, you have health, and all these have to be monitored by the Colonel to see that they are run properly, to get in and investigate, to find out how this is going and so forth. Everything is not left to them alone, but the Colonel has the responsibility to see to it that they are done well" (Colonel Cawley, interview of January 13, 1988).

The political hierarchy further consists of a Deputy Colonel and a Major (both offices are sometimes held by a single individual) as well as a Captain. They supervise the individual officers as authorities with extensive power and report directly to the Colonel (Colonel Cawley, ibid; see also Galloway 1981:109ff.). In addition to his duties as chief administrator, which include financial administration, the Colonel functions as the highest judge in civil (especially land) disputes and criminal proceedings. His authority as judge is based on Article 12 of the peace treaty: "That captain Cudjoe, during his life, and the captains succeeding him, shall have full power to inflict any punishment they think proper for crimes committed by their men among themselves, death only excepted . . ."[105] (quoted in Hart 1985:120).

Today this article is interpreted to mean that all criminal actions by Maroons perpetrated on Maroons can be sentenced from their own jurisdiction—the Council as judicial Senate and the Colonel as chairman of the Senate. Only murder is exempt; however, according to Mrs. Cawley, the mother of the Colonel (conversation of January 7, 1988), no case of murder has ever come before them. The Colonel does reserve the right to "delegate" his administrative powers to the state authorities, but many Maroons see this step as a sign of weakness and partial relinquishment of sovereignty (for example, elected Colonel Sterling of Moore Town, conversation of January 5, 1988). A politically powerful Colonel would more likely administer justice in criminal cases in conjunction with his Council, which also has judicial authority, than to yield one of his central areas of authority to the state courts.

"Most of the decisions are made by the Council. Yes, like a case of stealing, the person would be brought into the Council and the different officers give their views on the issue and a final decision would be taken and the Colonel would make that final decision" (Colonel Cawley on January 13, 1988). This "final decision" usually consists of a monetary fine, now that corporal punishment has been abolished and prison terms are not feasible because of a lack of a suitable locale and on economic grounds. Along with the penal sentence, judgments on potential civil claims for compensation on the part of the victim are also decided, for instance in the case of theft (see also Neumann 1966 for the customary law of the Maroons of Suriname).

Only if a condemned criminal fails to comply with the sentence does the Maroon administration refer the case to the state courts, which must apply Jamaican (state) law just like in any other legal case involving Maroons. If the defendant or the plaintiff feels discriminated against by the Maroon court and asks the Council for permission to bring the legal matter before the state courts, the Maroon Council generally grants this wish, which leads to stages of appeal from traditional Maroon courts to state jurisdiction. "What generally happens then, if he feels that that would be the better decision for him, well he is allowed to do so; we will not go against his will in that respect" (Colonel Cawley, ibid.). However, this type of request is quite rare, as Colonel Cawley explains with a laugh: "But many of the times many people settle with the decision of the Council, because the penalties out there are harsher than what we would really render to our own people. . . "

Criminal acts that occur outside the Maroon villages and involve at least one non-Maroon on either the victim's or the perpetrator's side do not fall under the jurisdiction of the Maroons. These acts are prosecuted by the Jamaican courts. At the instigation of the state, the Maroons aid in the investigation, and arrest suspects found in their jurisdiction, but coercive measures are set by the Jamaican authorities, since the Maroons have no direct role in the executive branch (Colonel Cawley, ibid.). In these types of cases, a great deal also depends on the personal diplomatic skill of a Colonel who is supposed to offer his "subjects" the greatest possible protection without affronting state authorities or breaking Jamaican law. Since he functions internally and externally as the highest quasi-state authority, his diplomatic abilities determine the condition of the fragile relations between the "state within a state" and the state. As a mediator between "his people" and the state authorities, he inevitably winds up caught in the middle. More radical, younger members of the community regularly demand from him an assertive foreign policy that does not always reflect the actual division of power. However, if he renounces too many rights and privileges by yielding too much to the official Jamaica, he places Maroon sovereignty and autonomy at risk. Then the Colonel endangers the internal unity of "his" community, which could lead to its dissolution.

Roy "Nigerian" Harris, the president of the Maroon Federation, a pan-Maroon organization founded in 1987 that advises on common affairs of the various settlements, has accused Colonel Harris of Moore Town of treason:

There is a death sentence on the Maroons; join with the federation now. Your own people is selling you. . . Mr. C.L.G. Harris has condemned the Maroons and is selling all possible secrets he can get to know to foreigners. It seems as if we do not have any future because we are surrounded at home and abroad. We now must have an open ban against C.L.G. Harris or any Maroon leaders who fail to act to save the people. (Roy Harris 1988, in a pamphlet)

Colonel Harris in turn contested the legitimacy of the Maroon Federation. A few days after the appearance of a newspaper report (in the Jamaican *Daily Gleaner* of February 12, 1988) about the election of Roy Harris as its president, he published an equally scathing rebuttal.

The public debate between Colonel Harris and his opponents within the community reflected a deep rupture in the social unity of the Maroons of Moore Town. The phenomenon, by no means limited to Maroons, that a central figure might split a society into loyal and disloyal citizens, produces arguably even more unpleasant consequences for the Maroon state within the Jamaican state than elsewhere. With the backdrop of the already fragile relationship to the state of Jamaica, internal conflicts carry the potential of bringing about the beginning of the end of sovereignty and autonomy.

Tenuous Ties:
The Maroon States and Independent Jamaica

Ethnic and social minorities throughout the world aspire to assert their rights with varying degrees of success. Considerably more complex is the process of interaction between the Jamaican state and the Maroons, who as *de facto* binationals are pressing not only for equality before the law with the "other citizens" but also to have their historically based minority privileges respected. In doing so they assume a confident attitude that does not resort to petitions and other actions that might seem like entreaties.

They insist on strict adherence to their inherited rights of sovereignty and tax exemptions, but they also wish to have direct representation in the state affairs that affect them and a stronger say in financial spending.

Nobody represents the Maroons in the parliament apart from people who are not Maroons, and the Maroons are not pleased about that. . . And perhaps that's the reason why we are not getting the help that we need; and the economic assistance that we should be getting: like roads, water supply and health services and so forth, because these are the things that we should get according to the treaty that was made between the British and the Maroons. (Colonel Cawley, interview of January 13, 1988)

The expenditures for the lacking infrastructure do exceed by far the savings from the tax exemptions and are therefore out of reach for the Maroons. Without sufficient access to the market—most transporters consider the potholed streets ruinous to their vehicles—agricultural products essentially cannot be disposed of properly, which has continued to impoverish the population as a whole and bring young people to the point of leaving the country. The only way out was the forced cultivation of "ganja" (marijuana), which helped to ease the economic difficulties before reaching the point of crisis (see Spence 1985:137ff., 178f.). It must be obvious how this very economic restructuring could only lead to further strain of the fragile pact of tolerance with the state.

Only with the explicit consent of the Colonel is the state police allowed to enter Maroon territory, at least in the view of the autonomists. Unannounced police raids to destroy the illegal agricultural product therefore always used to meet with civil disobedience by the Maroons, which usually was futile, according to Colonel Cawley. One serious incident occurred on March 31, 1988, when a policeman from the "Special Operations Division" in Kingston was beaten to death by angry residents of Accompong after he had "confiscated" ganja from the house of a Maroon without orders to do so, allegedly using his office for his own material benefit. During his flight, he had shot into the air several times. In its official position statement, the Council of the Accompong Maroons essentially absolved "its citizens" of guilt by designating their behavior as "unbecoming," but provoked by the policeman. The Jamaican newspaper *The Weekend Star* quoted the Council's position on page 28 of its April 8, 1988 edition:

> The Council and residents of Accompong regret the tragic circumstances by which Mr. McPherson met his death; we wish to assure everyone that the Maroons are peace-loving and law-abiding citizens who have governed themselves for over 249 years going into 250 years. It is the first time that such an incident has occurred in Accompong. We have ably demonstrated over the years, and

especially through our annual celebrations, that we are one of the best self-governing communities in Jamaica.

Many Maroons are aware that these types of incidents can easily escalate, not necessarily to an armed conflict as in Suriname, but could certainly tighten the screws of repression and resistance by several turns in the tension between themselves and the state authorities. For this reason, Colonel Cawley (in the interview of January 13, 1988 quoted above) also wishes direct negotiations with the Jamaican government that include the British treaty partner. According to the Colonel, true stabilization of mutual relations can only guarantee better cooperation between the "two states":

> But at the same time not to allow them to erode the system we have here and the peaceful way of life that the Maroons have. We want a better say and to have more voice in this country of ours. They said: Out of many one people, but that is not true to the Maroons, because they have not come to the Maroons and negotiated anything with the Maroons as yet.

The Maroon Colonel shows his awareness of the critical future implications of the "foreign policy" relationship to the state when adding to his remarks: "So they are doing some backdoor deals that the Maroons are not pleased about, but we are keeping cool because we realize that it will take some legal issues and some time to put things together before we can make a good approach."

Aggressive Symbiosis:
The Maroon Economy

Inevitably, the situation of long-term warriors poses unusual economic challenges in coping with the problems of physical survival. The dire situation of the Maroons led them to develop a complex utilization of resources that included the white plantations in virtually all Maroon communities in the African diaspora.[106] They devised a series of survival strategies, which together yielded an economic system that worked in an aggressive social environment. This system served to supplement their livelihood, which was based primarily on self-sufficiency, with plantation raids and "highway robbery" (Hart 1985:60). This counter-aggression

140

was doubly motivated, since it served not only an economic aim, but also fought to limit the expansion of plantations.

The unstable conditions that prevailed during the time of armed conflict required a high degree of flexibility. A strict or systematic division of labor by age or gender was out of the question under these circumstances. Even the "seasonal" (occurring at a time other than the rainy season) campaigns undertaken by the British against their black adversaries affected their division of labor and their economic activities in general, about which we have few concrete details.

The Maroons relied on the resources of self-sufficiency as a foundation for their social security. In the subsistence sector of their economy, which far outweighed their other sources of income, they diversified their techniques of food production to reduce their dependency on the productivity of any one economic type. With varying intensity they supported themselves with yields from their activities as hunters and farmers, employing shifting cultivation and provision grounds around the settlement where they also kept livestock. Since information on the economic activities of the Jamaican Maroons is sparse, a definitive statement on their predominant technique of food production is hard to come by; it is therefore also impossible to classify their particular type of economy.

By blending the various cultural experiences from Africa with the store of knowledge of the First Nations and the zoological as well as ecological knowledge acquired from exploration and intensive observation, the freedom fighters gained a specific range of knowledge they needed to tackle their economic as well as military problems. With this as a basis, they developed a spectrum of economic activities, which included the following forms of food production.

In their biome, the tropical rainforest,[107] they made use of a broad "food palette" of edible wild plants and animals fit for hunting. It is difficult to determine whether the Maroons in times of peace practiced a gendered division of labor known from other so-called hunters and gatherers, assigning the men the tasks of hunting and fishing, and the women the gathering of natural products. The extent of this form of food production in the economic picture as a whole is equally indeterminate. We can establish that special significance was accorded to it due to the necessities of a war economy which forced the Maroons to operate with guerrilla warfare methods. During their absences from the settlements, which could last for months, both individual Maroons with specialized military tasks and whole rebel groups were dependent on their knowledge and abilities of self-sufficient hunting and gathering. Women in particular had to compensate for the drop in production caused by the English scorched-earth policy by exploiting natural resources. Military and economic strategies complemented each other. Rebel groups quite deliberately used their hunting and fishing villages not only for temporary sojourns for hunting and fishing expeditions, but also as part of their defense system to mislead British military expeditions or as "camouflaged traps" in the event of a raid (Dallas 1803:67).

In the area of Maroon agricultural techniques, it is difficult to establish the ratio of extensive to intensive cultivation. Certainly a combination of the two served to offset losses incurred in war. One of the major problems consisted in finding a site for continual occupation that was optimally suited to their diverse needs of protection, defense, assault, and subsistence. In order to avoid changing settlements all too often, they used swidden cultivation, paying careful attention to space the extensively planted fields as far apart as possible so as not to forfeit all of the resources if discovered by the enemy (Martin 1985:266). The danger that the arable lands gained by slash-and-burn farming were too easy to spot made the Maroons dismiss the possibility of an even more extensive use of land with this form of agriculture (see Schafer 1973:158). It is quite possible that they coupled extensive planting with intensive farming methods and at least occasionally prolonged the use of suitable provision grounds with natural fertilization, for instance with bat droppings from nearby caves.

It was mainly women who cultivated the fields located near the villages with intensive farming by using the natural fertilizers from livestock in cultivation. The relatively small, permanently cultivated tracts could feed a relatively large populace, particularly in times of crisis[108] (Hart 1985:64f.). For both swidden cultivation and intensive cultivation, they preferred to use their multipurpose tool, the machete, which is employed just as often today; a horticultural method in which the ground is loosened to dig in the young plant (see Bargatzky 1986:53).

The most important "social security factor" of the free black communities is apparent in the subsistence sector of the economy here described. Nonetheless, their need for war material did not permit them to rely exclusively on the resources of self-sufficiency. At the Sunday market they sold their food surplus or traded spicy "jerk pork," wild honey, and handmade products such as hammocks for weapons, gunpowder, ammunition, and other essential commodities (Beckford/Witter 1985:40; Martin 1985:257; Genovese 1981:52; see also Roy 1986:116; Craton 1982:65). On these occasions, they could gather crucial intelligence about advancing troops and other planned military operations of the British from the slaves who dominated the marketplace.

The extraordinary strategic achievements of the Maroons in the economic sphere consisted in rationally coordinating and complementing economic activities with military interests. The circumstances of their existence had a considerable impact on any of their economic decisions. Toward the colonial perpetrators of this distress they developed an aggressively symbiotic relationship as a response to their economically repressive measures by viewing the plantations as a quasi-natural resource. As with all other economic activities, with this source of profit from raiding the "supermarket" of the plantation the overall principle was: cooperative work with subsequent distribution among all Maroons. The institution of collective land ownership with distribution according to need reflects the intersection of individual and collective interests. Solidarity was the highest priority in the precarious situation of the Maroons. The fact that it had to be brought about often enough with force, as the preventive punishment authority of the Colonels demonstrates, should quell any exotic notions of a society living homogeneously in a social equilibrium.

Once the peace treaties were ratified, the economic horizons of the Maroon communities changed fundamentally. The previously vital source of income plantation raids dried up instantaneously; at the same time, monetary compensation for turning over runaways, wage labor for plantation owners and the government (especially in road construction), and access to the market for most of their products opened up new avenues to improve their economic status. The subsistence sector of their economy grew accordingly smaller and the Maroons were more fully integrated into the monetary economy of the colony (Dallas 1803:104f.; Schafer 1973:155).

One additional historical event had far-reaching economic consequences for the free black communities. With the abolition of slavery in 1834 (1838), almost a century after the treaty granting independence to the Maroons, the hitherto available sources of income diminished. Besides the end of the hunt for runaways and the military mercenary service for the colonial power in rebellions, the establishment of rural settlements far from the hated plantations entailed an increasing competition for agricultural production. Since the Maroon settlements were isolated and the roadways were in a sorry state (even today they are far from properly maintained), marketing their products became more costly relative to their new rural competitors, who of course in contrast to the

Maroons did not locate their fields in the remotest corners of the island.

According to Colonel Cawley (interview of January 13, 1988), the economic situation of the Maroon nation has come to a head in recent years as a result of the generally worsening marketing conditions for agrarian smallholders. Their increasing poverty and the well-known consequences of rural exodus are assuredly neither Maroon-specific nor Jamaica-specific (see, for instance, Rodney 1980:198f.), but they hit the geographically isolated farmers in the self-governed (Maroon) villages much harder than the rest of the rural population because their marketing options are already more limited. The following two sections discuss some of the economic strategies and perspectives of this current situation and the social consequences.

"Full Belly tell Hungry Belly, Keep Heart"

Every year brings the same scenario: At the independence celebrations of the Maroons, state officials (usually of lower ranks) appear as festival guests and distribute nothing but sweet talk to the celebrating hosts with pompous speeches. They talk about Maroon spirit and pulling oneself up by the bootstraps. But most of those Maroons present know in advance that the government aid they seek will probably not be mentioned this year either, and that if a politician does not come empty-handed even with promises, there is a long way from his declaration of intention to the fulfillment of his announcements. Most young people have better things to do than stand for repetitive lip-service. Their future probably lies not in the "enclaves" of their parents and grandparents, but in urban centers in and outside of Jamaica.

They are slow to warm to the prospect of having to perch on the same narrow edge of survival as the older generation as formally independent farmers, especially since their needs are oriented less to the heritage of Kojo and Nanny and more to the "ideals" of national and international youth culture. Belonging to young culture, even in Jamaica, requires at least some status symbols, which could not be afforded from the available sources of income. Too many related problems prevent or complicate the market exchange of the (rare) surplus of foodstuffs. Spence (1985:178f.) enumerates the major difficulties of the Maroon farmers: a lack of money caused in part by a lack of credit availability (as mentioned earlier, the banks require private land deeds as collateral), an insufficient workforce for the large-scale cultivation of fallow land because of rural exodus, a scarce and expensive supply of artificial fertilizers and pesticides, and inadequate marketing options resulting from an almost total absence of infrastructure.

From the perspective of the government, this situation appears to cover up a kind of tacit starvation strategy along the lines of "no taxes, no social services, no new streets." Without a halfway serviceable roadway system from the Maroon villages to the nearest marketplace (such as from Accompong to Maggotty), the autonomists remain in a state of involuntary economic isolation.

> We find that the Maroons, they are people who are hard working and they can do a great deal if they are given the opportunity or opportunities are at their disposal. Today the Maroons want to be more progressive and so you find that we have to be thinking of negotiating with the Jamaican government as well as other foreign agencies to see how we can get the help that we need to develop our educational and social aspects of life here in Accompong. (Colonel Cawley, interview of January 13, 1988)

For the time being, the cynical Jamaican saying "Full belly tell hungry belly, keep heart" is a fitting commentary on the platitudes of the "officials" at the annual festivities.

"Me Go a Foreign": ## "Flight" from Maroon Enclaves

Although the economically most dynamic agricultural activity of the 1970s and early 1980s, namely the cultivation and sale of "ganja," managed to keep some young Maroons in the villages (see Spence 1985:135ff.), more recently even this source of income has dried up noticeably. The Maroons protected their territorial integrity against the scorched-earth policy common elsewhere in Jamaica. However, with the escalation of the international anti-drug campaign that originated in the United States (which includes "ganja," or marijuana, as does Jamaican law in its list of illegal drugs), the traditional treaty rights were ignored. Unable to practice their usual resistance, the Maroons had to look on helplessly as their crop was destroyed from the air by small maneuverable airplanes and helicopters spreading poison over large areas.

"After me finish Secondary [school] me go a foreign." Young people dream

145

of going off mainly to America; others contemplate England or Canada.[109] A striking example was the nightmare of a young nephew of Captain Currie. After he had spent several months in America, his corpse was returned to Jamaica; the abeng sounded mournfully to announce this arrival. When young people go to the metropolis (whether Kingston or New York), most of them experience the problems of daily survival rather than lack of status symbols, even for those privileged to find a place to live with relatives in the big city. Urban hustling that eventually leads to shady dealings is often the only short-term solution. "You stay hungry one day and maybe a second, but not a third one," as the president of the youth club of Moore Town (who is quite young himself) explained the situation to me (conversation of January 5, 1988) in summarizing the perspective of his generation.

Maroons of the older generation repeatedly express their concern about this momentous sociocultural development (for example, the historian of Accompong, Mann O. Rowe, conversation of January 5, 1988, and Captain Currie, conversation of January 8, 1988). "We refer to it as a brain drain from the community, because since they cannot produce the things and get money for it, you find that many of them have left the community and they have gone to Kingston as well as many of them have gone to foreign lands to see for the better living" (Colonel Cawley, interview of January 13, 1988). Without of course being able to offer ready solutions, Colonel Cawley hopes for a gradual improvement of the current situation for young people by employing traditional cooperative strategies.

The successful Maroon Cooperative Talent Incorporated (The Maroon Cultural Centre) under the direction of Roy Harris demonstrates one actual initiative of this type. The cooperative's explicit goal is to create work opportunities without the usual exploitative conditions. In the form of a permanent workshop,[110] the organization, which now boasts two hundred members, brings together a multitude of talents ranging from crafts (such as needlework) to repair work (refrigerator and oven repair) to artistry (woodcarving, painting, music) and agricultural operations, to name just a few examples.

In 1988, work began on a cultural center in Accompong to promote the creative talents of young Maroons. The goal of such cooperative efforts is to retain or cultivate the interest of young people in Maroon culture, thereby reinforcing their sense of identity. At the same time, these efforts create institutions that make it possible to handle increasing tourism to the former rebel villages without compromising the general good of the community and undergoing painful experiences of cultural "bulldoz-ing."

Will these isolated initiatives suffice to inspire more young people to stay put, or will the "American dream" result in cultural hibernation? Maroons respond to these questions with a shrug of the shoulders and a terse "me no know."

"Children of One Belly?"
The Kinship System

Ethnological analysis of the political, legal, socioeconomic, and lin-guistic characteristics of the Maroons shows that there are numerous unresolved questions, as we have seen. The kinship systems raise even more such questions. Uncertainty on this subject stems in part from the fact that until recently, white authors were not very interested in this per-sonal sphere of the free black communities or never reached sufficient familiarity to be able to learn even the most important categories of their familial systems. We should also not ignore the likelihood that Maroons were also not especially keen on having the intimate details of their social lives researched by white social scientists who would then divulge this information to a broad public. Knowing that an increase in information for the state (once colonialist, now nationalist) power also inevitably pro-duces an improvement of the instruments of control, it is plausible that they showed themselves unwilling to disclose kinship relations to *obroni* (strangers) (Müller 1988:133). Centuries of experience with the "divide and rule" policy suggest good reasons for the reluctance of the Maroons to transmit substantial insights into their internal affairs.

A factor that contributed to these particular (negative) conditions of research was the link between the genealogical concepts of the Maroons and the "First Time." As Price was to learn right from the initial phase of his fieldwork with the Saramaka Maroons of Suriname, knowledge of the formative phase of the Maroon communities is difficult to come by. During his first stay in Saramaka, only one topic was overtly taboo: "Stretching roughly to 1800, 'First-Time' is not more 'mythologized' or less accurately recalled than the more recent past, but knowledge of First-Time is singularly circumscribed, restricted, and guarded. It is the foun-tainhead of collective identity; it contains the true root of what it means to be Saramaka" (Price 1983b:6). For the Saramakas, First-Time knowl-edge relates to the older and larger social communities or clans, the for-

147

mation of which can be traced back matrilineally to an original rebel group as the oldest ancestors of the clans. Therefore, specialized knowledge about the past means power in a real sense, and is invoked to resolve land disputes and other rivalries by proving prior rights favoring one's own clan (see Price 1983b:7).

Applied to the Jamaican situation, this particular obstacle for passing on knowledge concerning genealogical and ancestral relations seems virtually irrelevant, for lack of a comparable clan organization, but other barriers to transmission are at work. Maroon historians, such as Mann O. Rowe in Accompong, are fully aware of the social power of their knowledge and therefore only allow so much of it to "flash up" in conversation as to prove their competence, but are on guard against transmitting all the knowledge stored in their memories. In order to pass along information, they also need the permission or an explicit charge by the "transcendental power"—the very ancestors who founded the Maroon genealogy. "Me 'ave fe get de duty. If dem nuh tell me fo do it, me cyaan't do it. Me 'ave fe go by the rule. So me a pickney. Dey teach me. So if dem tell me: Don't do dat ting, I cyaan't do it. An 'if yu went to me for a ting, an' dey no tell me fe gi' yu, me cyaan't gi' yu" (myal woman Mrs. Gladdys Foster, interview of January 10, 1988; see Glossary at the end of this book).

Despite these obstacles to research—especially mistrust of white and black outsiders, who were the traditional enemies—ethnologists and social anthropologists such as Richard Price have tried to gain acceptance as apprentices of the Maroon historians in order to follow the only culturally acceptable course to learn about First-Time knowledge. Their motivations are not only historical interest in the oral traditions that reach far back chronologically, but also what they reveal about the genealogical systems of

Gladdys Foster, former head of a revival community and myal specialist of the Accompong Maroons

the Maroons. Bilby (1984:11), in his study of the creation myth of the Windward Maroons, has emphasized the extent to which the principles of genealogical kinship rooted in the First Time continue to shape social relations among the Maroons today. Grandy Nanny occupies a central position in their social classification system. For the Windward Maroons of today, Nanny is considered not only the cultural heroine and successful spiritual and political leader, but also an "apical ancestress":

> Grandy Nanny is the "mother" of the Maroons, and all present day Maroons are her "yoyo"—meaning in the Kromanti ritual language "offspring" or "children." It is by virtue of their ostensible common descent from Grandy Nanny (the title "grandy" preceding her name itself Jamaican Creole for "grandmother") that all Maroons, regardless of whether or not actual genealogical ties can be shown to exist between them, are held to belong to a single family. (Bilby 1984:11f.)

Windward Maroons continue to base both their "familial membership" in the genealogically-based Maroon nation and their ambivalent and socially distanced, but essentially familial relationship to other Jamaicans on the mythic oral tradition of the familial rupture between Nanny and her sister. "The children of Grandy Nanny's sister may be only distant kin, but they are nevertheless kin" (Bilby 1984:17). The same vision of a blood tie that linked the defiant Nanny to her "pacifist" sister still forms the basis of the social relations between the two kinship groups, which arose from dual ethnogenesis.

In a similar vein, the biotic brother-sister relationship of Kojo and Nanny guides relations between Windward and Leeward Maroons, with the significant difference that there was no rupture between Kojo and Nanny as there had been between Nanny and her sister. Each year, Nanny is said to visit her brother and his living relations on the day preceding the official festival, January 5, in Accompong, to partake in the more intimate communal festivities of the deceased Old Time people with their living descendants (Mrs. Gladdys Foster, interview of January 10, 1988). Whether the Accompong Maroons enjoy a similar oral tradition reflecting the relations to non-Maroons is just as unclear to historians as is the actual genealogical position of Kojo himself. Unlike the Windward Maroons' relationship to Grandy Nanny, the Accompong Maroons do not define their connection to Kojo in terms of kinship. Instead, they generally use a military title, but in a ritual context they address him as "Master," reflecting his leadership role in the transcendental world. This terminological distinction is evident in Mrs. Foster's designation "Master Sister" for Nanny. There appears very little on the identity of the parents of Nanny and Kojo, although their common genealogical descent from the Ashanti supreme god *nyankopan* lurks through the oral tradition. It should be noted that Moore Town, Charles Town, and Accompong terms for "god and earth" (*nyankopan asase*) closely resemble West African Akan linguistic forms (for a discussion of this issue including the appropriate orthography, see Dalby 1971:41; see also a pamphlet of the Maroons Federal House of Assembly [Maroons Federation], which calls its members "Nanny, Cudjoe, Quao Nyankipon children of the true and living God").

There have been repeated efforts to confirm the findings of Dallas (1803:31), who claimed to have uncovered evidence of earlier kinship systems with a lineage or clan organization based on the diverse self-designations of the Maroons as Kyatawud, Kencuffee, and Yenkunkun (Schafer 1973:66; see also Dunham 1946:76, who speaks of a "Rowe clan"; also Dalby 1971:33 and Bilby 1984:13, who are less supportive of this view). Kopytoff (1976:49) has, however, insisted that no proof exists for a past or present lineage or clan organization among the Maroons of Jamaica such as it has existed among the Maroons of Suriname since the First Time. Essentially, the villages of the Maroons of Suriname,[111] which are inhabited by a few hundred people on average, are comprised of a social core of matrilinear relatives and their spouses plus some descendants of the lineage men (see Sally Price 1984:11). "Matriliny dominates descent ideology, with 'matriclans' and 'matrilineages' (the exact definitions of which vary from tribe to tribe) forming the basic units of the formal social structure" (Price 1983a:295).

The genealogy of the matrilinear kinship system of the Ndjuka (Maroons of Suriname) embraces only women who trace their heritage to a common female ancestor. According to Köbben (1983:321), virtually all legal, political, economic, and religious relations in the village are expressed in terms of kinship. The matrilineal descendants of the female ancestor Afo Tesa form the nucleus of the settlement. They are "the people of the belly" (*bé-sama*). The "fathers made them children" (*dada-mekepikin*) descendants of the men of the matrilineage, who are not themselves members of the lineage, but who live in the village, are the second group. The third category is formed of the affines (*konlibi*), those who came to stay. This category consists primarily of men. The Ndjuka sharply differentiate among these three categories and assign them rights and duties that vary by category (Köbben 1983:322).

Matrilinear groups combine several "bellies" (matrilineages), which together form a matriclan (*lo*). If, for instance, a "lo" consists of five "bellies," the kinship genealogy is traced back to the apical ancestry of five sisters. Matrilinear Akan influence is unmistakable, but patrilinear organizational characteristics of other African kinship systems are also evident (Köbben 1983:323f.). In one respect, they do differ from West African matrilinear societies: Every matriclan is traceable to a particular group of runaways, which included the sisters (linked by a biotic relationship) that established the lineage.[112]

One specific aspect makes ethnological consideration of Maroon kinship systems especially interesting and more useful than the justly criticized "kinship algebra." In contrast to the enslaved black people on the plantations, the free blacks could "order" their familial structures themselves. In the process, they could incorporate African "grammatical forms," as they did in so many other endeavors. The issue of whether recent kinship systems and familial relations build on surviving African concepts, norms, and behavior patterns, or should be attributed to the devastation of slavery is often discussed because of its implications for the all-important question of identity in today's Caribbean societies (see, for example, Higman 1979:41ff., Genovese 1981:53, and Hill 1980:83f.). A comparison to organizational structures of the Maroons, who stood to the slaves in an antithetical relationship of free to oppressed, could provide valuable clues (Besson 1995:196ff.).

A route of entry to a scholarly endeavor of this sort can be found by contrasting non-unilinear kinship groups of slaves in Suriname, who are composed cognatically from all bilateral descendants of a particular person brought from Africa with the matrilinear kinship groups of the Maroons of the same country (see Mintz/Price 1976:35ff.). More can be gained from an examination of the "children of one belly" kinship system and all its Caribbean features both for an intercultural comparison between various Maroon communities on the one hand and between Maroons and non-Maroons on the other as well as from structural analogies between individual kinship systems or elements in the Caribbean and similar identified forms in Africa.

"The Girl has Killed Hog":
Gender Imbalance in Maroon Communities

Although the isolation of the Maroon villages served to protect estab-lished sociocultural organizational forms, it posed an enormous econom-ic hardship and therefore an existential threat. When young Maroons were integrated into the urban service sector, as they inevitably were, the ongoing isolation of the Maroon enclaves lost much of its function of cul-tural protection. The consequent changes in family structures and gender relations are quite evident. Since it was mostly young men who left the country for urban centers, the result in the settlements was gender dis-proportion. Young women often live with children of an earlier relation-ship under their parents' roof, while their former partners only return to visit for the January 6 independence celebrations, if they return at all. The inevitable consequence of this continual separation of partners is the child-rearing system of "my mother who fathered me," which was ana-lyzed in a 1966 book of the same title by Edith Clarke. "I don't have to read that book because that's exactly what I experienced already in my own life," declared Henry Fitzroy, a young Maroon from Accompong liv-ing in Kingston, concerning his personal childhood recollections (conver-sation of March 20, 1988).

If the woman also moves to a big city with a male partner or alone, the children remain in the care of their grandparents (Hill 1980:83) or, if they are for some reason unable to care for them, are brought up by a mater-nal figure who is not a blood relation. Women like Mrs. Cawley (the mother of the Colonel) have brought up so many foster children that they are called "Auntie" by the entire community (Mrs. Cawley—"Auntie Bee"—conversation of January 12, 1988).

Frequently, male Maroons who leave the community to work else-where choose what they call "outsiders" (non-Maroons) as partners and return to the villages with them years later. In former times, only women were allowed to bring male "outsiders" into the village, not the other way around. Schafer (1973:233f.) sees the origin of this unequal gender treat-ment with the matrilinear "children of one belly" kinship system, accord-ing to which the (Maroon) identity of the mother is constitutive for the (Maroon) identity of her children.[113] This author reports that today, both men and women are able to cohabit with non-Maroons in their villages, with the stipulation that a man seeking entry into the community be required to pay an admission fee ("vooten") "to buy himself in" and undergo an initiation rite in the form of an entrance examination.

In any case, both men and women who return to the Maroon villages bring with them urban notions of the nuclear family, which has led to a gradual move away from the model of the extended family. In general, the woman moves to the house of the man to establish a nuclear family household with virilocal residence. "Man builds his own house to receive his wife. After the house built and finish, then the marriage come out" (Mrs. Hilda, interview of January 13, 1988). Maroon marriage ceremonies no longer differ from those of other Jamaicans. Even the "older heads" know of the old traditions to prepare for and celebrate a wedding only from stories, but have not experienced them personally (the storyteller Thomas Rowe, interview of January 12, 1988). Mr. Rowe can still recall from his youth that a hog was slaughtered to serve at wedding receptions, but his knowledge of initiation rites for Maroon girls (chronicled by Dallas 1803:115) comes only from oral tradition.

In these initiation rites, as soon as a girl reaches the age of matrimony, the parents would have a feast, the centerpiece of which could be the slaughtering of a hog.[114] This ritual served to announce that their daughter had now reached womanhood and could entertain proposals of marriage. The metaphor "the girl has killed hog" defined her new status as eligible for matrimony. As a kind of advance contribution to the future dowry, the guests would place a coin in the mouth of the young woman. Her own parents would give her a gold coin. Dallas reports that this ceremony also included dancing and drinking rum[115] (see also Cassidy 1982:221 and Schafer 1973:70).

Neat categorization of Jamaican Maroon communities into monogamous Windward Maroons and polygynous Leeward Maroons by authors from the colonial period, namely Edwards (1983:241) and Dallas (1803:108ff.), must also be taken with a large grain of salt as far as historical authenticity is concerned. Even frequent citation in modern literature fails to lend it credibility in the absence of new empirical documentation. Reading Edwards' (1983:241) "cultural descriptions" in their racist context sorely tempts us to dismiss anything he has to say on the subject: ". . . the Maroons, like all other savage nations, regarded their wives as so many beasts of burthen; and felt no more concern at the loss of one of them, than a white planter would have felt at the loss of a bullock. Polygamy too, with their other African customs, prevailed among the Maroons universally."

It strains credulity to imagine that the Windward Maroons punished every act of adultery by death so as to avert social unrest (Price 1983a:19; also Craton 1982:82), while at the same time polygyny was the norm among Kojo's Maroons (Dallas 1803:110; also Schafer 1973:69). Two passages in Namba Roy's ethnological novel *Black Albino* (1986:3, 28) offer a more plausible scenario. These passages describe the right of Maroon warriors to cohabit with another woman if they were unable to conceive children with their first wife.

In any description of gender and family relations between Maroons, the long course of their social existence must be taken into account. A "social jigsaw puzzle" thrown together from various eras, which builds on unreliable sources to start with, cannot address the question of the possible change of social structures during a societal history of nearly 350 years. Although definitive indications of dynamic developments for the formative phase seem virtually out of the question, oral traditions could provide valuable information at least for the last century. It would therefore make more sense to look into more recent developments of social structures with communicative approaches to gain a way of measuring its progressive changes occasioned by the "opening to the outside." The disproportionately high number of men who left the villages and the relationships between men and women need to be examined. Certainly a great deal of ethnological and other research remains to be done. It appears obvious that the historical source material has little of value to contribute to this pursuit.

Grandy Nanny's Symbolic Significance for Jamaican Women

"Old Nanny," as Burning Spear calls her in his "reggae homage" "Queen of the Mountain" (on the 1985 LP *Resistance*), is considered the personified symbol of black resistance against white oppression by the Maroons and others. In the historical perspective of Maroon oral tradition, she played the key role both in the armed struggle against the colonial power and in founding the Maroon nation. In our time, however, her symbolic force covers a broader target group and reaches into social spheres that are directly linked to the confrontation between black and white. As a personified antithesis to subjugation in reaction to repression, she inspires not only the insubordination of black people against the roles assigned to them in the western hemisphere, but also stimulates the potential for resistance of black women against their assigned roles within their group. In this sense, "old Nanny" lives in the collective consciousness of emancipation movements, with contours that vary accord-

Nanny of the Maroons on the Jamaican $500 bill

ing to the chosen emphasis of the particular group to be liberated.

It is obvious that Maroons choose to stress different personality and character traits from Black Power organizations or black women's movements. However, the fact that they all join in hailing Nanny as the symbol of resistance indicates a congruence of their goals, as the feminist drama and writing collective Sistren (ed.: Ford-Smith 1986:XXIf.) has noted: "The struggle of women as a whole within radical movements for the recognition of their own autonomy. . . must be matched by a struggle against racism and class privilege in the women's movement itself."

Among the Windward Maroons of Moore Town, Charles Town, and Scott's Hall, Nanny is *the* central social figure.[116] She is considered the apical (mythological) ancestress—"mother of mothers"—queen, "chieftainess," "goddess," and "higher science."[117] As an obeah-woman, she even surpasses the supernatural abilities of Kojo (myal specialist Mrs. Gladdys Foster, interview of January 12, 1988). Her *yoyo* (descendants or children) consider her original place of residence, Nanny Town, the holy place of Jamaica, which is associated with her obeah science and is therefore subject to certain taboos (Dalby 1971:48).

Most Maroon oral traditions about Nanny focus on her safeguarding role in war. According to these narratives, she was able to use her ritual powers to weaken the enemy psychologically and render her own warriors invincible. One of her alleged abilities was to determine the best moment for waging war; she could also keep a large cauldron boiling with her supernatural gifts at the foot of the precipice of Nanny Town, which would lure curious British troops into it, resulting in their demise (Mathurin 1975:36). By far the most popular account of Nanny's gifts, however was her reported ability to catch cannonballs between her buttocks and to fart them back with deadly force. Craton (1982:81) finds many African parallels to this myth during the long period of resistance to the Europeans, which might of course also bear testimony to the racist and misogynist attitudes of the colonial reporters (see Zips 1998a:203). The feminist writing collective Sistren (ed. Ford-Smith 1986:xvi) suggests that stories of this sort need decoding to sharpen women's awareness of social contradictions: ". . . the tale is offering a greater truth—one which states that the female body brings forth life. In so doing women can turn back death. And so these stories are invaluable in the effort to change the effect of oppressive forces on our lives."

The Maroons trace their own identity in part to the historical singularity of their "mother of mothers." By contrast, in modern feminist literature, Nanny embodies an African-Caribbean female model whose distinguishing traits are evident precisely in the manifold past and present struggles for black women's liberation. The rebel Nanny is now called "Ni" so as not to be confused with the opposite model of the domesticated, complacent servant who, in her capacity as "black mammy" and "nanny" of the manor house, loved her own oppressors. All Caribbean women who feel bound to the same traditions of African self-confidence and willingness to register opposition of the women are said to lay claim to "her" (Ni's) legacy. Ni's historical uniqueness could thus be relativized in the larger collective framework of experience of the insubordination of black women:

> Ni was not merely an exceptional woman. Her power was under-pinned by several factors—material and cultural. It drew on the tradition of the Ohemaa [the Ashanti Queen Mother]; on the control which African women had over agriculture in Maroon society; on the specific needs of the war effort as well as the circumstances of sexuality which existed in the rebel communities of the time. Other black women drew strength from these traditions too. Cubah, for instance, was to have been Queen of Kingston, if the rebellion in which she was involved had succeeded, and the earliest Maroons of the seventeenth century had a Coromantee Queen. The legacy of these women belongs to all Caribbean women who try to change oppressive circumstances in which they find themselves.[118] (Sistren/Ford-Smith, ed. 1986:xiv)

It is obviously inappropriate to the African-Caribbean women's movement to draw rigid contrasts between the clichéd images of women of the active woman rebel (Ni or Nanny) and the passive "black mammy" (nanny) (so often depicted in the melodramatic slave epics of Hollywood), which only solidifies existing stereotypes. It is time to dissolve oppositions that are only apparently absolute and ferret out the hidden potential for resistance of the rebellious Ni (Nanny) behind the better-known image of the domesticized nanny.[119]

To recognize her it may be necessary to readjust one's senses of the rules of resistance and the limits of power. It may be necessary to seek her out over the years in odd places beside the stove, sweeping the yard or crouched over a pan of clothes. It may mean coming to terms with ways in which ordinary women have determined their own struggles for themselves and the ways in which they have assessed their own victories and defeats. (Sistren/Ford-Smith, ed. 1986:xivf.)

The concepts of struggle, strategy, and women's resistance in general could be redefined to insure that the heroization of Ni's historical role does not obscure the "small" victories and defeats of black women in their diverse everyday struggles. Even if only few women entered into an open confrontation with their oppressor as had Nanny or Cubah, many women continue to share the experience of repression and their own revolt against it. This resistance, by turns overt and covert, was nurtured by the tradition of pride and self-respect of black women, and was never completely undermined even in the face of humiliation, force, and exploitation.[120] "This sort of heritage produced rebels and ensured that there would always be women among the rebels"[121] (Mathurin 1975:3).

Even when women did not take on the role of rebels in the strict sense of the term, they did rebel in many situations against their social status as enslaved women in particular within the framework of the living conditions of black people. Their economic resistance during the period of slavery, for example by refusing to work, by working in agricultural subsistence production, and especially by marketing agrarian products to provide for themselves cannot be separated from the larger context of societal resistance by both males and females.[122] This must also be true of their cultural insubordination, which was expressed in "making war with words," in obeah rituals to maintain their religious integrity (and, on occasion, to poison their white masters), or quite generally in preserving their identity (Mathurin 1975:7ff., 11ff.; see also Bastide 1983:196). Although suffering the brunt of economic and sexual exploitation, they did not resign themselves to the role of victim, but rather resisted oppression along the same lines as the "other sex." For this reason, we will not be focusing on gender-specific black resistance except in unusual cases that warrant separate treatment. In both qualitative and quantitative respects, there were no major differences between the manners in which men and women expressed their resistance, except when a logical division of labor was clearly mandated, notably during armed battles of the Maroons. Women and men rejected the systematic oppression of slavery and colonialism to the same degree and revolted together (Mathurin 1975:23ff.).

It is difficult to say whether it was primarily the change in gender relations in recent years and decades that worked to the disadvantage of women or rather changed viewpoints that were decisive in tracking down and attacking ingrained inequities. (Black) Women's Studies, feminist research, and critical gender approaches in the social sciences have become increasingly prominent and are now thematizing gender inequalities. Sistren is concentrating its dramatic[123] and literary work on the ways in which social inequity determines the horizons of black women: ". . . many of the same determining forces impact on the lives of the women: migration pulling like a magnet, female unemployment or underemployment, the failure of the educational system, rapid urban industrialization, inadequate housing, violence as the supreme and ultimate expression of power, manipulation of sexuality in order to dominate, the failure of present political structures" (Sistren/Ford-Smith, ed. 1986:xvi).

The situation of women in the Maroon villages strikingly resembles that of their counterparts in the rest of Jamaica. Maroon men seek work in the cities or in western metropoles in disproportionate numbers and leave their partners behind with instructions to "mind baby." Only in rare cases do these women receive adequate financial support when their husbands work abroad. The resulting dire situation means that women fail to get adequate job training, which widens the already substantial gap in their chances for a decent career.

Maroon women have reacted to social change in a variety of ways. Here, too, they have not resigned themselves to the role of the silently suffering woman sacrificing herself for her children. Instead, they have stepped up their economic, cultural, and political activities. Until a few years ago, they were scarcely involved in the political decision-making processes of the Maroon states. Today, they represent a full half of the

"Auntie Bee" Cawley (center), the wife of the former Colonel in Accompong, with her son Harris N. Cawley (left), himself a Colonel in the 1980s

Council members in Accompong (Thomas Rowe, interview of January 12, 1988). The increasing acceptance of women into the Council by Colonel Cawley was the expression of a need for their expanded participation in the political decision-making process. Reading between the lines of an interview with Colonel Cawley (on January 13, 1988), I find it evident that their political participation is an outgrowth of their growing social power: "Yes, in days gone by, many women were not involved in the decision making of the community. So since I came now and since we have prominent women, I thought it best that we should include women in the Council. So women have been brought in."

Although no woman has ever run for the office of Colonel in the history of the Maroon communities, their informal influence on the decisions of the Maroon "head of state" should not be underestimated. This influence applies not only to the social force of what Colonel Cawley calls "prominent women," but also to their familial proximity to the elected person of the Colonel, which is not simply reducible to the role of a representative First Lady standing in the shadow of her husband. McIver (1984:2) considers Mrs. "Auntie Bee" Cawley, the wife of a former Colonel and the mother of a more recent Colonel, to have been one of the most influential and powerful members of the Accompong Maroon community. Political continuity and social cohesion are defined by women like Mrs. Cawley, who claimed (conversation of January 8, 1988) that her son made important decisions only after consulting with her.

Women are making great strides in achieving gender equality in politics, but on the cultural level they already occupy a leading position. Their cultural "dominance," which is especially evident in the religious sphere and during the annual celebrations of independence, is also confirmed by Thomas Rowe (interview of January 12, 1988) when answering the question as to whether young Maroons could learn the Kromanti language and other cultural traditions from him: "No. . . you have other people in the culture who you can learn from, as my sister, who is the head, who is the governess fe de culture."

The long-standing tradition of Maroon women as religious authorities and ritual specialists, going back to the most renowned *obeah specialist* Nanny, also symbolizes their central significance for the preservation of cultural identity, which should not be misinterpreted as cultural or political conservatism. Rather, the achievements of Maroon women in keeping their culture intact characterize the cultural dynamics, as is particularly evident in their economic crisis management.

Maroon women have reacted to the gender imbalance of the Maroon community caused by the rural exodus of numerous young men by recourse to their traditional domain of agricultural subsistence production. They have also steeped up their involvement in sidewalk vending (*higglering*)[124] and other forms of marketing farm commodities (Mrs. Hilda, conversation of January 12, 1988; also Colonel Cawley, interview of January 13, 1988). In Accompong, some women have also opened small grocery and dry goods stores to insure the living standard of their families.

In Maroon communities, women and men have always contributed in equal measure to the social, economic, political, and cultural survival of the "states within a state." The last few years, though, have seen rapid social change, and male Maroons in particular have been acknowledging the extraordinary achievements of women (according to Colonel Cawley, ibid). McIver (1984:73) correctly sums up the situation in the following remark: "After Nanny there were other Maroon women who struggled to defend the unity and identity of their people." This historical fact justifies interpreting Nanny's personality traits as an expression of the pride and the assertiveness of African-Caribbean women. Only then can the stories of "old Nanny" be understood as a component of the historical experience of black women in the Caribbean and their symbolic power for the critical struggles women are now facing.

"Condemned to Die?"
Traditions in Decline

It is the same old song heard around the world. With magnetic appeal to the younger generation, westernized concepts of "modernity" are displacing the world view and related cultural traditions of their elders. Cultural and social anthropologists often consider the loss of traditions deplorable and try to preserve them. With the deepening of their historical perspective, they themselves tend to become specialists in competition with the indigenous bearers of knowledge. In other words, they gain the symbolic capital of historical knowledge by traditional means of oral transmission. In several respects, scholarly engagement with Maroon culture has been no exception. However, their past experience with *obroni* (outsiders or non-Maroons) has put them on their guard when it comes to comprehensive transmission of their knowledge to "strangers."

Knowledge is power, and communicating knowledge communicates power—perhaps even power over the informer's own society. Maroons hold to the principle: "He that keepeth his mouth, keepeth his life." Those who violate the norms of secrecy lay themselves open to the retaliatory measures of their dead ancestors. Ritual knowledge, which is an important component of cultural identity, should therefore remain restricted to the small circle of "legitimately" initiated Maroons and be guarded from the prying eyes of foreign visitors. Maroons employ various strategies, which are not even recognizable as such to the outsider, to screen their secret knowledge from the outside world. "Non-Maroons are not permitted to learn of these things. There are supernatural sanctions against imparting Maroon knowledge to outsiders, and thus Maroons have developed patterned ways of 'dodging' the queries of meddlesome outsiders" (Bilby 1981:77). According to Bilby, the Maroons use a special word, *jijifo*, to designate this shrewd evasion of the need to answer questions politely. *Jijifo* derives etymologically from the Twi expression *gyigyé* (a collective term for various forms of deception). The idea is to mislead the questioners by evasion or deceit (see Thomas Martin 1973:134ff.; also Price 1983b:14ff., who had similar experiences among the Saramakas of Suriname).

In the light of this system of protection, particular information and attitudes of Maroons can be interpreted in at least two ways. If, for example, Colonel Harris of Moore Town experiences difficulties in translating a Kromanti text, as with the appointment of a new Lieutenant on the day honoring Nanny, October 16, 1985, and has to locate a "prompter" from among the crowd, who can communicate at least some sense of the contents of the inaugural address spoken by him, it can mean that the Colonel himself has forgotten the meaning of the text, that he does not wish to reveal its contents himself, or that he is proscribed from doing so. The conclusions we might draw from these interpretive variants directly contradict one another. The first possibility suggests a substantial loss of meaning of formerly significant cultural traditions; the others speak to its continued vitality, manifested by the very intention of maintaining its secrecy. In other words, the first possibility would demonstrate that the Kromanti formula had degenerated to an empty phrase, having already lost its actual meaning; the latter possibilities, that feigning lack of knowledge would be an indicator of the unaltered power of specialized knowledge and thus a cultural affirmation of the inalienable Maroon identity. Stymying scholarly interpretive efforts in the religious and ritualistic complex is, understandably, an important evasive strategy of the Maroons.

This evaluation of the particular stance of the Maroons toward the outside world regarding their First-Time culture Kromanti seems fundamental. Outsiders should not be overly hasty and base their judgments of social reality on first impressions. It was certainly striking that whenever I steered the conversation to Kromanti language or dance (since it was highly unlikely that they would broach these topics themselves), the Maroons answered curtly and evasively, for example with the question: "Kromanti? How do you spell that?" Mrs. Gladdys Foster, a myal specialist, is the exception in this regard. During my very first visit, she sought communication with the "Master" (Kojo) by libations such as pouring out rum and "blowing rum" (spraying rum from the mouth) to get his permission to talk to me about myal. After she had poured the tenth libation on the floor in front of her wooden house, she addressed Kojo with the following words: "Ten bokkle more. Master, is de ten fe yu, sir. And I give yu ten. Me de beg yu, loose me hand now. Choose de man deh, choose yah man deh." Once Kojo had given his explicit approval to her, she was able to communicate parts of her knowledge to an outsider without fear of reprisals from Kojo.[125]

Numerous reports in a similar vein (see, for example, Bilby 1981:76ff.; Thomas Martin 1973:134ff.) should suffice to lead us to two inescapable conclusions, namely that we should respect the Maroon desire for self-protection expressed by their secrecy, and that it would be misguided to pronounce their culture dead. Apparent disappearance or simple lack of visibility does not necessarily indicate that cultural traditions have died off, but more likely that they are elusive to the casual observer. Now that travel agencies organize so-called educational and cultural Cockpit Tours to the Maroon enclaves, sometimes even in collaboration with the Maroon administration, which welcomes the additional revenue, these protective measures seem warranted. When Maroons put on music and dance performances for tourists in front of the monument to Kojo, they are quite deliberately offering a folklore demonstration devoid of meaning. Kromanti language and dance are reserved for transcendental interaction with the dead. First-Time Maroons are firmly against *obroni* snapping photographs. The issue of whether the changing situation in the course of increasing tourism, migration, and other forms of interaction will lead to a weakening of the social power of the "dead"[126] and therefore of Maroon identity as a whole is moot even for cultural specialists of the Maroons (Thomas Rowe, interview of January 12, 1988; see also Bilby 1981:90).

Entrusting very young Maroons with important tasks—both the abeng blower and one of the drummers of Accompong are fairly young—obviously gainsays this notion. The "older heads," steeped in the Kromanti tradition, have preserved their authority and respect from all sides right up to the present day, which is evident from the lack of any serious conflict between the generations. Building on these foundations, they can fulfill their role as guardian of the collective identity as Maroons.

Historians, Storytellers, Healers, and Spiritual Mediums as Preservers of Collective Identity

Stored away almost exclusively in the mental "archives" of a very small number of specialists, both men and women, is the knowledge that is kept concealed from outsiders. Their task is not only to preserve it mentally, but also to pass it on and disseminate it in a cautious manner. Passing knowledge on means schooling apprentices. Dissemination encompasses the duties that normally fall to specific areas of expertise, namely public lectures for historians, public readings for storytellers, medical and psychological treatment for healers, and contact to the transcendental world for spiritual mediums. The two complexes of tasks, namely transmission and dissemination, also differ substantially in their teleological orientation. As an oral tradition in the narrow sense, the former activity intends passing on comprehensive personal knowledge and the social status inscribed in it. It involves the teacher as a representative of the elder generation and an apprentice of the next generation. The lat-ter set of public activities, by contrast, involves the community at large through individual performance and participation by all. Both forms pro-vide the means to maintain historical continuity and social cohesion.

In this system of "mental archivization" of knowledge and its oral tra-dition, a great deal of responsibility falls to the individual specialist, since the portion of cultural or social knowledge he or she preserves is destined to be lost to posterity if the specialist forgets it or dies. If he or she wish-es to avert losing these abilities and transmitted knowledge, a reasonable portion must be passed on in time in order to share the responsibility with the collective or a successor, which requires a basic willingness to apportion at least part of his social power. Taking on and storing tradi-tional knowledge in turn demands a high degree of collective interest, which nowadays competes with other cultural phenomena. For example, most young Maroons know more reggae texts than Anansi stories or Maroon songs. In any case, for the aforementioned reasons, only a rela-tively general and fundamental portion of the complete store of knowl-edge is preserved collectively, while highly specialized knowledge, espe-cially from the First Time, is accumulated in the heads of individual experts (see Price 1983b:8ff., who notes this in reference to the Maroons of Suriname).

Colonel Cawley (interview of January 13, 1988) does confirm that a portion of specialized knowledge is passed on by experts to the next gen-eration, but not nearly enough for his liking: "They mostly conserve and that is what we are losing out on. There for instance you have the herbal-ist Marilou Rose, and she knows a lot about bushes, and if you are sick, she could tell you what kind a bush to use for that special kind of sick-ness. But over the years now, she has not imparted such knowledge to people and we find that much of that had been lost."

This loss of knowledge has adversely affected the detailed specialized knowledge of pharmacology that had been cultivated for ages (Price 1983a:10; also Montejo 1968:105). Although a general, collectively pre-served segment of their "house medicine" is still intact, the waning degree of medical knowledge threatens the continued existence of tradi-tional Maroon medical practices. The construction of a clinic financed mainly from outside the community and the search for a doctor trained in western medicine are concrete evidence of this development[127] (Colonel Deputee Williams, conversation of January 5, 1988).

Just as the art of healing is systematically learned by so very few, expert knowledge of history is also exclusively limited to a small circle of professional or self-taught historians. Only Maroons are eligible, since particular abilities and attributes can only be transmitted "in the blood" and necessarily exclude outsiders (Bilby 1984:14). Both the range and the precision of knowledge distinguish an expert as an exceptional historian. Not only one's individual potential, but also the social position and reputation of informants and of teachers (usually relatives) determine the value of one's knowledge. Many narrative expositions of history are documented with source material about the informants and the origin of the oral tradition (see Price 1983b:8ff.).

Besides historians, it is the storytellers "who know things."[128] They too function as mental "archivists" to preserve the continuity of oral tradition. Of course their primary task is not the preservation of the oral tradition, but communicative cultural and symbolic recounting of the stories of Anansi (also called Ananse), "old witches," *duppies* (spirits), and seafarers. A strongly symbolic status fell most of all to the "fictitious" Akan cultural icon Anansi among the African-Jamaicans, and especially among the Maroons (Patterson 1973:250ff.; also Barrett 1979:34). As a spider with the human capabilities of cunning and trickery, he has personified an identification figure in Jamaica for a long time, owing to his arsenal of tricks in outsmarting stronger opponents (Peter Martin 1985:168ff.). "Doing an Anansi" still means achieving a victory or advantage by outwitting another.

In the social activity of storytelling, which is as much a means of expression of the culture as a whole as an individual ability of particular storytellers, the stories can also serve moralizing, therapeutic, and didactic functions (Abrahams 1983:158ff.). Anansi does not always win. If he behaves reprehensibly in the eyes of the storyteller and his public, he must often pay the price for his deceptions in the stories, to the delight of the audience, which identifies in this case with his adversary. The following text is an example of this type of story. It was told by Thomas Rowe on January 11, 1988, and is reproduced here as an unabridged transcription of the tape. The title of this story, which is one of the most popular of his repertory, is "Whitebelly mek Br'er Anansi kill him mother":

> Once there were two friends. One was Anansi and the other was Whitebelly. So dem have a family to maintain and life was very hard. So one day Whitebelly say to Anansi: Bredda Anansi, me can't take the hardness; you know. Me have fe do something that me can have food fe feed me family. Anansi say: Yes, Whitebelly, go run and get a machete and get a file. And he clear a nice piece of land, and

he plant it with corn.

In the meanwhile now Anansi, him walking up and down, doing nottin' until the corn strive good and just start to bear now, put out the. . . we call it the corn baby. Anansi pass one day and him see Whitebelly in deh. And him say: Bro Whitebelly, you corn strive good, man, and it start to bear too. But if you want some big ear a corn, go through and brek out all a dem likkle small one deh, and you will get some big ear ah corn. And Whitebelly tek him saying and he got through and him take out all the corn baby. And was waiting now to get some big ear ah corn. And instead a getting big ear ah corn, dem corn trees dem dry up. So him realize now that Anansi trick him. So him go away and him study, until him come to a decision now, that him going mek Anansi kill him mother. So him go all about and him borrow moneys from people, what is pure silver; until when him get enough one mawnin' him come out, and him cry out seh: Ma dead, Ma dead, ooiiihh. And the people come in, everybody come in, and they help him and they prepare for the funeral. . .

So the mawnin' now of the funeral; so they build the coffin and bore some hole in a de coffin and him cork it. So when the minister now come with the body to the grave, 'im say, ask the people dem to lift up the coffin fe him and him spread a white sheet underneat and 'im say: Ma, what yu got fe gi' me, gi' me. Mek everybody see it. And 'im pull de cork out underneat de bottom a de coffin an' money pour out pon the sheet, money pour out pon the sheet.

Anansi was there now and he see that. Him say: Bwoy, look how Whitebelly Ma dead, lef 'im rich; and 'im travel back to him yard. And when him go there, him madder was inside the kitchen. And him go right inna de kitchen, and him take up the mortastick, and him lick the old lady inna her head. 'Im say: Dead you old buke, dead. Dead you riches gi' me, too. And the madder just pick you one dead. And when the madder dead now, him bawl out: Ma dead, oihh. Ma dead, ooeeh. And the people dem come in and them help him, too. And dem prepare for the funeral, same as what dem do for Whitebelly.

But Whitebelly now and the people dem, they talk up before, so dem know what going on. So 'im do everything same as what 'im see Whitebelly do. And when the body was to go down inna de grave now, 'im get 'im sheet and him spread it underneat an' him ask de man dem too to shake the coffin fe him, and they would be

shaking till now. Not a money come out. An' him feel sad and dis-
made that him go home.

And after a few days pass, Whitebelly invite him to a feast. An'
when him [Anansi] go 'round, and when he was eating, drinking
and when it sweet him, him say: Bro Whitebelly, a who cook dis yah
sweet sweet food? Whitebelly say: No, Ma cook i'. Him [Anansi]
say: No, man, the man a dead long time. Him [Whitebelly] say: No,
man, mind a kitchen. And when him go inna kitchen, 'im say: Come
mek me go show you. An' when 'im [Anansi] go inna kitchen an' go
see Whitebelly madder in deh, 'im does make so: . . . whoops. . .
and 'im never go back in de house fe go finish de feast. 'Im just run
outta de house, an' Whitebelly never see 'im again. Yunno, so it
does not pay a man to be too trick. Yes, so.

This story, which also appears in Tanna (1983:34 and 1984:86ff.),
reveals several metaphorical shifts. After Anansi tricks Whitebelly into

*Mrs. Cora Rowe, today one of Accompong's most respected moral authorities,
with her father in the 1930s in a pose of "traditional" Maroon defiance*

167

destroying his harvest, the latter takes revenge with a second trick by suggesting to Anansi that the (feigned) death of his mother has helped him gain unimaginable wealth. The envious Anansi then kills his own mother, as Whitebelly had anticipated, and only then learns that Whitebelly had outsmarted him. Disgruntled by his futile undertaking, he notices while dining at Whitebelly's house that Whitebelly's mother is still alive, while his "source of food" was destroyed by himself—in the same way that he had convinced Whitebelly at the beginning of the story to destroy his food supply for no good reason (Tanna 1983:29).[129]

Identification with Anansi therefore depends on his actual role in a given story. Although Anansi's traits can be compared to those of the Maroons, the fictional figure of the stories is not elevated to a cultural hero (Thomas Rowe, interview of January 12, 1988). For the cultural identity of the Maroons, the existence of the stories, the individual narrative abilities of the storyteller, and the social participation of the audience are more important than identification with the hero of the stories.

The storyteller of Accompong, Thomas Rowe (interview of January 12, 1988), attributes the continuing cultural significance of this declining art to an oral tradition going back to the days of the "old time people":

> Well, from time to time we understand that the older Maroons is this storytelling, and we call it Kromanti; is because dem they tek as entertainment, you see, because they were living in the woods without any other form of entertainments, so then at nights or whenever time dem 'ave little time, dem would sit and tell the younger one the story. Yes, then they would mek up the fire and dem sit around it, dem smoke dem pipe, dem tobacco, yu know, dance and sing Kromanti songs and entertain themselves. For the tradition now, it follow, coming right down, even though some change, because the younger ones, they are not so much interested in the old time things.

Of course, the verbal art of the old stories has found an overbearing competitor in reggae and the spontaneous art of "deejaying" or "toasting." But the sustained interest of some young Maroons in traditional culture as well as in modern trends shows that younger generations are obviously not ready to trade in their Maroon culture for urban culture. Social prestige is still bound up with the function of the *abeng* blower or "hornman" of the Maroons. Such a position, with its inherent symbolic recognition, continues to attract young people. The abeng, which had been used by the Akan of West Africa as a means of communication,[130] was similarly employed by the early Maroons to dispatch a "sophisticated vocabulary" (Schafer 1973:63). The abeng could inform villages as to the numbers of enemy troops, their weapons, and the routes they had taken (see also Campbell 1985:20f.). For this reason and others, the abeng represents perhaps the most important symbol of Maroon identity today.

Nonetheless, or perhaps precisely for this reason, it not only serves the purpose of symbolizing cultural identity, for example during celebrations that are open to the public. Its use on particular occasions shows that it is both expression and medium of Maroon cultural identity. Even if the two abeng blowers of Accompong are no longer in a position to transmit complex messages or to use tone variations to call particular individuals by name in the tradition of their ancestors of the First Time (Dallas 1803:89), their participation in, for instance, calling a meeting of the Maroons to announce a death,[131] digging a trench, announcing the return of a body to its home town as a final resting place, and for ceremonial purposes is considered indispensable.[132] The further use of the abeng as a means of alerting the community of danger and as a call to defense during police raids of the ganja fields qualifies as a parallel to the First Time.

The various cultural specialists can do justice to their role in preserving the collective identity of the Maroons because they maintain a connection to the first rebels who had founded the community. They view themselves as a temporary last link of a chain of oral traditions and are able to enter into direct interactive communication with the dead. To preserve their link to the dead, they need a means of communication intelligible to their ancestors. Besides the "speaking musical instruments," the drum and the abeng, they also use the verbal language of their forebears. "The ancestors have their own form of speech, quite different from that of living Maroons, and it is this which must be used in order to communicate with them. Any Kromanti Play, then, must involve not only the language of the living, but that of the dead as well" (Bilby 1983b:38).

Kromanti, the language of the dead, is used almost exclusively to communicate with dead ancestors during a Kromanti play (see Bilby 1979). Kromanti performances always aim for the participation of one or more "spirits" in healing the sick and other related purposes. These spirits' transcendental powers, related to the living ascendant, take possession of one dancer to be used as a spiritual medium. Participants in the ceremony who are not visited by an ancestral spirit can communicate with him solely in the language of the "older heads," which contains numerous Ashanti elements (Dalby 1971:38). Communication among the living employs everyday "Jamaica talk," which strongly resembles the colloquial speech of the "other" Jamaica. Both Maroons and African-Jamaicans have about 250 words of African origin in use (Cassidy 1982:21), yet the African influence cannot be reduced to a purely lexical aspect. The languages of Africa shaped verbal forms of expression throughout the Caribbean in many aspects[133] (Warner-Lewis 1979:108).

With the "Jamaica talk" Maroons use exclusively for everyday speech, they have the linguistic tools at their disposal to communicate with their neighbors and all other Jamaicans. One result is the long-term, relatively conflict-free relationship between the Maroons and the other residents of the island, disturbed only by sporadic government interventions. With a nearly identical common language, both parties always have the opportunity of playing down divisive factors, in the sense of "we are one black people," and of emphasizing the uniting theme of "we look the same, we speak the same, we are the same." On the other hand, the traces of a second, quite fragmented "ritual language" of the Maroons, comprehensible only to insiders, allows them to assert the uniqueness of their own identity. If we trace back the genesis of this identity to its source, the Maroons feel that this distinction reflects the old contrast of freedom of their "older heads" with the lack of freedom of the enslaved on the plantations. The collective identity of the Maroons is still grounded in this distinction, and is expressed in the Kromanti plays and the social unification with their ancestors in the course of such a feast.

"For Maroons Only. . . ": Kromanti Plays as a Mainstay of Collective Identity

Other than on special occasions, such as the annual public independence celebrations, non-Maroons are excluded from Kromanti ceremonies, since the Maroon spirits who take possession of the dancers react to the smell of "different blood" with extreme aggression. Their existence, their participation, their active intervention, and their aversion to "outsiders" are all part and parcel of the social reality of the Maroons. Once they have been allowed to attend a Kromanti ceremony, all outsiders are due to experience the authenticity of the visitors from First Time in the bodies of the living.

When an obroni attends a Kromanti Play he must be handled with extreme caution, for nothing will so enrage a possessing

Maroon spirit as the presence of an outsider. This point cannot be exaggerated. Upon sensing the presence of an obroni, whether a niega or any other outsider, the granfa will invariably become violently inflamed, and the life of the outsider will be in peril. Almost immediately the possessed fete man (now called granfa) becomes agitated and begins to sniff his own armpits—a gesture which is recognized by the other Maroons present to signify that he 'smell' a 'different blood' in the vicinity. The granfa instantly calls for an afana (machete) and starts to rant and rave about the obroni in his midst. . . he shrieks out obscenities directed at the obroni and the living Maroons at the ceremony who are responsible for his presence. (Bilby 1981:78f.)

In the days of war of the First Time, every "outsider" in the proximity of the Maroon settlements spelled danger. Anyone who had not been sworn to secrecy[134] was not entitled to leave the village, for reasons of security, since treachery was always foremost in their fears. The outcome for such outsiders tended to be death. The spontaneous death threats and instantaneous attacks of the ancestor spirit granfa, dwelling in the medium of the fete man, reflect the social conditions during the period in which the spirit had lived.

Even at official ceremonies to commemorate Nanny Day in Moore Town (October 16, 1985), which were organized to solidify and expand a stable relationship to the "outside world," the "dead" were troubled by the presence of "outsiders." One militant granfa in particular, who had chosen the body of a fete man camouflaged in foliage for demonstration purposes and to symbolize old war strategies, could barely be restrained by Maroon bystanders from attacking all obronis in sight. Not only whites count as *obroni*, but also *niega* (a generally pejorative designation to classify all African-Jamaicans who have no Maroon blood flowing in their veins), and consequently also the officials who are sent by the government to pay honor to the Maroons.

This strict ban on those with "different blood" on any other ceremonial occasion reflects the persistence of Maroon "nationalist" exclusivity. In the same way that outsiders are lumped together as obroni[135] or niega (when only black Jamaicans are involved), the Windward Maroons view themselves as a nation of *Cottawoods* (*Kyatawud*). This nationality can only be passed on "in the blood" if both parents are Maroons. Cottawoods have access to the acquisition of knowledge, special attributes, powers, and abilities that are reserved exclusively for "true Maroons" (Bilby

1984:14).

Whichever etymological version of the derivation of Cottawoods one prefers, the cultural content is closely linked to the Kromanti ceremony (see also Barrett 1979:117). If the term is traced back to the word "Scatterwoods" (Bilby 1984:20), it refers to the first Maroons, who, living scattered in the woods, began the war against the slaveholders. Those old guerrilla fighters attend the Kromanti ceremony as "transcendental relatives." At this ceremony they can fulfill their active role of healing the sick or putting in a good word for an individual or the community as a whole only if they do not have to fight against *obroni* in attendance.

Cottawoods could also be derived from the *cotton tree*, which is the typical site of the dead. The dead are said to wait here to be called into the bodies of the living with drums or the abeng horn. The fact that participants in the Kromanti play use this expression as soon as they recognize a manifestation of a "dead granfa" in the body of a *fete man* (Schafer 1973:249) is evidence for this derivation. However, even if the wooden Ibo drum *cotter* or *cotta* (Brathwaite 1981:21; see also Patterson 1973:234 and Cassidy 1982:268) is used to explain the etymology of the term for their national identity,[136] there is clearly a close connection to the Kromanti ceremony, in which the drum represents a means of communication between the drummer (*okraman*) and the dancing "dead." One of the two drums used by the Windward Maroons of Moore Town, the *cutting drum*,[137] communicates with the dancing ancestor as a "speaking musical instrument," after it has invited the ancestor out of the realm of the dead to the ceremony with drumbeats, together with the accompanying *rolling drum* (see Bilby 1981:74f.).

In the final analysis, it seems less relevant to opt for one etymological variant than to underscore the affiliation of the term of national identity (*Cottawoods*) with the Kromanti ceremony as the social event that maintains the cohesion between living and dead Maroons. It follows that the group identity of the *Cottawoods* is inextricably linked to the Kromanti dance. The special feature of the secret ceremony is its pronounced African character, which can be explained as the "conservatism of the dead."

When it comes to shaping their spiritual life, the Maroons are not free to modify and further develop religious rituals and convictions at their own discretion or to adjust ritual observance to conform to changing external factors, although they have considerable latitude in other areas of their culture. Not only their own spiritual life is at stake, but also that of their deceased ancestors. For the latter, active participation in cultural developments essentially ended with their death. Their participation in the "life of the living" in the Kromanti ceremony depends largely on the continued intelligibility of cultural forms of expression. Consequently, the drum rhythms, speech, songs, and dance movements must conform to the historical perspective and the religious, cultural, and philosophical foundations of the time in which the old ancestors were alive. However, success in safeguarding the old traditions depends upon the dedication of the living. Only in close interaction with the living can the integrity of the Kromanti dance be protected. As long as they are convinced of the supernatural powers of the dead, including the fear of judgment, they will refrain from any incisive changes in the Kromanti dance.

If for whatever reason they do opt for some departure from tradition, they interpret any subsequent undesirable incidents as punishment meted out by the dead and in the future hold to the will of their ancestors expressed in these sanctions. "I remember one day, they did change the day of the celebration. . . and whole heap a tings did happen up here, one year they did not keep it on the 6th and a lot of things did happen" (Mrs. Foster, interview of January 10, 1988). According to Mrs. Foster, grave violations of the rules even result in the death of the person responsible. Anyone who incurs the wrath of the ancestors should count on some form of retribution, such as being stricken with illness (Bilby 1981:77; Dalby 1971:37).

In comparison to other aspects of the Maroon culture, there is a distinct conservatism in the religious-spiritual sphere. This conservatism stems from the will of both the deceased and the living for the continued social participation of the ancestors and the requisite preservation of "old" forms of communication. In order to invite and summon the earliest ancestors—the first Maroons—into the circle of the living, the message must be delivered in "the deepest language," their old "African" Kromanti language.[138] Even the second ritual language (known as "deep language"), which is employed to communicate with the more recently departed, is not useful for reaching the oldest Maroons who were born in Africa; they understand only their own language (Bilby 1983b:39f.).

Since virtually all First-Time Maroons were brought up in one African culture or another, it is not surprising that they drew on their African experiences to realize their goal of reconstructing a meaningful new culture in the forests of Jamaica. Without reproducing any one specific African culture, they created a new entity, for which their diverse African experiences were formative. After their death, they insured the preservation of their cultural values and forms of expression by interacting with

their descendants. The safekeeping of "the dead" must be held responsible for the correspondence of Maroon and West African traditions, especially in the ceremonial aspects of talking drums communicating with
ancestors and deities: "Among the Akan and the Yoruba, drum poetry
also appears in invocations to spirits of various kinds. Longer Akan
poems sometimes open with stanzas calling on the spirits associated with
the drum itself—the wood and its various components—or invoke certain deities or ancient and famous drummers" (Finnegan 1970:493).

Parallels to the (Windward) Maroons are striking: In the Kromanti ceremony there is obviously also an association between the *Cottawoods*
(participating dead) and the old expression *cotta(-wood)* for the drum;
both drummers are called *okraman*, derived from the Ashanti word *o-
kyeremá*, and they invite their ancestors to the dance on their talking
drums, which, like those of the Ashanti, consist of a pair of drums, one
male and one female (Dalby 1971:43). They play three types of Kromanti
songs, which include not only the "old war songs" and the "new war
songs," but also the "jawbone songs" (Beckwith 1969:193). According to
Cassidy (1982:275), jawbone refers to the Ashanti practice of fastening the
lower jawbones of their massacred enemies to their drums as trophies. In
the Kromanti ceremonies of the Windward Maroons of Moore Town and
Scott's Hall, which do not always reflect the practices in other Jamaican
Maroon communities, there is a selection of Akan cultural forms of
expression pertaining to battle and war, owing to the close integration of
music and social life in African contexts, which is expressed by corresponding changes of musical practices as the way of life evolves (Nketia
1982:244). The Maroons as abducted Africans continued this organizational principle by reworking their experiences of armed combat in their
music and thereby providing the means to produce a cultural expression
of resistance. Although it is distinguished by an unmistakable West
African character, the Kromanti ceremony was a creation of the Maroons.

The Kromanti ceremony's significance as a bastion of Maroon identity
stems from its African-Caribbean-Maroon originality. By its complete
integration into the spiritual life of the Maroons, it functions as a guaran-
tor of group identity that embraces the living and the dead. Moreover, it
reinforces the exclusivity of the religious and philosophical tenets of the
Maroons, which are based on interaction with the transcendental world
and reverence of ancestors. By following a course that is the diametrical
opposite of that of the Christian churches[139] and insisting not on conversion but exclusion of all non-Maroons, it avoids direct confrontation and
battles for the "souls" of the Maroons. As a side effect, the rules of preclu-

Fort Kormantine: the first British castle on the Gold Coast

sion spare the religious complex of the Kromanti dance from the sub-
verting influence of *obroni*, whether by means of the usual intolerance
Christian denominations had toward African spirituality or by a syncretic process. Through these protective cultural barriers that the first
Maroons constructed and still oversee in harmony with the living, religious observance remained by and large spared from both negative influences (Bilby 1981:80).

The Kromanti ceremony as the core of Maroon cultural identity also
builds the visible foundation of Maroon spirituality, the major aspects of
which will be covered in the next chapter. "The Kromanti 'language,' the
music, the songs, the dance, the whole belief system articulated through
Kromanti Play, and the imperative of secrecy attached to it, are the crucial
features which, joined together, form a distinctive Maroon cultural identity. It is therefore difficult to conceive of the continued, long-range existence of the Maroons as a distinct people in the absence of the Kromanti
tradition" (Bilby 1981:90). However, no one is more aware than the
Maroons themselves that their sociocultural existence stands and falls

with the protection and preservation of their religious traditions. "Ashanti kuto"[140]—"Ashanti only," the Maroons of Scott's Hall declare when dealing with matters not intended for the eyes and ears of outsiders. A code word of the Maroons of Charles Town, "Ashanti Kromanti," announces who is meant by Ashanti, namely those Africans who were transported to Jamaica from Fort Kormantine on the west coast of the old continent and became Maroons in Jamaica.

"Clear Road Oh, All de Force a Come": The Social Community of the Living and the Dead

Pride is written all over the faces of the Maroons who dance and sing their way through the main street of Accompong on the day of independence. "Clear road oh, all de force a come"—the living and the dead. They confidently celebrate their identity as Maroons before Jamaican television cameras, in the presence of national and international guests. The living participate in the historical successes of their ancestors, who are honored in numerous speeches. The "dead" participate in the independence and the religious freedom of their living descendants, as manifested in the Kromanti songs. Before an assemblage of government officials, missionaries, and domestic and foreign visitors, the Maroons demonstrate social cohesion, a strong cultural identity, and historical continuity. During public, highly symbolic celebrations, their omnipresent uncompromising habitus reflects the real achievements of these relatively small communities, namely to have defended their political, philosophical, religious, and cultural systems successfully time and again against every form of colonization and to have kept the social community of all forces—living and dead—intact.

In this aspect they differ from most other African-Jamaicans, who have managed to preserve particular African basic religious values, but have been exposed to religious Europeanization for generations. Even before the British plantation owners had to acknowledge them as human beings and allow them to convert to Christianity, the white masters had devastated many of their cultural forms of expression and suppressed their African religions (Thomas-Hope 1980:9). The Christian missionaries persisted in doing so, employing universal methods of repression (see, for example, Wernhart 1980:140ff.), albeit by different means. Just like the white slaveholders, the "colonizers of the interior" also feared the power of African religiosity in moral harnessing and organization of "armed" resistance to the existing system.

The role of the Christian mission in stabilizing slavery stems from its rejection of active resistance and determined suppression of African religious expression (Patterson 1973:208; Erskine 1981:38ff.). The two aspects cannot be seen in isolation. The stigmatization of socioreligious African protest as paganism and as superstitions causing eternal damnation combined with the missionary assumption of a divinely ordained status quo that man may not cast aside[141] (see Lewis 1983:200ff.).

The history of the African-Caribbean slave revolts shows that fear on the part of whites was not unjustified. Nearly every revolt involved obeah-men or women, who had often organized the uprising and given the rebels a religious impetus to fight (see, for example, Schafer 1973:163). This tradition of socioreligious resistance lives on today along with the antagonistic relationship of European-Christian and African religiosity. Critical voices, such as those of the Rastafari, attribute the ongoing motivation of the African resistance to a structural continuity between colonial and neocolonial strategies of exploitation and oppression. Since the days of slavery, the bigotry of the rulers has been apparent in missionary attempts to pacify the oppressed pseudo-religiously: "The world which confronted them was one in which an economy was built by the destruction of their bodies while the planter instructed the church to preach to their souls" (Erskine 1981:38). The ultimate failure of these efforts is evident in the continuity of black cultural defiance and resistance. Long before Bob Marley and Peter Tosh declared: "preacher man, don't tell me heaven is under the earth," many black people have been rejecting the ecclesiastical appeasement policy in the form of Christian salvation. Adherents of the myal movement in the so-called Great Revival (of African religion) in about 1860 are said to have retorted sarcastically to the missionaries, who promised milk and honey after death, by asking whether God actually operated a cow pen in heaven[142] (J.J. Williams 1938:173).

By contrast, religions of African origin offered the uprooted black family not only consolation, but also the mental foundations of resistance and thereby constituted the earliest form of protest against living conditions in the alien new world of oppression:

In black religion as it was practiced in early Jamaica, both the myal-man and the obeah-man—usually native Africans—were able to give to the black family an impervious courage deriving from the belief that the God of their ancestors was on their side in their search for freedom. . . The myal-man and the obeah-man in preparing black people to fight and destroy the harsh world of oppression would often administer a mixture of gunpowder, grave dirt, and human blood, which was supposed to make one indestructable. The implication of this practice was that black people believed that the world which was crushing black people was not final or permanent but that, through the power of myal and obeah, black people could find freedom in history. (Erskine 1981:46)

Unlike the established church, which was controlled by the plantocracy, obeah and myal specialists reflected the African-Jamaican pursuit of liberty. Wherever their ideology of resistance took hold, their religious practices in individual cases often had a crucial role in a successful uprising against the plantocratic system, which opened a bridge to the Maroons for the rebelling runaways. Numerous obeah specialists had already constructed this bridge with the free rebels for "secret service operations" (see Dallas 1803:34). In the enclaves of the freedom fighters, black religion was a fundament of cultural identity, working to counter attempts at cultural annihilation and a mental arsenal of weapons in the struggle for independence. "It supported the values and goals of Maroons, gave them confidence, helped to motivate them, and promoted solidarity among them" (Hogg 1960:20).

In order to do justice to the emancipatory quality of the religions of African origin as a foundation of cultural and armed resistance, conceptual sensitivity is required. Terms from the ideological vocabulary of white religions should not be employed in describing black religions (see Kühnel 1986:140). Although clear-cut terminological discriminations such as superstition, pagan cult, idol worship, and devil worship have long since been banished from scholarly language, other stigmata such as magic, witchcraft, medicine man, belief in spirits, and possession by spirits are far more tenacious. Even if it would be ill-advised to adopt radical solutions in certain situations in the interest of intercultural intelligibility—expressions like spirits of the dead or being "possessed" are also used in this book occasionally—the following remarks will essentially define the concepts on their own terms rather than continuing to use vocabulary with lingering negative connotations.[143] If we read the old sources, such as Edwards (1983:239; first published in 1796), a change of terminology and perspective appears imperative: "Concerning the Maroons, they are in general ignorant of our language, and all of them attached to the gloomy superstitions of Africa (derived from their ancestors) with such enthusiastic zeal and reverential ardour, as I think can only be eradicated with their lives."

Even on this point Edwards was misinformed. Not even death was able to uproot their "enthusiastic zeal" and "reverential ardour" for their religious traditions. Why should they give up their connection to the transcendental powers of their spiritual universe,[144] which they perceived to be the indispensable foundation or *conditio sine qua non* of their struggle for freedom (Price 1983a:10)? Nonetheless, on the plantations, religious movements provided the focal organizational structures of black people and thus constituted the organizational basis of the African-Caribbean counterculture within a European-dominated system (Schuler 1980:32).

Although the religious rituals of the slaves were sharply curtailed by judicial or ecclesiastical prohibitions and plantocratic control, and had been forced underground, they could never be stopped altogether and most certainly not destroyed[145] (Morrish 1982:40; Kühnel 1986:141). The freedom attained by fighting put the Maroons in a position to structure their spirituality according to their view of life and revive their religious traditions without direct repression. "Good over evil" governed the principles of social regulation as socioreligious dogma and inspired their military and cultural resistance to the Europeans. The obeah and myal specialist possessed the power and the means to surmount negative forces—whether they originated within the community or entered it from the outside (Schuler 1979:65f.).

Like the Akan *o-bayifo* (a frequent etymological derivation of obeah man from the Twi language [of the Akan]; see Cassidy 1982:241ff.), the Jamaican obeah specialist was doctor, philosopher, and priest all in one. However, he was not the sole member of the community who could function as a medium to the transcendental world. Any community member was in a position to assume the role of communicative mediator to receive a "guest" from the spiritual realm[146] (Brathwaite 1981:12). The community of living and dead coexisting in an expanded social structure is still a social reality today, which therefore (as mentioned earlier) is also described as such. I am thus dispensing with the usual subjunctive formulations to indicate scholarly skepticism. In the conviction that the unity of the Maroons with their ancestors can be qualified neither as abnormal behavior nor as superstitious ritual and most certainly not as a sociopathological disturbance or devil worship—as Christian voices in Jamaica in particular still loudly proclaim even today (Kühnel 1986:142)—I treat the religious ideas and practices as the basis of their cultural identity and of their ultimately successful struggle for freedom. This struggle has never ended and could only be ended by the social end of the Maroons, as is reflected in the old war song "Clear road oh, all de force a come." Even if no scholarly prognosis can be made about the future course of the autonomous communities in their ongoing struggle for existence, an emotional optimism in this regard seems in order in view of self-confident Maroon demonstrations of power at their celebrations of independence. The call to "Clear road oh, all de force a come" speaks for their perpetual cultural opposition. Anyone who dares oppose them has to count on the resistance of a community that unites the living and the dead.

"The Power of the Dead": Ancestral Spirits as Active Participants

"The dead," as the Maroons call their deceased forebears, do not end their existence in this world. While their human bodies might be lifeless, at least one part of their spiritual power is transformed when translocated to the "other world." The spiritual part of a dead person changes his abode from the endosphere to the exosphere. From there, the *duppy* (spirit)[147] can return to its former domicile, but must have the body of a living person to accomplish this, since his or her own "physical shell" is lifeless and lies buried. If a living person receives the spiritual "guest," the Maroons call his situation "to be in myal," that is, to be visited or "possessed" by a dead person. Because of the reciprocal connection between the living host and the "dead guest," which exists even prior to and beyond the actual "possession," "visiting" seems to describe the interactive process better than the usual reductionist "taking possession."

The characteristic element of belief in survival beyond death in the African religiosity is manifest in the continued participation of the "dead" in the life of the community (Parrinder 1980:22; Morrish 1982:24). The widely-shared Jamaican belief in the existence of *duppies* is evidence of the African roots of their basic religious tenets (Brereton 1985:50). This basic religious assumption of the power of the dead is expressed in myriad ways in everyday life in addition to its ritual function in burial ceremonies and in the practice of obeah and myal. In particular the "nine night," the climax of the funeral rites on the ninth day following the death of an individual, is designed not only to distract the attention of the living from their painful loss and provide them with pleasure, but also serves to entertain the *duppy*, who participates in the funeral party before crossing to the exosphere.[148] Once again, the dead person can partake of the pleasures of life: singing, dancing, telling stories and jokes, gambling, and consuming good food and rum (Cassidy 1982:255; see also Patterson 1973:196ff.). Loud, boisterous, and lavish celebrations during the nine night woo the dead in the other world so as to keep them allied with those still in this world (Morrish 1982:63f.).

The custom described by Gardner (1971:198f.) of cutting off the suit pockets of the dead before they are buried to prevent them from filling their pockets with stones and returning as ghosts to tyrannize the living is probably no more than a colorful anecdote about the world of the *duppies*.[149] "Mind Duppy!" is called out as a warning to careless people about to pour a glass of water out of the house during the night without first warning a *duppy* who might be sitting there unaware of the involuntary shower awaiting him. This warning is probably not intended altogether seriously. These anecdotes portray spiritual forces in anthropomorphic form.[150]

Through their experience in the other world, the ancestors have access to an expanded horizon which encompasses knowledge unavailable to their living descendants. Their "long arm" reaches back from the other world into their former sphere where they can influence the course of events. By maintaining communication and unity "in myal" the living can utilize the power of their ancestors to solve their own problems. The authority of the obeah and myal specialists as primary contact persons of the "dead" is also based on this ability.

Maroon cultural specialists, such as the historian Mann O. Rowe, nurture their close connections with the exosphere and keep the powers from the "other world" in a good mood with frequent libations. Mann O. Rowe never takes a sip from his rum glass without sharing his drink with the "old time people," which he accomplishes by emptying several drops onto the ground "for the dead." If the amount of liquid seems insufficient, he pours a bit more so as not to seem stingy to those from the "other world." In return, he expects a similar degree of generosity on the part of the "dead" in communicating knowledge from their exclusive domain.

Schafer (1973:228) correctly concludes: "Maroon concepts of religion center mainly around reverence for the ancestors." This reverence reflects the African conviction that death has no ultimate power over life, which can transfer its spiritual energy from this world to the other world and thereby preserve it (Schuler 1980:72). "The spirits of the dead, called duppies, jumbies, or bigi-men, are closely linked with the living and have a great deal of influence in daily human affairs. They possess the power to bring either good or evil. Close contact is maintained between living Maroons and the ancestral spirits. Duppies may be manipulated by the living for their own purposes" (Bilby 1981:55).

If the supernatural powers of the ancestors are required for whatever reason, the living go to the burial ground of the dead or the place where they once lived, for instance to "old town" near Accompong, to establish contact with them. With a bottle of rum for the ancestors, they seek their help, their advice, or simply their participation in certain affairs. As "globetrotters" between "this world" and "the other world," duppies have a vital social importance and can assume the roles of marriage witnesses, judges, healers, soothsayers, and guardians, or take on regulatory powers, as a kind of "supernatural police." The living know the wishes, needs, emotions, and personality traits of their ascendants, which closely parallel human characteristics[151] (Bilby 1981:55), and go to great lengths to cultivate their good will. "So sometimes like a day to come now they would come and say: Colonel, it is going to need a bokkle of rum, because we have to go to old town or we have to go to Peace Cave. And I say: Pretty fine, what are you going to do? And then they would tell me some of the things that they have to do, you understand what I mean, to marry up or cure up the old ones, and so forth" (Colonel Cawley, interview of January 13, 1988).

The social community of all Maroons who ever lived comes about with the visit of one or several ancestors in the bodies of the living. When they all join together, they live through their central religious experiences (Turner 1980b:49f.). In the literature, there are isolated references to the existence of the divine Accompong (Akuampon) or Yankipong in the religious system of the Maroons, who, as the almighty creator, may well be identical to the Akan *(o-)nyànkopan* (Dalby 1971:41; see also Dallas 1803:93 and Gardner 1971:184). In any case, according to Bilby (1981:55), no direct communication with Yankipong (also called Tata Nyame) is possible for the Maroons: "Yankipong is generally seen as being remote from the living and unconcerned with everyday human affairs."[152]

The ancestors see to the concerns of the living and intervene often in their social life even without being summoned by their descendants. They exercise social control as they see fit with mediators they select and with whom they actively communicate. One can only go "down deh"—to old town—if called by the dead, but not at the whim of the living. The medium assigned to carry out the will of the ancestor, such as Town Master Kojo, must unconditionally obey the superhuman authority in order to escape punishment himself for lack of obedience, even if the master orders the death of another individual. The living person, limited as he is to endospheric horizons, is incapable of recognizing the higher purpose of the delegated action and therefore has no grounds to oppose it:

> Then suppose yu get a calling fe went down deh, you wouldn't go? If a de life call yu, yu cyaan go. If a de dead sen' yu, yu can go. If a de dead sen' yu, yu can go. For 'im [Kojo] a go sen' yu an' tell yu, yu 'ave to go an' do. Just so. . . If de master will fight an' come to yu, yu'ave fe fight fi him. For 'im a converter. Master converter. Master don't do no killing. . . Is de soldier dem. . . but 'im no kill. But 'im hire soldiers. . . 'Im call dem 'im dawg. . . 'Im used to run dem come, do de work, but 'im no kill yu. Just so it go." (Gladdys Foster, interview of January 10, 1988)

From this description we can gauge the degree to which the "secular" endospheric power of the political authorities is restricted by the exospheric influence of the "dead," embodied by the spiritual mediums in this world. Social prestige is also derived from the reciprocity of the regular complex relations between particular ancestors and the living partners, which is expressed in the respect of the other community members and imbues the mediums to the world of the ancestors with symbolic capital and political power. They may go beyond acting merely as delegates of the "old (dead) people" and otherwise participate in their authority by themselves confronting the ancestors with their wishes and soliciting "supernatural" aid in fulfilling them. If they succeed in involving them in their political agendas, thus augmenting their own say significantly, the political authorities "of this world" will sometimes find it difficult to assert their secular power. At the very least, however, the individuals equipped with abilities of mediation can sway political consensus and create important correctives in steering society. This symbolic capital rests on the social recognition of the ancestral powers conferred to living actors.

"Drink, Have a Drink, Have a Drink, I Will Drink with You": Communication Between Two Worlds

In order to realize their potential power in the endosphere, the Maroon dead make regular use of living mediums, whose tasks are to receive and translate messages from the other world. Only certain individuals who have been sought out by the spiritual beings because of their special ability and specialized knowledge are considered permanent mediums between the two spheres. They function as mediators between the worlds of the dead and the living, which, of course, are not divided by any absolute boundary. The living can enter into the "other world" at any time when they die, and the dead may make ephemeral visits to their former environment by "possessing" the body of a medium known to them, normally for the duration of a myal dance. Both the living and the dead are in a position to invite for a myal dance in order to initiate a communicative relationship according to Maroon spiritual concepts. The living community is unable to see the spirit of the dead, but clearly recognizes the effect of his visit on the medium.

Myal specialist Gladdys Foster (interview of January 10, 1988), describes the physically demanding union with an ancestor. Communicating messages from the beyond with a dance requires a person to dance on his head, feet in the air:

> In de myal business, I was de head a it. . . For me gone up and down. . . Wid de myal, I dance it. I was a dancer. . . Anywhere a message to go out, they come to me. they send me out. Me 'ave fe gi' 'im. . . For de myal is dis: if 'im send yu a desso, yu 'ave fe go. And if it gi' yu a message yu 'ave fe carry it. An' when dem come, dem tell yu wha' fe say, yu 'ave fe say it. An' tell de people dem de understanding. . . For very, very bad ting, yu know, when dem tek yu. Yu dance 'pon yu head. Yu go dung 'pon yu head an 'yu two foot can go up so. And yu dance 'pon yu head. Dat is myal.

Although the ancestral powers (called *evil* in the following text)[153] treat the body of their human host quite roughly, they protect him from injury and even from the reddish muddy earth when they jump onto his neck, begin to ride him, whirl him around, and throw him on the ground or into the air with wild leaps:

Evil dance wid yu. An' when de evil dem come 'pon yu, dem sit dung yasso—'pon de neck. An' dem wheel yu, an' if 'im wheel, 'im wheel, yu have fe wheel wid 'im. Dem sit 'pon yu. Dem no run no way, dem sit. . . An' when yu go dung 'pon yu head, yu 'ave fe spin yu head so, de head de 'pon dirt. Yu two foot can go up so; dem dance. An' ebryting wey dem tell yu, yu have fe explain dem. Dat is myal. So it is a really good ting. An' if yu cyaan manage it, yu 'ave fe lay down on the groun'. Dey 'ave yu. An' yu dance 'pon your head. Yu dance to wheel. An' yu explain, tell de people dem, wha' happen. Anyting going happen, they will tell yu. Yu 'ave fe explain an' tell dem. Just dat. . . Dem protect yu." (Gladdys Foster, ibid.)

With their mediating abilities, the religious specialists utilize the spiritual power of the dead for their social community. They transform the energy from the other world to this world in an effort to protect individuals and society as a whole and to battle misfortune, sorrow, illness, and antisocial behavior (Stewart 1984:102). Without the aid of the dead, the living are incapable of seeing into the future, making prophecies, protecting the community when evil threatens, healing the sick,[154] and solving crimes. Their political power is therefore limited by the spiritual

Today, many Jamaicans, including Maroons, make the journey back to the Motherland. The bottle of Jamaican rum presented to the ancestors at the shrine of the slave dungeons in Cape Coast Castle tells the story of an individual's connection with his or her forefathers.

authority. The mediums, who act as communicative adjudicators for the community, help enforce the social authority of the ancestral spirits.

In contrast to the Colonel and other political authorities, mediums derive their power not from the living, but from their ancestors. They are thus entrusted with their "office" for life, and cannot be discharged by living Maroons. For this reason, too, their role in the spiritual life of the Maroons can hardly be compared with that of a priest of the European Christian tradition. They are chosen directly by the ancestral spirits and not appointed by a hierarchically superior office holder within an ecclesiastical organizational complex. Moreover, they do not lead the community in worshipping a (supernatural) deity, but bring about unity with the ancestors, whose essential humanity is confirmed by visiting the living. The religious experiences in the course of this interactive relation between endosphere and exosphere cannot be depicted with the terminology of the Christian concept of worship or by the adoration of a supernatural power. Instead of honoring the ancestors by religious acts or rituals, the living invite them into their circle for a communal activity, the mediums functioning as communicative linkages (Brathwaite 1981:16).

The medium empties "ten bokkle rum" onto the floor in order to invite the Master (Kojo) to share a drink and some conversation:

> I'm going to pass a drink to you, Master. Djink, 'ave a djink, 'ave a djink, I will djink with you. And if yu give me that pint of that ol' rum, I will djink with you. . . Tek djink and if you want me to give you the odder one, I will gi' him the odder one. Mhm. . . Mh. . . I-sah, I-sah. . . One bokkle more yah yah, two bokkle more, ah de more yu djink, ah de more yu want. Three bokkle more, three bokkle more, yah yah, yah. . . Nine bokkle more, ah de more yu djink, ah de more yu want. Ten bokkle more. Master, is de ten fe yu, sir. And I give yu ten. . . So. . . Mhm, mhm, mhmmhm. . . . (Gladdys Foster, interview of January 10, 1988)

The "dead" have two communicative options open to them. They can speak to the medium as in the text cited above (expressed by the affirmative, understanding "Mhm" of Mrs. Foster) or directly to the community in their own language through the mouth of the medium, which the living call "cutting an unknown tongue" (Cassidy 1982:150). In both cases, the aid of communicative mediators is required, which shows the degree of social power associated with the command of the Kromanti language (see Dunham 1946:156f.). Words and messages of the ancestors, as the

186

community receives them in the translation of the medium, are said to have apodictic force.

When Mrs. Cawley and her husband, then Colonel of Accompong, first visited Charles Town, a village of the Windward Maroons, the residents gave them a frosty reception until a woman "in myal" confirmed their identity as Maroons:

> When I went to Charles Town. . . a lady. . . came there and she heard that the Maroons from Accompong is there. She came to know us and she just stand up talking, and I just felt that heavy breeze, just came down on the two of us. And she just picked from me, and she began to dance and she danced and went on the kitchen top. The kitchen was thatched and after when she up there, she bawl: They are real Maroons, they are not any spy. . . And she dance and dance until she dance off her shoes. The two shoes drop on the dirt. . . And then after now, everybody came into us. They did kind a doubt us before, you know. They didn't talk with us so nice, until after the woman dance and tell them that we are real Maroons. . . She talk some other languages that I don't know. It may Kromanti. . . Some of them understand it, but I could not understand the other language. . . And after that everybody come into us. And everybody glad to see us, yu know, and making much of us. But before they fear us." (Mrs. "Auntie Bee" Cawley, interview of January 10, 1988)

The mediums between this world and the other world do not invariably use their "direct line" to the exospheric powers to the advantage of the individual and society. In principle they may also bring about deleterious consequences for individuals or groups when converting the energies of the dead. If there is a conflict of interest between individuals or in the community as a whole, the contact person of the ancestors can intervene to settle it unilaterally, which explains the continuing criminalization of certain African religious practices and forms of expression—especially obeah—in Jamaica today.

"Him Kill One Hundred and Wounded Ninety Nine": Obeah and Myal in Jamaica

It is a matter of debate whether the Christian mission of the 18th and

19th centuries in the Caribbean belongs to the antislavery or the proslavery ideology (many social scientists opt for the latter view; see Lewis 1983:199). By contrast, the fundamental role of the African religion in black resistance is incontestable. Obeah and myal[155] as integral elements of a more comprehensive religious system that united several similar African heritages formed the bases to organize black counterculture in the underground of the plantations and especially in the Maroon enclaves. Likewise starting point of cultural resistance and mainspring of the open rebellion against white tyranny, they ensured the psychic survival of the enslaved majority and the physical survival of the minority of Maroons and runaways, whose struggle was crowned with success.[156]

Herein lie the actual roots of the criminalization of African religion by the plantocratic legislation (Brathwaite 1981:14f.). The legal rehabilitation of the still-vital African-Caribbean religiosity in Jamaica has yet to occur. Obviously, this is due to the dogmatic condemnation of obeah or communication with ancestors as "devil worship" by church organizations, which vigorously oppose their Africa-oriented competitor, and to the apprehensions of the legislative agencies of the "rebellious element" of obeah and myal. In stark contrast is the fact that the government made Nanny—the most prominent obeah practitioner of Jamaican history—a national hero. Missionaries and government officials come to Moore Town for Nanny Day, the annual holiday in her honor.

Nanny's obeah knowledge is said to have been of crucial significance in the armed struggle against the English. Her religious actions aimed at rendering her own fighters invincible and neutralizing the opposing troops.[157] Not until Tacky's Revolt in 1760 did the whites recognize the potency of obeah in the resistance to slavery, which was reflected in the anti-obeah law that followed on the heels of this revolt (Act 24. Sect. 10, 1760). Until then, they had laughingly dismissed this "silly superstition"; in the aftermath of reported poisonings and of the heroism of the invincible rebels they labelled it a threat to the system of the first rank[158] (see Williams 1970:113; Patterson 1973:192; Gardner 1971:189; Barrett 1979:74). From a plantocratic perspective, they were surely not wrong in doing so, as evidenced by the "poisonings" that were often suspected but rarely proven as well as by the active participation of obeah specialists in the black resistance[159] (see Vestdijk 1941:116, 267; Williams 1970:179).

However, the importance of obeah is not limited to its function as a means of organizing the revolts and as the "spiritually psychological arsenal of weapons": "[It] offered to its followers comfort and consolation in all of the major crises to their life experience, from the daily oppressions of slavery on to the nature of life itself and even to the nature of death and the afterlife—granting them an importance in spiritual life denied to them in the political and economic life of the societies in which they lived out their daily lives as the despised and rejected" (Lewis 1983:198). These philosophical and religious aspects of obeah and myal as well as their social implications for the internal organization of black communities were long ignored by most (white) authors. Obeah and myal were degraded to an exotic pagan custom with concepts such as black magic, witchcraft, and warding off evil spirits.[160]

Beckwith (1969:107; first published in 1929), who typified her era, provides a telling example of the deep disdain white authors held for African religion and its Jamaican forms of expression. In the following passage, she describes "two classes of obeah men": "The first class, generally African by birth, are dirty, ignorant, and deformed in some way—with a lame foot or a wall eye, for example—who accept a small fee for their services. The second class, well-dressed, intelligent, dapper, who make a pretense of 'duppy-catching,' do nothing without a large fee. The first class seem really to believe in themselves. The second are conscious of their own fraud. The first class are perhaps self-hypnotized and often exhibit senile dementia concealed under a show of profound authority." It can be assumed that the objects of this criticism preferred to be ridiculed as "incompetent charlatans" and "demented old people" than to experience the full weight of racist persecution and "anti-African exorcism" from the Church. Only in the protection of their anonymity could they fulfill the spiritual and practical needs of black people (on the plantations and subsequently) and operate in the service of resistance.

Neither plantocratic legislation, which made any "communication with the devil" and "any other superstition" as well as the use of blood, feathers, bird's beaks, dog's teeth, broken bottles, grave dirt, rum, eggshells, and similar paraphernalia punishable by death or forced deportation from the island, nor the missionary counter-propaganda could seriously threaten the existence of black religion in Jamaica: "It was in religion that Europeans worked hardest to influence black culture in the eighteenth and nineteenth centuries, and yet it is in religion that the survival of African culture is most noticeable in twentieth-century Jamaica" (Erskine 1981:29).

Even attempts to represent religious views of life as an expression of (lacking) intelligence did nothing to alter this fact. "It is true that as the Negroes became better educated and more intelligent, the spiritist beliefs (upon which obeah practices depend today) lose their hold upon the mind. . . But the fact that the trade remains lucrative proves the persistence of the belief, and there is no reason to suppose that the practitioner is in every case more intelligent than the great mass of the people who employ his skill" (Beckwith 1969 [orig. 1929]:107ff.). These descriptions, which can be explained by the Eurocentric and racist syndrome, are overwhelmingly opposed in current ethnohistorical, sociological, and religious-anthropological research. The sophisticated use of poisons from plants as a tool of resistance under the prevailing circumstances of plantocratic oppression and control should alone suffice to set right the racist paradigm quoted above, which has acquired some new facets in the recent western "voodoo and zombie euphoria."

Numerous deaths of Europeans attributed to tropical diseases during the time of slavery are now ascribed to the radical resistance of obeah specialists. Many of them had comprehensive knowledge of poisonous plants and were able to mimic a natural cause of death by administering precise doses of a poison[161] (Williams 1970:113ff., 136ff.; see also Patterson 1973:265). They thereby impressively demonstrated to "their" community the mortality of the white tyrants and provided evidence of their own power, upon which they could also base their claim to exercise social control functions. Moreover, they constituted a unifying factor in the latent rupture between slaves ready for battle and loyal slaves who feared reprisals for possible treachery or other antisocial behavior with supernatural sanctions. Since it was difficult to prove that poisoning had taken place, and it was even rarer for an obeah man to be pronounced guilty and executed, the impression grew among the other slaves that the power of the whites was inferior to that of the black religious leaders, which they expressed with the pervasive saying: "Buckra could not kill Obeahman" (Gardner 1971:190; see also Martin 1985:205f.).

Individual revenge and resistance against the oppressors were crucial to psychic survival. The ritual protection of the oppressed granted by the ritual specialist with the help of the exospheric powers and materialized with the donation of a "fetish," served the same purpose. Besides this, the obeah and myal specialists contributed to transferring the African religions and philosophies into the diaspora, where they kept them alive at least in fragments in the underground of the dictatorship and prevented the complete religious deracination of black people in Jamaica. They thereby also met the need of the enslaved for social order within the black community, which seemed largely irrelevant to the whites, as long as "their human capital" was not damaged. As a result they only paid attention to the concerns of the exploited when murder or bodily harm threatened "their possessions." All other forms of "aberrant" behavior, such as theft, treachery, rape, or disloyalty among themselves, were rarely prosecuted if not taken up by the obeah specialists (Erskine 1981:29).

Owing to the wealth of information that came to their ears alone, they had an easier job of prosecuting alleged criminals with their obeah abilities, often without the aid of the exosphere (see Gardner 1971:189). When the news "obi set fe him" made the rounds, the psychological pressure began to work on the guilty party, who henceforth interpreted all negative experiences in the causal framework with the dreaded obeah (Williams 1970:112). "Obeah as a belief-complex works on the mind, and can sometimes be fatal, as the records of Anthropology show. It works upon the imagination and can carry one to the ultimate consequence of fear—death" (Barrett 1979:77).

Mr. Reid—an obeah man from Accompong—referred to this aspect of his work with no small degree of pride, as Gladdys Foster (interview of January 10, 1988) reports: "When me dance an' go up Mister Reid yard, Mister Reid say, 'im kill one hundred and wounded ninety-nine." During the time of war against the English, obeah and myal—possibly at times even practiced by one and the same specialist—collaborated in the interest of the community. As two aspects of a more comprehensive religious system, which among the Maroons was not subject to complete destruction by the persecution of the whites (as on the plantations), obeah and myal are likely to have been closely linked in many ways. "Perhaps the real difference between obeah and the myal cult is that whereas the obeah-man was a private practitioner, hired by a client for a specific purpose, the myal-man was a leader of a cult group, devoted to organized religious life" (Erskine 1981:31).

Especially in the older literature, obeah is demonized as "black magic," and continues to be demonized today by both the government and the Church, which says more about their own mentality and prejudices than about the African religious form itself. Of course there are dubious "obeah practitioners," who exploit the vitality of "African religiosity" to make their living with "hocus pocus" in urban centers. In the rural areas and some cities of Jamaica, however, obeah men and women still play a complex role as an African-Caribbean antithesis to a Christian religious view. With strategies similar to those during the period of slavery, specialists protect themselves and their clients from persecution by the government, which also recalls anti-African attitudes of the slaveholders. The strict "information blackout" toward outsiders should not lead us to underestimate the high status of "science" (obeah knowledge) in the spiritual life of Jamaica (see Barrett 1979:75). To solve weighty problems or in times of crisis, many Jamaicans still turn to obeah and myal specialists for help or advice.

In the Maroon enclaves, these specialists are still leading practitioners in the religious system, which exists side by side with Christianity. They continue to enjoy awesome respect within their communities and beyond, and are reputed to possess superior spiritual powers because of their connections to the old Maroon heroes (Bilby 1984:15). Their abilities are usually termed "science," which has no negative connotations. "Tan deh. . . 'im a de higher science" means something along the lines of "Don't speak his name, watch out, he has the highest abilities." The same message can be expressed in other terms: "If yu went dung the hill an' call 'im name, no man good, de people cut yu neck fe 'im. 'Im can do the work, 'im know something yah man" (Mrs. Gladdys Foster, interview of January 10, 1988). Thus, outsiders who dare to call the name of a "scientist" in old town—the resting place of the dead—face the wrath of the dead (de people), who would cut off their necks.

Obeah and myal should not be viewed as basically antagonistic powers, at least for the Maroons, as some authors (for instance, Patterson 1973:188) would have us believe in a binary opposition of black (evil) and white (good) magic. Both aspects of the religious system, or rather its practitioners, probably worked together in many regards. At the very least, they pursued the same goals, such as support of armed resistance, preservation of cultural identity and continuity, and maintenance of the social order.[162] If we go on this assumption, which appears justified by the common spirit of resistance in times of peace and war, participation together in certain ceremonies, and the relatively stable internal peace of the Maroon communities, then the opposition of obeah and myal appears limited to just a few situations (see Erskine 1981:31ff.; Dunham 1946:132; Bilby 1981:55).

Perhaps the most important situation in which obeah and myal specialists stand on opposite sides as antagonists occurs when spiritual powers of the "scientist" are used to the detriment of an individual, which can only be averted by the myal dancer. From the information of the myal dancer Gladdys Foster, however, even in this case there is no basic adversarial relationship, unless the myal specialist considers the sanction of the obeah specialist unjustified. If the person who was pursued by the obeahman by spiritual powers really was guilty of an antisocial or otherwise forbidden conduct, the myalist does nothing to save him. The nail which is hammered into the cotton tree by the obeah professor[163] and which is intended to rob the person in question of his soul is in this case not pulled out of the tree in a liberating gesture (see Rashford 1985:55). "Gustin and Issa thief some Ganja. And after them thief the Ganja, dey went dung fe go tek me out. An' when me go dung deh, me see two nail. . . Dem say: There are two nail fe draw out. Me say: Don't draw it. Dat nail a fi Gustin and that one a fi Issa. Nobody touch it. An' ten now it dideh. . . Issa dead, Gustin go 'way. If Gustin come here. . . 'im gone. . . A jus' so it go" (Gladdys Foster, interview of January 10, 1988).

In a certain sense, the myalist functions as an appellate authority within this system of social control based on spiritual sanctions, determining whether the measures of the obeah professor are just, and, depending on the outcome of this supervisory check, either confirms the "sentence" or suspends it with the aid of spiritual powers. In the above-mentioned case of the theft of an agricultural product (ganja), to which strongly antisocial implications are attached in the agrarian community of Accompong, Mrs. Foster decided alongside the obeah-man and demanded that the nails remain in the tree, with fatal consequences for one of the two thieves (the second was able to flee the country).

The social cohesion of the Maroons has always depended on the interplay of obeah and myal. Therefore, the above interpretation cannot automatically be extended to the urban situation in Jamaica, where religious elements continue to be torn out of context and are subject to social marginalization and criminalization by the government. Since these negative assumptions are by and large absent in the independent Maroon "states," a complex interactive relationship exists between the two aspects of African religiosity, which assumes antagonistic aspects only in particular situations. Only then does the myalist intervene correctively in the "science" of the obeah specialist or in some cases confronts him directly.

"Me Dance Myal fe Pull Nail": Myal as Counterforce to Obeah

In times of crisis, when a relatively homogeneous aggressor in the form of the plantocracy administration and colonial power confronted the black people of Jamaica, obeah and myal always fought on the same side (Williams 1970:214). As religious "subsystems" within a philosophical and spiritual context, they did not oppose one another as antagonistic forces. The specific political condition of the Maroon communities, which had to assert their autonomy and cultural integrity constantly against external authorities (first the colonial power, then the state) precluded antagonism. Their social existence, which was in a state of permanent peril from external aggression, depended on perpetual unity undisturbed by internal conflicts.

In some situations, a dialectical relationship between obeah and myal practices has had significance for social control. Still, if the "obeah professor" violates the customary law or the moral values of the society by his concrete practices, the myalist is expected to reverse the consequences of obeah actions as a counterforce and intervene as a corrective. Only he functions on the same level between the endosphere and the exosphere and thus has at his disposal the suitable spiritual "tools" to work apotropaically. His activity is virtually always socially approved, which is not necessarily the case with obeah specialists, who often act in their own interests or for the private interests of others for pay. Scientists are brought in, among other reasons, to prophesy future events and influence them favorably, to heal diseases, or to support their clients in court by influencing the judicial decision-making process with their transcendental abilities and precluding negative witness statements (Cassidy 1982:243).

On a regular basis, members of the "lower" social strata avail themselves of their services, which gives them a socioeconomic role as protector, doctor, and advocate of the financially needy. Within a given social stratum, these activities are not considered antisocial. Only when they are recruited for "mystic malevolence" or aspire to it voluntarily, obeah scientists have to count on opposition, which can be carried out by another religious specialist. If the obeah-man nails the shadow of a living man to the cotton tree without a reason that is acceptable to the community,[164] the myal dancer has the task of lifting the unjustified mortal spiritual sanction on the same spiritual level (see Brereton 1985:50). "In short, the obeah-man has *put* obeah on someone, and the myal-man says he will *pull* it"[165] (Cassidy 1982:244; see also Morrish 1982:46).

In a public ceremony,[166] a "four-eyed" myalist (see Williams 1970:154), who has one pair of eyes for this world and one for the other, pulls the nails out of the tree and returns the living person's shadow to him, thereby restoring his vitality:

They nail you inna de cotton tree. . . the obeah man dem. When town master come to me fe dance myal and pull nail outta cotton tree, me foot swell so. And when me dance an' go call him, de man dem hear and dem come out. . . When we start go dung now. . . dey walk a river road and me tek the old road. . . an' when me reach by the cotton tree. . . dem come, mek dem mek a fire heap road, an' when de fire road a burn, an' when me wheelin', me say: Drop! Me hav' fe call your name, tek your nail, an' when dem drop de fingernail, me draw it. Me hav' fe tek it an' put inna fire, bring you back to smaddy. So it go.[167] (Gladdys Foster, interview of January 10, 1988)

In this case of "shadow catching" by the actions of the obeah-man and in similar situations in which the scientist abuses his power, according to the majority consensus of what constitutes justice, the myalist attacks only the negative consequences of obeah, but not the root of the specific evil, namely the "obeah professor" himself. Usually the "perpetrator" is not found out: "Who put the people in the cotton tree? Nobody no know who. It can be Simon or Booster or Mister Reid. It can be the three a dem, obeah man dem. Dem do it. Yu see, nobody know the direct one, what do" (Gladdys Foster, ibid.).

Sometimes the myalist goes beyond apotropaic measures and directs the powers bestowed by the transcendental forces of the ancestors directly against the obeah-man. Gladdys Foster reported (interview of January 10, 1988) killing the obeah-man Mr. Reid in this manner. The cause of the direct confrontation was the theft of an amber, an object with ancestral power, which was coveted by both myal and obeah specialists. An amber is said to have various uses, probably owing to its electromagnetic power.[168] Since only the dead may properly grant someone possession of an amber and give instructions for its use, its utilization in the context of obeah and myal activities represents the participation and support of the ancestors. "Yu keep amber, but a dem hav' fe gi' yu. It deh all inna grass, according to where dem put it. If a amber a gi' it to you, dey say to you, seh: Tonight, yu went topside Charlson yard, yu will see amber, tek it an' jus' so it go, yu see amber, yu can tek it, for dem gi' it to you, an' carry it go a yard. And then teach yu. . . yu know what to do" (Foster, ibid.).

If anyone appropriates an amber without having it bestowed by the dead, that person must die, according to Mrs. Foster. Raul ("Raul getting dead by the amber") and Mr. Reid, the obeah man, are two examples. Although Mr. Reid already possessed a legitimately acquired amber bead to practice his science, he also stole one belonging to the town master, which probably means Kojo: "Mister Reid did have it. Thief it. When the house burn dung, Mister Reid went down there, tek the amber bead, tek town master amber, wey 'im work with it. Town master gi' him amber fe himself. 'Im got the amber and kill young people dem. Reid. Allright. Him got the amber, wha' 'im tek from town master, 'im cyaan't use it, for 'im no know how fe use it, but 'im got it a yard."

Especially once it was established that Mr. Reid also had nailed at least one "innocent person" to the tree, Mrs. Foster was assigned the task "in myal" of getting back the stolen amber and neutralizing Mr. Reid. For this purpose, Kojo gave her three shrubs (soccabobbie) as weapons: "An' when me wheel an' go way, dat time master gi' me three soccabobbie, you know it."

Thus prepared for the fateful meeting, Mrs. Foster began to interrogate the obeah-man to establish the unlawfulness of his possession of the amber. Only someone who has received it from the dead is instructed in its use by them. In the reverse situation—if someone is incapable of appropriately putting the amber to use, he must have stolen it—the perpetrator is considered convicted: "An' when me say: Reid, come; 'im say: Yes sir. Me say: I was looking for you long time. 'Im say: You was looking for me long time? Me say: Yes. Me say: Reid, you know what me come about. 'Im say: No. Me say: Where is me amber bead? 'Im say: I have it, sir; 'im go tek it out. . . How you come by it? 'Im say: A him tek it. Me say: You cannot use it? Him say: No. Me say: Why? 'Im say, 'im don't know how fe use it."

With this confession from Mr. Reid, the necessary condition to carry out the sanction was met. Mrs. Foster complied with her task of "execution of the sentence" by throwing Kojo's weapon—the three soccabobbie—at the feet of the obeah-man: "An' when me wheel so an' come back, 'im sit 'pon 'im bed and me outta door, me fling the soccabobbie so, an' me lick 'im 'pon im foot. 'Im stretch the odder foot gi' me. Me fling the odder one an' lick 'im. Me say: Reid, you number call. 'Im say, 'im don't know the meaning of the number, dat call. Me say: Your time is expired. 'Im say; 'im don't know it. I say: You supposed to know it."

Mr. Reid really should have known it. According to Mrs. Foster, he was dead nine days later. She was barred from attending the funeral by the "dead," so as to avoid confronting Mr. Reid's "power beyond death." "Me say, me lick 'im Friday, and me go to Spalding Saturday. An' when me go a Spalding, the odder Saturday de people dem, me come 'pon, tell me seh Mister Reid dead. So 'im live. . . 'im did nine day after. Nine day. After nine day 'im dead. An' I don't see the coffin, and I don't see the grave. For I could not went deh. Dem tell me, not to go 'round deh. An' me could not go. So anything dem gi' you command, you cyaan't do it."

From Mrs. Foster's account of her drastic confrontation with the "higher science man," we can infer the meaning of the concrete situation for the relationship between the two socioreligious complexes. It was not the killing of young people with the aid of the legitimately conferred ambers, but the illegitimate possession of the stolen amber that caused the sanction to be imposed. While carrying out the harsh, but authorized social control by the obeah specialist, the myalist obviously does not have an antagonistic relationship to him. For the analytical conceptualization[169] of the "ideal" relationship of obeah and myal, this means a potential antagonism, which can arise in particular situations, but is not inscribed in the religious and philosophical system. The Maroons consider obeah and myal two mutually compatible religious aspects within a larger spiritual context, which is based on the interaction between living and dead Maroons. Although they operate with different means, usually separate from one another, they do essentially pull together for social survival while preserving Maroon identity.

Annual Celebrations of Maroon Independence

All of Jamaica's large Maroon villages organize annual independence celebrations, which also function as commemorations of the cultural icons Nanny (in Moore Town, Scott's Hall, and Charles Town) and Kojo (in Accompong).[170] No other event enjoys a comparable status in the life of the Maroons. In addition to the entertainment value of the several days of "spree," their multilayered religious, political, economic, familial, and psychological implications give this event its special cultural significance. The festival signals a process of re-evaluation, redefinition, and renewal of existing relations to the outside as well as within the societal network.

The communal experience during the Kromanti dances, as the ceremonial focus of the festivities, confirms the feeling of social cohesion. Music and dance, characterized by the participation of the "old ancestors," present their African character. They symbolize the historical meaning of Africa as the birthplace of the First-Time people in the outlook of the Maroons. It is therefore not surprising that a statement concerning African social and religious festivities or ceremonies also applies to the meaning of musical activities for the Maroons: "The performance of music in such contexts, therefore, assumes a multiple role in relation to the community: it provides at once an opportunity for sharing in creative experience, for participation in music as a form of community experience, and for using music as an avenue for the expression of group sentiments"

(Nketia 1982:22).

The collective experience of their own cultural creativity unites the community with the "double connecting link" of the Kromanti ceremonies. First-Time music and dancing together serve as a communicative medium to the "dead" or "older heads." In addition, they relegate to the background the competing identities of the Maroon emigrants as Kingstonians, Londoners, or New Yorkers, at least for the duration of their visit to the old neighborhood, emphasizing instead their Maroon identity. "The Maroons today held their traditions for many hundreds of years and every year there is a general celebration where all the Maroons from all over Jamaica will come together to Accompong and celebrate. The celebration unites the Maroons and keeps them aware of what is happening and where the Maroons are going today. . . You find that people who live in the foreign, they always come specially for the celebrations from England and from the United States. Every year we have some visitors, Maroons, who are out there, who return to come to the community to celebrate in this thing. . . Each celebration a lot of them come to just pay respect to their old ancestors and so forth" (Colonel Cawley, interview of January 13, 1988).

However, more than renewing social contacts and familial bonds is at stake in the family reunions. An economic component also predominates in the relationship between (Maroon) hosts and (Maroon) guests. The emigrants, who typically left their community for reasons of financial exigency, are expected to contribute both money and commodities (especially technical apparatus and "foreign-style" clothing). These contributions are an indispensable component of the reciprocal relationship between hosts and guests. In the words of Colonel Cawley (ibid.): "Today in Accompong, many of the citizens are living elsewhere and they want to contribute to the well-being of the Maroons here." Anyone who is not in a position or frame of mind to have relatives partake of his possible superior economic position, must *de facto* forgo the independence celebration, which will mean a sacrifice of his social prestige (Bill Peddy, conversation of January 9, 1988).

This is not the sole economic aspect of the festival. The official representatives of the Jamaican government are also hoped and expected to contribute gifts in the form of political concessions and especially public funds. Quantifiable grants for road building, medical care, and cultural events are a barometer of the current quality of political relations. Of course, other clues from the area of symbolic interaction are also indicators of the relationship between Maroon "states within a state" and the

Jamaican government. All symbolic interactions are subject matters of careful evaluation, such as both the number of the government envoys and their rank in the political hierarchy, the length of their stay in the Maroon enclaves, and the content of their speeches before Maroon gatherings. For days after the festival, the diverse interpretations of the process of interaction with the various agents of the Jamaican goverment provides ample material for passionate discussions. The regular delegation of the second and third rank of politicians, their trifling addresses without concrete economic pledges, and their brief stays—while the government helicopter waits to transport them back—are taken as a provocation and evoke cynical commentary.

Nonetheless, the Maroons value the presence of the official delegates at their independence celebrations as a symbolic recognition of their quasi-autonomous existence, and the majority clearly do not want to miss it. Moreover, the annual state visits confirm the legitimacy of Maroon sovereignty, which is demonstrated on this occasion in a political and cultural context before the eyes of the "private" Jamaicans who attend and on television to the Jamaican public. With these reciprocal recognitions, neighborly relations to other Jamaicans can also be renewed in the spirit of the oral tradition of the "Two Sister Pikni" myth. The reggae and dance parties over the course of several evenings, which are organized in Accompong for this occasion, help along this latter goal. They also represent an important source of income within the economic context of the celebration. All non-Maroons who do not want to miss this unique street festival and the appearances of popular new "cultural heroes," namely deejays, have to pay the price of admission in Accompong. The numerous peddlers selling ice cream and snacks and the professional gamblers bring in additional money.

In a way, the complexity of the interactions during the festivities reflects a concentrated picture of the complex structure of relations between Maroons who stayed and those who left, between dead and living Maroons, between Maroons and private non-Maroons and non-Maroon officials representing the government. But even this characterization of the Maroon relationships among one another and to the outside world are, strictly speaking, nothing more than a fiction for the sake of simplicity, since none of the "listed groupings" exists as a homogenous community. The Maroons are aware of the instability of these relations. During the reunion for the independence celebrations, they can carefully gauge any changes and attempt to influence them accordingly.

Dance with the Dead

From the complex structure of relations that the interaction during the independence celebrations suggests, the relationship to the ancestral spirits as the fundamental part of the Maroon identity predominates. The double purpose of the festival emanates from this relationship: Whereas the official part of the festival in Accompong, which is also open to all non-Maroons, is dedicated to the achievement of peaces treaties and foundation of Maroon sovereignty, a part of the ceremony, reserved for "true born" Maroons, celebrates an intimate "birthday party" for Kojo, the signer of the peace treaty. Only Maroons are invited to the barbecue in "old town," the city of the dead where Kojo lies buried. Ample quantities of chicken and pork are roasted, but the attendees get only the liver to eat. All other parts of the meat are reserved for Kojo and the "old time people"[171] (Gladdys Foster, interview of January 10, 1988).

Besides this barbecue in "old town," several other festival ceremonies are also strictly private affairs, intended only for the established descendants of the ancestral spirits. During the night of January 6, three men have to get Kojo's personal bottle of rum, which is stored in the Peace Cave, and serve a drink for their hero at three specific locations, before the rum is sprayed to the "dead" as a drink to welcome them. "Peace Cave, you hav' fe went deh, from inna night, an' do the duty up deh. So ongly three men . . . do de duty an' put de djinks inna de way, dem hav' fe put it. A three part, wey dem have fe put rum. . . which part master djink, they put de rum roun' deh" (Foster ibid.).

On the eve of the official festivities, the Maroons play and sing their Kromanti songs in their "family" circle, surrounded by dead and living relations. In Accompong, an ancestor is "incarnated" on this occasion in the body of a female dancer. The drummers, dancers, and other participants effusively greet the guest from the other world. They are ecstatic about this visit, which reinforces the community with the mighty ancestors who managed to wrest a peace treaty from the English colonial power. Likewise, the wild dance of the "dead" in the body of a living person proves the vitality of the exospheric allies. When the ancestor tosses the human "host" into the air or throws him on the floor (*chop down*) and rolls him back and forth between the dancers, the drum speaks with the old Maroon in the "old African tongue." Kromanti phrases of the spiritual mediums alternate with the drummed texts. The rhythms of the talking drum, as a linguistic surrogate, represent the linguistic structures of Kromanti. Rum is sprayed on the abeng, the drums, and the myal dancers

Mr. Johnny (Gyani) "Kujee" Chambers visited by an ancestor during a Kromanti dance under the Kindah tree

"to feed the spirit" (Schafer 1973:232). The man who serves Kojo's rum to bid welcome to the ancestors takes some rum into his mouth and sprays it in the air. It is the evening on which Nanny comes for a visit from Moore Town and thus, as Kojo's sister, symbolically completes the family circle that also embraces the other Maroon villages.

On the actual day of the festival, the ascendants in Accompong are far more reticent. Too many outsiders represent a potential enemy element. After the celebrations and Kromanti dances of the previous evening, they are not necessarily "incarnated" in the bodies of myal dancers on January 6. At an earlier counterpart festival in Moore Town on October 16, the transcendental powers were certainly not restrained from active participation in the Kromanti dance by the presence of some non-Maroons. Three dancing men were selected as mediums and "visited" by the dead. Their common identity is manifested in their union in a single body.[172] Still, the presence of non-Maroons ("strange blood") requires "inhospitable" actions to control the dead. Maroon spectators who are initiated into the rules of the Kromanti dance as apprentices of the medium but are not themselves "possessed" grab hold of the ancestor, who sits in the neck of the dancer, and prevent the ancestral spirit from taking over the visited body altogether. If the spirit were to do so, he might use the visited body as a physical weapon to attack "different blood" (see Schafer

1973:230).

In any case, the presence of the deceased ascendants, perceptible only to the Maroons, marks an ideological dividing line to all non-Maroons, whose "border" is of course defined according to classification along ethnic or political lines. Although close familial relations are assumed to the members of the different Maroon villages, other African-Jamaicans are considered very distant relations. Visitors from abroad, regardless of their skin color, are considered foreign guests unless they come from Africa, which allows for the prospect of a spiritual, cultural bond, and potentially even a blood relationship.

Each group evaluates the various phases or situations during this gathering in a characteristic manner. The Maroons of Accompong see the secret ceremonies, inaccessible to outsiders, as a preparatory component of the "family festival," which in principle becomes public on the eve of January 6, but expects no invited guests outside the circle of Maroons. All non-Maroons and Maroons may partake in the official celebration on the festival day, but the divergent historical and cultural identity of the hosts remains the focus of the events. Only on the "reggae night" of the following evening does the clear line of demarcation become blurred by the communal participation of the young people in this cultural form of expression. This event allows the Maroons to let down their barriers between themselves and everyone else, which were demonstratively emphasized and celebrated in earlier phases of the festivities.

"They were Attacked by an Army": Spiritual Authority of the Maroons

Despite the enormous missionary efforts of various Christian denominations, numerous aspects of African religiosity were kept alive in the Maroon villages, and, to a lesser degree, in the rest of Jamaica as well. One simple reason should be emphasized here: Maroon science, obeah and myal, which entailed communication with the exospheric powers and the integration of the ancestors into the social life, suited black attitudes and interests, whereas missionary Christianity—at least before it was reinterpreted through the prism of black historical experience—basically served white interests. In the philosophical view of the Maroons, Christianity was a foreign entity that was difficult to reconcile with the history of resistance and protest against European oppression and was therefore close to impossible to integrate (see Erskine 1981:29ff., 69ff.).

202

Since the ruling Jamaican elite seems to be the successor in interest of the colonial power from the perspective of the Maroons, spiritual forces still remain operational in cultural resistance even today. They not only bolster the pride and defiance of the Maroons, but also curtail the aggression of governmental agencies, which tend to avoid confrontation with the descendants of the first freedom fighters. The survival of African religions in the consciousness of most Jamaicans is largely responsible for this. Like the Maroons, their occasional Jamaican adversaries in police uniforms also believe in the existence of spiritual powers. Moreover, the "Maroon scientists," particularly of the self-governed territories, have the reputation of possessing extraordinary abilities. They are considered capable of retaliating for any encroachment from the government with "supernatural sanctions" aided by Kojo and other "older heads." These psychological implications of the orally transmitted narratives of the invincibility of the transcendental powers that collaborate with the Maroon obeah specialists is evident in the palpable respect of the "foreign" guests at the annual festivities.

However, even government agencies seem to shy away from direct confrontation with the spiritual forces of the Maroons, if we are to believe the account of Colonel Cawley (interview of January 13, 1988):

> There is a lot of spiritual powers that have been among the Maroons over the past years, because I remember once that some officers intruded on the Maroon territory and they [the Maroons] took the Abeng and the horn and the report was made that the officers felt something that was coming up on them, as if it had been a bullet, and they became so scared. . . that they ran and left their machetes and different things in the bushes and went back to the station and left their Jeep on the road. It was something, that. Yes, because the spirits of Kojo had interfered into the whole setting. So the Maroons still hold more firmly to the fact that the spirits do something.

With no small degree of amusement, Colonel Cawley describes the psychological effect of the blowing of the abeng on the police who had come under orders to destroy the ganja fields of the Maroons. Even before the living Maroons showed up, they are said to have been alarmed by the sound of the abeng and thought they were being attacked by the army of the transcendental powers. Overcome with terror, they took flight:

The Abeng is blown and is used many times to alert the people. And it has been used three times since I am here as Colonel for the past five years. When the police comes in the bushes. . . what alerted the people so much was the sound of the Abeng. They just go to the Abeng blower. And from it is blown, everybody knew that they were there, raiding the people's fields, and so a group of people get up within minutes and they were marching to the area and that is the time. . . the police run from the fields because, they said, they were attacked by an army. . . Oh my, it was something, and those policemen, if you should see them today, they can give you the frightful experience they had. . . Even before we reached the spot where they were, while they were in the hills coming, and the Abeng was being blown and the people were coming through the hills, the police, they were fling out of the field when they were half a mile away because, they said, they were attacked by an army. So the army went before the people reached there. Oh yes, there is a deep belief that the Maroons have about the spirits that people communicate with.

Although Colonel Cawley's report of this event was punctuated by several outbreaks of hilarity, the event itself was threatening for the self-government and territorial sovereignty as well as for the economy of the Maroons. This event also points up an important component of cultural resistance, namely that both sides concurred as to the superiority of the Maroons, based on traditional military strength kept intact by the participation of the ancestors. In a certain sense, both sides interpret the encroachments as violations of the "blood treaties" and consequently as a direct affront to the cultural icons Kojo, Nanny, and Accompong. Possible retaliatory measures of the virtually unarmed Maroons could hardly dissuade the police task forces, who had access to high-grade technology, from carrying out raids on illegal agricultural products. They seem to fear spiritual retribution, about which they have been warned with oral traditions reaching back for centuries, coupled with recent reports and stories.

In the absence of effective weapons systems, (alleged) spiritual powers serve a protective function by keeping the government agencies from violating the norms established legally in the peace treaty. Moreover, they enhance the pride and determination of the Maroons, which, through various mechanisms of symbolic interaction, inhibits the state from attempting forceful integration and dispossession of the self-governing communities.

Their tradition of resistance, which in Jamaica is now only cultural and no longer military,[173] has several points in common with modern socio-critical intellectual currents and philosophical movements and cultures such as Rastafari. For these recent agents of cultural resistance, spiritual powers as such may also signify the mainspring of their social conduct, even if they live less by the power of communication with their ancestors and opt to build on the power of the word. They are connected spiritually with the Maroons in their willingness and determination to protest oppression in any form, be it religious, cultural, or economic. This link in spirit was demonstrated recently with the massive congregation of Rastafari in Accompong on January 6, 1997 to pay honor to the "original freedom fighters" in the African diaspora. The continuity of black, Africa-inspired resistance in Jamaica, which the following chapter will thematize, is expressed by the reggae band Culture in the song "A One a We" (on the LP *Culture at Work* 1986), in which many heroes like Marcus Garvey and Malcolm X are depicted as standing side by side with the Jamaicans fighting for their rights.

VI

"Chant Down Babylon": Cultural Resistance in Jamaica Today

Johnny Chambers, one of the most renowned singers and dancers of the Accompong cultural group

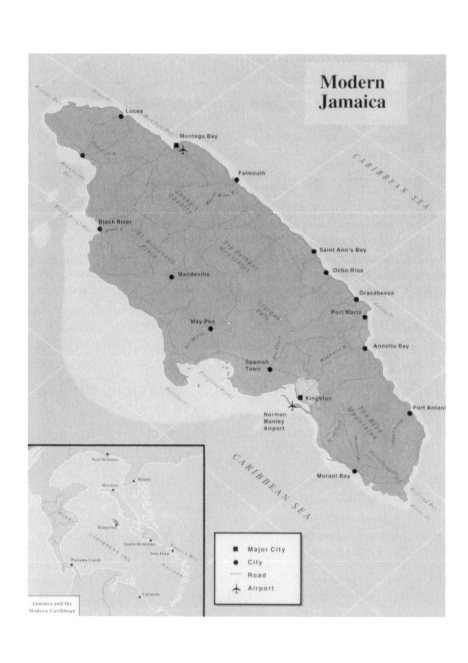

Modern
Jamaica

What has really changed since the days of the Maroon wars, since the formal abolition of slavery, or even since the end of the colonial era? Did anybody offer any form of reparations? Quite the contrary: Those whose ancestors had had to pay with their lives over the course of three centuries for the exploitation of their own labor did not receive any compensation to help them launch an emancipated existence. Instead, payment was made to those who were themselves part of the tyrannical dynasty and who had profitted from the fruits of slave labor. The English Parliament awarded the slaveholders rather than the slaves a monetary compensation of twenty million pounds sterling following the so-called emancipation in 1833 to indemnify them for the loss of "human property"[174] (Gaspar 1984:45).

Few colonial acts more clearly reveal the true mentality of the ruling Europeans. They continued to view "their black subjects"—according to ancient Roman law—as objects and not as human beings. Lacking land and jobs, these people had no real basis for existence. The ex-slaves were now free—free to starve or to continue working for their "ex-massas" under essentially unchanged conditions. One notable difference was that they would now be required to pay rent for the dormitories in the barracks and for the small provision grounds. A whole series of legislative and administrative measures was to limit their formal freedom and prevent the "mass flight" from the plantations that was feared by the plantocracy and by others. The Colonial Office hoped to achieve de-Africanization and a corresponding Europeanization of the African-Caribbean societies with the massive employment of British administrators, teachers, and priests (Hall 1985:70f.). They expected this strategy to yield a "development" of the "black workforce" according to the economic interests of the metropolis of the slaveholders.

Under no circumstances could ex-slaves become citizens with equal rights. In a way, this policy continues to flourish even today. Work on the sugar cane plantations still pays a pittance and has the lowest prestige (P.E. James 1960:17). Communal dormitories housing as many as thirty workers per room (the rent for which eats up part of their week's salary, which is barely enough to sustain them), "day laborers" cutting sugar

209

cane in the blazing midday sun, and unimaginable work conditions in the sweaty, noisy, and polluted work environment inside the sugar and liquor factory: all of these conditions suggest that not much changed with the abolition of slavery (see Padilla 1960:24). However, in the "tamarind season"—when there is nothing to harvest besides tamarinds—many peasants with large families have no choice but to continue working for the white owner even for close to nothing. On Hampden Estate, the owner flies over the plantation in his private airplane to supervise the operation, not wishing to come in contact with his workers. "It's pure, pure slavery, nothing else," comments Rasta Jah Greenie (reasoning of August 19, 1985).[175]

Perhaps the living conditions on the plantations should be viewed as an extreme case, but they remain symptomatic of the continuity of a social system that still crowds together the majority of its members on the narrow space underneath the bottom step of its social ladder. At its top stands the Queen of England, just as in Kojo's time. The symbolic value of this position can hardly be overstated for the recent culture of protest in Jamaica. However, the ladder is beginning to wobble because many are shaking it. Celebrity deejay Yellowman (in the song: "Throw Mi Corn," on the LP *Galong, Galong, Galong*) sarcastically comments on the contested legitimacy of her rulership that the Queen sits down upon the throne but never knows what's going on in Jamaica.[176]

Marcus Garvey, Leonard Howell, and Bob Marley were born into this social setting, the structures of which are still far too reminiscent of the old days. Their ideas of freedom, independence, socioeconomic reorganization, and cultural reorientation are shared by many lesser-known African-Jamaicans. Marcus Mosiah Garvey, "the black Moses," revered by many Rastas as a prophet, was the first to postulate the wish for sweeping changes: "We have been camouflaged into believing that we were made free by Abraham Lincoln. That we were made free by Victoria of England, but up to now we are still slaves. . . and the new Negro desires a freedom that has no boundary, no limit. We desire a freedom that will lift us to the common standard of all men, whether they be white men of Europe or yellow men of Asia, therefore, in our desire to lift ourselves to that standard we shall stop at nothing until there is a free and redeemed Africa" (Garvey, August 1921 speech in New York, in A.J. Garvey 1982:95).

Marcus Garvey championed the cause of rising above the traumas of de-Africanization. He was a pioneer of the Black Power movement and of Rastafari philosophy. His basic principles, such as the central thesis

"Africa for the Africans at home and abroad," have lost none of their validity even today for many in Jamaica and elsewhere. For people like the first leading Rasta activist, Leonard Howell, he left behind a legacy of emancipatory thought to develop the Rastafari cultural revolution. Even from prison he sent inspiring messages to his followers: "We have gradually won our way back into the confidence of the God of Africa, and He shall speak with the voice of thunder that shall shake the pillars of a corrupt and unjust world and once more restore Ethiopia to her ancient glory. Our enemies have seemingly triumphed for a while, but the final battle when staged will bring us complete success and satisfaction" (Garvey, message from an Atlanta prison in August, 1925; in A.J. Garvey 1982:324).[177]

The prophecy of the coronation of Ras Tafari Makonnen as His Imperial Majesty Haile Selassie, which was a symbol of the liberation of black people, is also attributed to him: "Look to Africa, where a black King shall be crowned, for the day of deliverance is here" (Garvey; quoted in Tafari 1985:21). The modern phase of Rastafarian philosophy and culture was ushered in with the fulfillment of the prophecy when the King of Kings (Negusa Nagast) was crowned (Black Starliner Inc. n.d.). These vibrant and challenging perceptions of a completely transformed self-consciousness and a new world view culture were to shake up the colonial basis of Jamaican society.

As Ethiopia, its 225th monarch, and the whole continent of Africa advanced to the center of identification in Rasta consciousness, Europe and its colonies, including Jamaica, were rejected as the centers of slavery and colonialism. Standard English began to be identified as a Babylonian language; Dread Talk and Rasta Highalogue were therefore used instead (Pollard 1983; Birhan 1980 and 1983). Rastas now saw themselves as black Israelites in modern Babylonian captivity. They thereby created an interpretive framework that could be accepted in the course of several decades of essentially unaltered social structures and rampant poverty by broad cross-sections of the social strata; firstly those scattered at the bottom of society in the urban ghettos, then also young people of the middle class caught in an identity vacuum.[178]

Rastafari began in Jamaica, then took hold among millions of people throughout the world as an African-Caribbean cultural revolution, owing in part to reggae texts such as "Chant down Babylon" by Bob Marley (on the LP: *Confrontation* 1983).

Abeng: Mouthpiece of the Oppressed

When slavery ended, the planters exerted economic pressure in their attempt to confine as many ex-slaves as possible to the plantations. In addition to judicial limitations on land allotments and the introduction of high taxes on land, anti-vagrancy laws also restricted the quest for freedom of those who had been newly emancipated. The plantocracy could further count on the help of the British Colonial Office in the satisfaction of their interests. The regulations of the apprenticeship system, which would supersede slavery without much of a break in continuity, and required ex-slaves to work forty hours a week at *de facto* slave labor for their "former" masters, sufficed to clarify to the apprentices the status envisioned for them (Augier/Gordon/Hall/Reckord 1986:182f.). With no prospect of qualitative change, they had only two real options open to them: to accept these conditions and keep working for minimum wage— "a penny a day"—or to use the land that was hard to cultivate and unsuitable for the plantation economy, known as "rock stone and hill side," as their basis for survival (Beckford/Witter 1985:40ff.).

The free Maroon settlements and ways of life offered models of a counterworld to the veiled form of slavery. Many farming communities were constituted in accordance with their example and led to sociocultural developments that deviated significantly from those on the plantations, in the coastal regions, and in the cities (Murra 1960:77). Although these communities could never attain the independence and privileges of the Maroons, the somewhat similar way of life became a symbolic impetus for a renaissance of non-European traditions and a mechanism to revitalize African cultural forms of expression. The massive uprooting that began with capture in Africa and continues into the modern-day school system cannot be undone. However, breaking away from the plantations, the symbol of European domination, was a first step toward reestablishing a connection to African roots that had been violently severed in various ways over the period of three hundred years of enslavement, but nonetheless persisted in thoughts and feelings.

Just as the abolition of slavery was far from insuring a meaningful liberation from the basic characteristics of this system, geographical separation from the plantations did not signify an end to economic dependency. If planters did not wish to assume all the risks and hardships of a meager subsistence economy, they had to adapt to the needs of the international market and grow cash crops for export. The white sugar planters soon recognized the profitability of the emerging large-scale banana production and put an end to their initial ignorance concerning what they called the "backwoods nigger business." Together with multinational concerns such as the United Fruit Company, they "skimmed off the cream" and left the watery remains to the rural producers (Beckford/ Witter 1985:50ff.). With all of the usual consequences of monocultures, their dependence on factors beyond their control and foreign interests continued.

The forces that had turned Jamaica into a sugar colony were the same as those that now fostered conversion to a "banana republic." In the knowledge that "banana republics" do not spring up on their own, but are made (see Rodney 1980:199f.) to exploit the budding dependence of the "small people" on the dictates of market prices and on political control, various kinds of resistance to the manipulation and exploitation that seemed to have no end in sight arose in Jamaica. This continuity of oppression, from original enslavement to modern political and economic paternalism, has kept alive the memory of the most successful opposition in Jamaican history—the Maroon struggle for liberation (see Price 1983b:12, which deals with the situation in Suriname).

Marcus Garvey was proud of his Maroon heritage, which motivated him in a manner that was described as follows by his wife Amy Jacques Garvey (1974:33): "The Maroon blood was stirring in his veins, and he felt that it was time for him to carry on the struggle for which the patriots of old had sacrificed."[179] Nanny, Kojo, and other exponents of this struggle evolved into symbolic figures of national identity and into a mental challenge to take up once again the "old" struggle for freedom, independence, and self-determination. "It is this sort of struggle that requires the swampland genius and bush intelligence as well as the studied cunning and sophistication of the guerrilla warrior" (Nettleford 1978:183).

Both quotations reflect the immense symbolic force of the earliest militant representatives of Black Power. The Jamaican Black Power movement made explicit reference to this symbolism by naming its newsletter *Abeng*. In the spirit of the old Maroon tradition, this newsletter, which was initiated at the end of the 1960s, radically confronted the political, economic, and cultural influences of "the West" and criticized the ruling power structures in virtually all social spheres, from education to the dependency implications of the banana industry and the fictive idyll of the "island in the sun." As a mouthpiece of the "black sufferers," *Abeng* articulated Garvey's ideals of black pride, recognition, equality, and power. Working from a "fundamentalist ideology," to use a now-common notion, its authors launched one frontal attack after another on the colonial bases of Jamaica. On the other hand, their unremitting attack on broad sections of society scared away a large part of their potential readership. Although *Abeng* did not survive long as a periodical, it remained to the end, according to the intentions of the editors, "a horn to blow" (Nettleford 1972:132ff.).

This ambitious project represents an example of how reminiscing on one's own historical experience may produce a more dynamic medium for social critique than adopting "foreign" ideologies. Quite deliberately the name "Abeng" symbolized the black experience in the conflict between Africans and Europeans as it has persisted since these cultures first collided. Turning to models from their own past and present, such as Nanny, Kojo, Accompong, Paul Bogle, Marcus Garvey, and Bob Marley implied a carefully directed attack on indoctrination with Eurocentric imperatives. These foreign norms of conduct frowned upon everything African as backward, and idealized everything European or American as progressive. Identity and pride—as preconditions to liberate one's own cultural creativity from the stigma of inferiority imposed by outsiders—are supported by the recognition of individual energies nourished by interaction within their social fields. Thus individual achievements are closely linked to the collective experiences of the group as a whole (see Nettleford 1978:183ff.).

The rich metaphorics of cultural African-Jamaican forms of expression sometimes veil their implicit social reality from outsiders. Jamaicans recognize the references to the present condition in its historical context as well as the fundamental critique evoked by comparison to the past. In Bob Marley's "Slave Driver Catch a Fire," the symbolism forges connections to the symbolism of Maroon resistance, but at the core it remains social criticism of the present, which, moreover, articulates the call for change. As Nettleford (1978:4) postulates: "The war of the Plantation is nowhere ended."

"Death to the Black and White Oppressors": Nyahbinghi—Spiritual War against Babylon

The international spread of reggae by Rastafari brethren has led to a common misperception that reggae is the true Rasta music. Some artists also use reggae and Rasta as synonyms or speak of them in the same breath. Many "Dreadlocks Rastafari," especially from the Nyahbinghi Order, reject this equation. "Reggae music is some sort of mix-up, mix-up business. Only Nyahbinghi music is divine and pure Rastafari music" (Winston, reasoning of September 10, 1985). They accuse at least some reggae singers and musicians of commercializing their culture and thus of "hybridization" with Babylon. They claim that reggae is just a business venture and that only Nyahbinghi songs serve to praise Jah ("giving I-ses [praises] to His Imperial Majesty"). Only these hymns could chant down Babylon through the power of words, sounds, and power, without the artificial electric energy of loudspeakers (Ras Colwin, reasoning of August 18, 1984).

For the Nyahman (Rasta of the Nyahbinghi Order), Nyahbinghi represents an "ancient duty" to fight against evil. Since Cain slew his brother Abel, it has been necessary to practice Nyahbinghi, a spiritual war against evil (Bongo Hu-I, reasoning of September 19, 1985). Nyahbinghi is neither sect, cult, nor ritual, but an indispensable part or even the very foundation of Rastafari philosophy and culture (Burbie, reasoning of September 23, 1984). Its origins in Jamaica go back to Leonard Howell and other original Haile Selassie followers, who, either from a newspaper article (in *The Jamaica Times* of December 7, 1935) or "through meditation and divine inspiration," as Rasta elders maintain, learned of the founding of a pan-African secret society called Nyahbinghi under the leadership of Haile Selassie. The Rastafari brethren in Jamaica wanted to lend spiritual support to its goal of driving Mussolini out of Ethiopia and of freeing all of Africa from European colonialism through "words, sounds, and power"—enacted with drums, songs, and spiritual energies.

In Howell's Rasta commune *Pinnacle*, founded in 1940 in the mountain region of Sligoville near Spanish Town, the community of Rasta brethren and sistren numbering approximately 1,600 developed Nyahbinghi as a form of cultural expression. Pinnacle was organized on a collective basis and resembled the Jamaican Maroon villages: "Rasta life at Pinnacle had all or most of the Maroon characteristics" (Jah Bones 1985:17). Its residents lived from agricultural products such as ganja, tomatoes, and yams, which they also sold at the local market. Like the Maroon villages, Pinnacle increasingly assumed the contours of a state within a state under the political and religious leadership of Leonard Howell. The government authorities responded with police brutality to crush "this new security risk." Upon Howell's release from prison after serving a two-year sentence (see Owens 1976:16), he reacted with Maroon-style enhanced security measures. Sentries, who now grew dreadlocks and called themselves Ethiopian warriors, secured the entrances to their settlement with an alarm system that announced the arrival of outsiders

215

with the beating of gongs in much the same way that the Maroons had used their abeng (Smith/Augier/Nettleford 1960:9).

After the smashing of Pinnacle by the police in 1954, most dreadlocks Rastafari moved to Kingston, where they experienced more than ever the violent destruction of their housing and ganja. Many of them consequently embraced Nyahbinghi, the spiritual war against Babylon, as their existential basis (see Jah Bones 1985:17ff.).

"Nyahbinghi means war, but the weapon it uses is love, because only love can conquer evil. But if love can't conquer the evil in a person, then the final Judgment will be dreadful, which could be no other than death to black and white downpressors" (Ras Colwin, reasoning of August 18, 1984). Nyahbinghi as a philosophy finds cultural expression in so-called "Grounations celebrations" and "Issemblies" of Rastas, which last for days or weeks. They are devoted to the praise of Haile Selassie and to "chanting down Babylon." They also promote the unity of Rastafari and provide the opportunity to develop doctrinal positions in reasonings. Furthermore, these gatherings represent a coveted respite from the "earthical runnings" (the everyday torments) in Babylon. By the experience of mutual respect and affection, Nyahbinghi gives the power necessary to await final redemption by repatriation to Africa in peace and love (Emsley Smith, reasoning of October 28, 1986; also Sonny, reasoning of August 13, 1984).

Nyahbinghi Issemblies take place on special occasions, notably on Haile Selassie's birthday, the anniversary of his coronation as the King of Kings, or to commemorate his visit to Jamaica. They can also be convened for other reasons, such as a state visit of delegates who supported South Africa's apartheid regime or are associated with the colonial order (the Queen of England is one example). The latter instances, of course, are not planned in honor of these delegates, but in order to oppose them spiritually. Just as Grounations serve to honor Haile Selassie, they concentrate the participating powers of the individuals to a collective energy of cultural resistance. When the two enormous bass drums Gun Court and Armageddon stress the heartbeat rhythm of the smaller fundeh drums and combine with the staccato attacks of the repeater players, the weapons of Rastafari work with "their full power." Night after night, the threatening cascades of the Nyahbinghi drums accompany the hymns to the destruction of Babylon with Jah Rastafari's Last Judgment:

In a de Armagiddeon
Earthquake and lightning,
In a de Armagiddeon
Fire and thunder. . .

In the tabernacle, the holy place around the altar of Melchizedek, dancing Rastafari brethren and sistren conjure up the destructive but cleans-
ing power of the cosmic fire. A "fire man" makes sure that the meter-high
bonfires behind the entrance to the congregation grounds not diminish.
They symbolize both the elemental and purifying power of the
Armagiddeon and the fires whose light led the children of Israel back to
the Holy Land out of Babylon. Words are completely ineffectual in recre-
ating the intense atmosphere of Nyahbinghi conventions: "For I would
even try to explain the conception of I and I worship, word could not
express it. But one would hav' to be involved in a physical location of the
Nyahbinghi. Simple it is not an individual system of worship, but rather
collectively. Each and every one would hav' to be involved to give thanx
continually and praises on to King Rastafari, Jah Rastafari, Selassie I,
Almighty God, the Omnipotent. . . when I and I chant. . . being accompanied at all time by I and I instrument to destroy wicked, the
Nyahbinghi drums" (Ras Historian, reasoning on the music cassette
Rasta/Jamaica, ed.: Michels 1980).

Nyahbinghi conventions, during which several hundred or even thousands of dreadlocks Rastafari from all parts of Jamaica gather together,
are a crucial component of the Rastafari Livity. Nyahbinghi, however, is
not exclusively a ceremonial occasion, but a philosophy that blends concepts and contents that would appear irreconcilable to an outsider, uniting love, peace, dignity, self-respect, and non-violence with hostility, spiritual war, destruction, and Armaggideon. In their view, "death to the
black and white oppressors" also implies love for black and white "non-
oppressors." Spiritual war, destruction, and Armagiddeon are therefore
necessary to conquer evil and to let the good live in peace, dignity, and
self-respect. Physical non-violence is an unconditional order; otherwise
one will become guilty oneself and go down with Babylon. "To chant
down Babylon" means to participate peacefully, but forcefully in the
essential struggle against oppression: "to free the earth for perfect Love,
Iya" (Ras Colwin, reasoning of August 18, 1984).

Even if many Rastas of the theocratic Nyahbinghi Order, which wor-
ships Haile Selassie I as the immortal, secular, and divine ruler, do not see
reggae music as their medium of expression, countless reggae composi-

tions point to Nyahbinghi to reveal the true roots of their creativity in both their music and lyrics.[180] Winston Rodney, known as Burning Spear, has called Nyahbinghi the source of his inspiration (interview of March 26, 1987): "The feelings of Nyahbinghi coming through the music and the music is coming through the feelings of Nyahbinghi. One Order." Neither the music and lyrics of a Bob Marley or any other reggae star who uses Rastafari themes can be understood without Nyahbinghi, the roots of their expression and their vibrations (Freddie McGregor, interview of July 9, 1987).[181]

Whatever course reggae ultimately takes as a commercialized form of communication of cultural resistance in response to Jamaican and international market demands, the drums of the Nyahbinghi will offer a constant medium of expression to "chant down Babylon."

Sounds of Defiance

These days, African symbols are ubiquitous in New York and most other American metropoles. Young African-Americans use them to express their critical distance from white America. They posit their "Old World," Africa, as an antithesis to the alien "New World." Forms of expression that developed in the Caribbean symbolize the process of the re-Africanization of black people in the diaspora. Jamaica stood front and center in this process (Chevannes 1981). Reggae texts like "As long as you're a Black man, you're an African" (Peter Tosh) hit a nerve of a generation that regarded Martin Luther King's dream of integration and equality within American society as pure fantasy.

When reggae went international, Rastafari, the major performers of this music, suddenly had a mass medium at their disposal. Their manifestoes in the form of song carried on the communicative exchange of black people about the commonality of their historical experience on an artistic level. Since the beginnings of their public activity in Jamaica in the 1930s, Rastafari have pursued a goal of solidarity along the borders of the collective black memory. Bob Marley, the "first superstar of the Third World,"[182] became the charismatic representative of Rastafari philosophy. With reggae music, his medium of communication, Marley and other performers globalized the central doctrines of Rasta consciousness (see Yawney 1993). The international success of reggae helped to decentralize the Euro-American music industry (Cooper 1993:176; and 1986). For the first time, a peripheral style of music was able to achieve a breakthrough

Hornblower in Saltpond Ghana (1994).
One of the horns used by the Akan is still called abeng

in the market for popular music. The big music from the small island (to paraphrase Third World in their song "Reggae Ambassador") pioneered what is now called "World Music."[183] Despite the inevitable pressure to conform on the part of the producers, reggae asserted its contextuality to the diaspora experience of slavery, colonialism, and resistance (Zips 1993a:291).

On the occasion of the Maroon program for the Folklife Festival of 1992, the Smithsonian Institution, together with Folkways, compiled and published an anthology of Jamaican Maroon songs, the title of which was *Drums of Defiance*. Drawing on this metaphor, which expresses the determination and spirit of resistance of the Maroons, I call reggae music "sounds of defiance." In doing so, I hope to show that reggae as well as traditional Maroon songs are defined by the collective memory of Africa in rejecting the cultural colonization by European values. In Jamaica, other musical expressions of this nature include the Kromanti songs of the Maroons, the Burru and Kumina music of smaller religious communities, and the Rasta music proper of the Nyahbinghi (see Nagashima 1984:67ff.). "The world wide popularity of Jamaican popular music has been built on a foundation of Rastafarian social, political, and spiritual values. Much has been made of the 'African roots' of Rastafarian reggae. Yet, surprisingly, attention has rarely been paid to the actual deeper roots of this music, the rural Afro-Jamaican traditions that have nourished Jamaica's popular music from its inception. The very deepest of Jamaica's African musical roots are to be found in the island's Maroon communities" (Bilby 1992).

To investigate Caribbean influences on contemporary African-American ideologies, it is necessary to adopt an historical perspective. Africa is the focal point on many levels—historical, sociopolitical, cultural, mental, and symbolic. The musical expression continually refers back to this context. Before the gradual abolition of slavery in the nineteenth century, only Maroon communities could realize cultural orientation to the African experience in the framework of a far-reaching social formation. That ability has earned them recognition today as a pre-nationalist liberation movement (Clarke 1974:23) and as "pioneers of black nationalism" in the diaspora: "The roots of black nationalism go back to the seventeenth century slave conspiracies, when Africans, longing for their homeland, banded together in a common struggle against slavery, because they knew that they were not created for servitude. . . The central claim of all black nationalists, past and present, is that black people are primarily Africans and not Americans. . . Nationalists define their identity by their resistance to America and their determination to create a society based on their own African history and culture" (Cone 1992:9).

The historical achievement of the Maroons consists in having created communities based on their own African foundations, consistent with later notions of black nationalist self-reliance. They also define their identities as free black nations on the basis of their successful struggle to resist the colonial powers. It would certainly be inappropriate to try to shift Jamaica's social conditions in the seventeenth or eighteenth centuries to the contemporary state of affairs in the Bronx or Brooklyn. Nonetheless, young African-Americans stress their commonality with descendants of the first African freedom fighters in the diaspora. For the rap band XClan from Brooklyn, the way to Moore Town, the major town of the Jamaican Windward Maroons, was not too far to film a music video there. As messengers of the Blackwatch Movement, an African-American organization for the ideological dissemination of black nationalism, Afrocentricity, and pan-Africanism, XClan demonstrates a collective consciousness with the Maroons which goes beyond symbolic implications:[184] The drums of the Maroons seem compatible with the contemporary sounds of defiance, and the scratches, breaks, and spoken raps of hip-hop.

In the historical and political arena, the survival of several Maroon communities over the course of centuries proves the basic potentiality of political autonomy and cultural self-determination. Also, the Maroons see their cultural identity as African, shaped by their concrete experiences in the Americas. They thereby fulfill the two major criteria of the African-American independence movements, which can be subsumed under the heading of black nationalism: the pursuit of national self-reliance, and an orientation to Africa while rejecting Euro-American cultural imperatives: "All black national movements have in common three characteristics: a disparagement of the white man and his culture, a repudiation of Negro identity, and a concomitant search for and commitment to the Black (African) heritage" (Lincoln 1991:52).

For the exemplary meaning of the Maroons as a model for other black nationalist ideologies, the success of their national self-government was decisive. Marcus Garvey, who referred to his Maroon heritage, may have recognized a microcosm for his visions of the free African national state in the first free black communities in the "New World." In any case, he viewed the primary goal of black people as the pan-African realization of the historical Maroon success—"the establishment of a separate nation 'so strong as to strike fear' into the hearts of the oppressor white race" (Lincoln 1991:62). To describe this attitude, his wife Amy Jacques Garvey (1974:33) found these words: "The Maroon blood was stirring in his veins, and he felt that it was time for him to carry on the struggle for which the patriots of old had sacrificed."

Of course the historical practices of the Maroons were not simply reproducible, since they were dialectically linked to the structures of plantocratic rule. It strikes me as more appropriate to seek the ideological effect of the successful resistance of black people in the Caribbean on the African-American struggle of emancipation in the twentieth century, notably black nationalism. Marcus Garvey's appeal stemmed from his ability to refute the negative stereotypes of Africa at least for his growing following. With his motto of "Up, you mighty race" he recalled eloquently the historical accomplishments of Africans. In addition to political and cultural achievements, he emphasized black resistance to European colonizers on the African continent and in the diaspora: "Garvey proudly recalled for his followers, though not always with complete accuracy, the stirring heroism of such black leaders of American slave rebellions as Denmark Vesey, Gabriel Prosser, and Nat Turner. The struggles of Zulu and Hottentot warriors against European rule, the histories of Moorish and Ethiopian empires, and the intrepid exploits of

Toussaint L'Ouverture against the French in Haiti were not neglected in the effort to make Negroes conscious and proud of their racial heritage. Garvey delighted in references to the greatness of colored civilizations at a time when white men were only barbarians and savages" (Cronon 1981:47).

"Africa Must be Redeemed": Marcus Garvey's Afrocentricism and Pan-Africanism

By using history as a focal point, Marcus Garvey pursued his political goal of solidarity among black people on the foundation of their common experience. His discursive strategies set out to transform the negative image of Africa that centuries of white racist indoctrination had created even in the consciousness of the descendants of enslaved Africans. Garvey reacted to the institutionalized relations between black and white with provocative radicalism. He countered fundamental legally protected discrimination of black people by white America with his demands for a total reversal of social reality. Instead of white supremacy, he insisted on black supremacy, using the argument of the biological, cultural, and moral superiority of the "Negro race"; he responded to the discriminatory exclusion of black people by American segregation policies with the wish for voluntary and definitive separation of the abducted Africans by their repatriation to Africa; he countered biological prejudice, racist attitudes, and stereotypical claims of cultural primitivity with statements that anticipated the spirit of the slogan "Black is beautiful" in the 1960s (see Redkey 1974:388ff.).

With his "ideology of Africanness," Marcus Garvey implicitly referred back to his Caribbean experience. The intentions of the black freedom fighters against slavery had already been separatist in the sense that they aimed at territorial sovereignty and political autonomy, and thus sought complete liberation from white rule and nation-building on the basis of solidarity and ethnicity. In this difficult process of constructing new social systems, an orientation to African religious concepts and social practices provided the backbone of cultural identity. Marcus Garvey faced a similar problem as his historical predecessors in the black resistance, namely of bringing together heterogeneous interests within the black population strata. People of African heritage in the diaspora were not a homogeneous group with identical experiences and shared expectations (see Zips 1993).

222

Crucial to Garvey's political ambitions was his detection of a common denominator for an international black mass movement spanning all social strata. He found it by using Africa as the subject of his vision of a "Grande Nation" and made it virtually synonymous with "Negro," using the parlance of the time. He gainsaid the legal and social lack of power among black people by pointing to the glorious history of Africa. His program of "race power" targeted the recovery of racial pride as a condition for the fundamental transformation of power relations: "He taught his people to dream big again; he reminded them that they had once been kings and rulers of great nations and would be again. The cry 'Up you mighty race, you can accomplish what you will' was a call to the black man to reclaim his best self and re-enter the mainstream of world history" (Clarke 1974:8).

Garvey proclaimed nothing less than the international struggle of all blacks for a united, decolonized, and independent Africa. With the founding of the New York branch of the *Universal Negro Improvement Association* (in 1917), an organization that he had launched three years earlier in Kingston, Jamaica, he set in motion a propaganda machinery for his political claims. By publishing the *Negro World*, the New York UNIA created the basis for the mediation and effective representation of black interests. The public appearances of the *de facto* self-appointed Provisional President of Africa,[185] accompanied by the mounted private police of the UNIA, the Universal African Legions, sharply contrasted with the legal status of African-Americans at the turn of the century. Garvey did not strive for a peaceful arrangement with the white rulers. His rhetoric did without diplomatic assurances. There was no place for accommodationist statements with the intention of gradual social integration of black and white. Outspoken statements against the white establishment served primarily to create a distinct social distance of outsiders, that is, the white race, and thereby indirectly encouraged internal solidarity: "We do not want what belongs to the great white race, or the yellow race. We want only those things that belong to the black race. Africa is ours. To win Africa we will give up America, we will give up our claim in all other parts of the world; but we must have Africa. We will give up the vain desire of having a seat in the White House in America, of having a seat in the House of Lords in England, of being President of France, for the chance and opportunity of filling these positions in a country of our own" (Garvey 1982; orig. 1923:II, 107).

Garvey's pan-African visions went well beyond the historical legacy of the Caribbean Maroon communities and the Haitian revolutionaries. He also connected to the discourse of the early pan-Africanists of the nineteenth century in the Caribbean and the United States. His political ambitions—the liberation of Africa from colonial rule, creation of an African superstate according to the American model, and the attempted repatriation of the descendants of the slaves, with the slogan "Africa for the Africans, those at home and those abroad"—already belonged to the major themes of Martin Delany, Bishop Henry McNeal Turner, and Edward Blyden. The fact that Garvey is frequently called the "Father of Black Nationalism"[186] is based less on the innovative achievements of his emancipatory thought than on his ability to create a huge following. For the first time, a black interest group attained the dimensions of an international mass movement.

In the United States, Garvey quickly gained the respect of wide circles of frustrated African-Americans who had fought for America in World War I. Their efforts were hardly rewarded. Instead of recognition and social equality, they experienced continued legal and social discrimination. A flare-up of lynching by white mobs made any vague hopes of social integration grow even dimmer. Emigration from the racist south to the northern metropoles brought only a transfer of the problems. Ghettoization and lack of career prospects created a climate in which Garvey's symbolic capital—his discursive strategies fueled with effective rhetoric—brought him immediate political success (Kinfe 1991:34ff.).

He also knew how to communicate his openness to a wide range of ideas as pan-African ideology, recreated from the blend of fundamental theorems of black nationalist predecessors. From Booker T. Washington he adopted the central proposal of creating black institutions as a basis for cultural and economic independence, group solidarity, and racial pride. He also drew heavily on other black authors, such as Dr. Robert Love of Nassau, Dr. Albert Thorne of Barbados, E. Casely Hayford of what is now called Ghana, and Duse Mohammed Ali of Egypt in the framework of the paradigms he mapped out. From these readings, combined with his personal experiences during his journeys to many areas of the African diaspora, he developed a version of black history as his vision for the future, which he called "His Story" (see Martin 1986:111ff.).

Garvey's major weakness, namely that he had been both capitalist and communist, Muslim and Christian, monarchist and democrat, was also his strength. Without any concern for their original coherence in the context of a political ideology or established philosophy, Garvey recontextualized particular aspects of seemingly irreconcilable systems of Marxism/Leninism, monarchism, and even of National Socialism for the

African or African-American experience. "Garvey foreshadowed the unwillingness of a later generation of black activists to be restricted by establishment political ideologies (sometimes even to the point of random eclecticism) by insisting that he felt free 'to pick out the best in every government whether that government be monarchical, democratic, or Soviet!'" (Martin 1986:52).

The UNIA thus remained open to diverse interests and routes of entry, even if these were not used by all segments of the black community to the same degree. The black middle class, which considered "going by the book" the only realistic possibility of attaining social compatibility between blacks and whites, responded caustically to Garvey's motto "Africa must be redeemed": "He believed in his program and he had a childish ignorance of the stern facts of the world into whose face he was flying. Being an islander, and born in a little realm where half a day's journey takes one from ocean to ocean, the world always seemed small to him, and it was perhaps excusable for this black peasant of Jamaica to think of Africa as a similar, but slightly larger island which could easily be taken possession of" (DuBois 1974:111).

Despite the controversy between DuBois and Garvey, waged with extreme acrimony and punctuated by frequent personal insults, the two men are grouped together these days: "No longer are we looking whitely through a tunnel lit with the artificial beams of Europe; we now are able to experience the Afrocentricity that the great prophets Garvey, DuBois, Fanon, Nkrumah, Muhammad, Malcolm, and Karenga had predicted for us" (Asante 1991:1). From a distance, the difference between DuBois and Garvey does not seem as insurmountable as the words the two opponents chose to garner the support of Africa-America would have us believe. For DuBois, pan-Africanism and black emancipation in the United States were complementary goals; Garvey rejected any aspiration to liberation within America as a misleading illusion. As a convincing substantiation of his politics, which were more combative than those of DuBois, he always pointed out the historical experience of the diaspora (see Kinfe 1991:110f.).

The intellectual and artistic Harlem literary renaissance of the 1920s also insured wide exposure to Garvey's ideas. Garvey's influence on some poets, including Claude McKay and Langston Hughes, proved so strong that the literary movement of which they were a part is sometimes referred to as "literary Garveyism" (Martin 1983). Some authors (for instance, Zora Neale Hurston, Eric Walrond, and Claude McKay) published regularly in the UNIA newspaper *Negro World* (Martin 1986:25,

92ff.). At least implicitly, most writers of the Harlem renaissance supported pan-African thought and the fundamental ideas of black nationalism. African-American art and politics combined in a manner that earned the name "cultural revolution" (see Rampersad 1992:ix).

Together with the new musical styles of jazz and of fine arts associated with Harlem, the Black Renaissance initiated a process of rehabilitating Africa in the self-consciousness of black people in the diaspora. Based on this sociopolitical program, the Black Renaissance was basically in harmony with Garvey's historical perspective and his efforts on behalf of building solidarity with a shared African experience at its core. Without mentioning Marcus Garvey by name, the historian Arthur A. Schomburg (1992:231, 337) wrote in the 1920s:[187]

> The American Negro must remake his past in order to make his future . . . For him a group tradition must supply compensation for persecution, and pride of race the antidote for prejudice. History must restore what slavery took away, for it is the social damage of slavery that the present generations must repair and offset. . . Fundamentally it has come about from the depreciation of Africa which has sprung up from ignorance of her true role and position in human history and the early development of culture. The Negro has been a man without a history because he has been considered a man without a worthy culture.

Some poems of the Harlem literary renaissance may be compared in their radicalism to today's rap texts by Public Enemy and Boogie Down Productions. Words of defiance, as found, for example, in the poem "If we must die" by the Jamaican-born poet Claude McKay (1928:53), express the existential threat of African-Americans in American society, which is dominated by whites; they also express readiness to resist:

> Like men we'll face the murderous, cowardly pack,
> Pressed to the wall, dying, but fighting back.

These types of literary "prophecies" accorded with Garvey's political justification for the separatist claim of his "back to Africa" program. If black women and men should attain positions of power within American society, the direct competition with the white power structure, according to Garvey's assessment of the future at that time, would lead to a violent confrontation. Integration, he predicted in the 1920s, would inevitably result in a race war in the United States within fifty or one hundred years (Martin 1986:23f.).

Garvey's "Back to Africa" variant of black nationalism, with its paradigmatic elements of black separatism and African (racial) pride, pan-African solidarity, and political independence, inspired numerous black activists in the diaspora and in Africa. Despite the many setbacks that befell him, owing in part to his own organizational blunders, even DuBois, one of his sharpest contemporary critics, foresaw a dynamic quality in the "agitation of the islander":

> He is today a little puppet, serio-comic, funny, yet swept with a great veil of tragedy; meaning in himself little more than a passing agitation, moving darkly and uncertainly from a little island of the sea to the panting, half-submerged millions of the first world state. And yet he means something to the world. He is type of a mighty coming thing. He voices a vague, formless but growing, integrating, human mind which some day will arrest the world. (DuBois 19;74:114)

XODUS

Like the earlier emigration movements of Martin Delaney, Edward Blyden, and Bishop Henry McNeal Turner, Marcus Garvey failed because of pressure from the white economic and political power structures. The UNIA steamship company *Black Star Line* went bankrupt. After a series of trumped-up charges, Garvey was sentenced in 1923 and 1925, lost his residence permit in the United States, and was deported to Jamaica. Long before Garvey's death in 1940 in London, the UNIA had been deprived of its former influence in the black populace. Garvey died without ever setting foot on African soil—having expressed the wish to be buried in Jamaica (see Whyte 1974:342ff.).

Despite the negative propaganda during his lifetime and after his death, the seeds of resistance he sowed in discourse and practice grew in the action of his successors: "An impressive array of tendencies within the black revolution of the 1960s and 1970s have identified him as a formative influence. Whether it is the Muslims, with Elijah Muhammad's Garveyite origins, or Afro-Americans in mainstream electoral politics, or Malcolm X, whose father was a UNIA organizer, or Kwame Nkrumah and Jomo Kenyatta in Africa, or the Rastafarians in Jamaica—it seems that there is a Garveyite lurking in the past of many a contemporary political activist or organization. . . It took the Black Power revolution of the 1960s with its revival of Garvey's red, black, and green, his race pride, his self-reliance, his separatism, his anti-imperialism and his revolutionary nationalism, to belatedly return to Garvey the recognition he deserves as a major, if not the major black figure of the century" (Martin 1986:360).

Elijah Muhammad, the founder of the Nation of Islam, which is influential today especially among young African-Americans, held views about black supremacy and strategies of black liberation and separation that were closely allied to Garvey's concepts. As a former member of the UNIA, he used the UNIA's Liberty Hall in Chicago in the early 1930s, after Garvey's deportation to Jamaica, for his first public meetings of the Nation of Islam. He thereby provided continuity to the political and programmatic goals of Marcus Garvey (Barrett 1977:114; see also Martin 1986:76f.; also Clarke 1974:372). "Repatriation to the Motherland" was also a priority for Muhammad. Unlike Garvey, however, he did not consider repatriation the only means of achieving separation between blacks and whites:

> The Honourable Elijah Muhammad teaches us that the race problem can easily be solved, just by sending these 22 million ex-slaves back to our own homeland where we can live in peace and harmony with our own kind. . . If this white government is afraid to let her 22 million ex-slaves go back to our country and to our own people, then America must set aside some separate territory here in the Western Hemisphere, where the two races can live apart from each other, since we certainly don't get along peacefully while we are here together. (Malcolm X and Haley 1987:286f.)[188]

Just a few years after his conversion to the "Lost Found Black Nation of Islam" in 1947, Malcolm X was appointed minister of the prestigious Mosque No. 7 in Harlem in 1954. He also became the major spokesman for Elijah Muhammad, the "Messenger of Allah." In his capacity of "Messenger's Messenger," Malcolm X spread Muhammad's message of black separation. Muhammad, like Garvey, believed ". . . that the Black man can hope for neither peace nor dignity while he lives in and is dependent upon white society" (Lincoln 1991:62). Lincoln (1991:74) summarized the difference in their approaches to black nationalism as follows: "Marcus Garvey wanted to found a black nation in Africa. Elijah Muhammad thinks America will do."

Garvey's pan-African nationalism went beyond the central UNIA slogan "Repatriation is a must!" For him, the crucial issue was the liberation of all Africans, whether it took place in the diaspora or in the "Motherland." He made it clear that repatriation was not for all descendants of the enslaved Africans, but initially only for a select elite under his leadership. Its task was to found a Black Nation as a bridgehead for the pan-African anti-colonial struggle for liberation on the African continent: "At this moment me thinks I see Ethiopia stretching forth her hands unto god. . . It falls to our lot to tear off the shackles that bind Mother Africa. . . Climb ye the heights of liberty, and cease not in well-doing until you have planted the banner of the Red, the Black, and the Green upon the hilltops of Africa. . . We say to the white man who now dominate Africa that it is to his interest to clear out of Africa now, because we are coming. . . 400,000,000 strong" (Garvey, quoted in Cronon 1981:183f.).

Elijah Muhammed had witnessed the practical failure of Garvey's call for pan-African "African redemption." Roughly four decades after Garvey's political peak in about 1920, Muhammad considered it naive and presumptuous for African-Americans to take the lead in pan-African liberation. At this point in history, the decolonization of Africa by African nationalist freedom movements was well underway. The policy of the Nation of Islam was therefore patterned on existing African (and Asian) models and propagated a black state on United States territory:

> Many of my people, the so-called Negroes, say we should help the nations of Africa which are awakening. This has been said as if we owned America. We are so foolish! What part of America do you have that you can offer toward helping Africa? Who is independent, the nations of Africa or we? The best act would be to request the independent governments of Africa and Asia to help us. We are the ones who need help. . . Separation of the so-called Negroes from their slave-masters' children is a MUST. It is the only solution for America and her slaves. (Muhammad 1965:35ff.)

Soon after leaving the Nation of Islam in 1963, Malcolm X founded his own organization, which he called *Organization of Afro-American Unity*, as a counterpart to the *Organization of African Unity* (OAU). The programmatic descriptions of the goals of his *Black Nationalist Organization* expressed all of the differences in content that had made him turn away from Muhammad's Nation of Islam (see Clarke 1990:335). With his theory of "domestic colonialism," according to which African-Americans in the United States represented a colonialized nation, he created a common basis for action with those who shared this outlook: "Malcolm argued that black people should identify with the majority of the world's oppressed and downtrodden peoples and elevate the black freedom struggle to the level of an international struggle for human rights" (Allen 1990:36).

In the final year before his assassination in 1965, Malcolm X sought a political alliance with African states with his OAAU in the framework of the international anti-colonial movement. He reformulated both Garvey's repatriation or "back to Africa" concept and Muhammad's goal of separation:

> There are an increasing number of Afro-Americans who want to migrate back to Africa. . . The idea is good but those who propagate the idea in the past put it to the public in the wrong way and because of this didn't get the desired result. The one who made the greatest impact was the honourable Marcus Garvey. And the United States government. . . put him in prison and charged him with fraud. . . A spiritual 'Back to Africa.' If our people would try to migrate back to Africa culturally, first try to migrate back culturally and philosophically and psychologically, they would stay where they are physically but this psychological, cultural, philosophical migration would give us bonds with our mother continent that would strengthen our position in the country where we are now, and then we'd be in a position to influence that government's policies. . . . (Malcolm X 1989:120)

His murder even enhanced his aura of an "apostle of defiance" (Kerina 1990:114). Many claimed bits and pieces of Malcolm X's world view for their own related interests. For this reason, his rich legacy of political manifestoes, from over ten years of propaganda activity for the Nation of Islam and from his short career as an independent black activist, became increasingly fragmented by the following generations of Black Power activists. Quotations by Malcolm X, even if they were torn out of context, served to identify black consciousness: "Like a secret handshake or password, the reverent quotation of Malcolm had identified the speaker as (1) repudiating the 'Negro revolution' or integration into American society and advocating instead the Black Revolution and struggle for Black

Shaddy Rowe, a member of the Accompong community combining Maroon and Rastafari livity

Power; and (2) repudiating nonviolence and advocating instead the fight for freedom by any means necessary" (Boggs 1990:50).

This fragmentation may have contributed to the fact that Malcolm X's cultural creed of "back to Africa" was at best reduced to a symbolic meaning. Africa, in the diaspora abbreviation "Afro," degenerated in the black consciousness of the 1970s to a myth. Afro hairdos, dashikis, and other "Afro" clothing as well as African paraphernalia (which was often pseudoparaphernalia) enhanced the myth to an unprecedented degree, but fell markedly behind the political significance of Africa for the black revolution as Malcolm X or Marcus Garvey had envisioned (see Allen 1990:168). Solidarity with Africa and the enlightenment of African-Americans with African history and culture, completely neglected by Eurocentric curricula in American schools, were indeed part of the standard themes of the Black Power movement, as was the uniting experience of slavery and colonialism. Still and all, Africa seems to have been relegated from the center to the margins of divergent Black Power discourses.

Beginning in the mid-1970s, Rastafari, a philosophical current from the Caribbean, helped restore Africa from cultural and political marginalization in the outlook of African-Americans. Its identification with Africa rested on a process of consciousness raising that had been revitalized primarily by Marcus Garvey:

In its "modern" context Rasta is striving as a matter of natural duty—a spiritual obligation—to identify with Ancient Ethiopia and Egypt. Given the history and experience of slavery, cultural rape and colonialism Rasta sought to reject and even discard the culture of Europe, which was forced on the African descendants of the Americas and the Caribbean. To these people Ethiopia became once again the foundation of their spiritual and cultural existence. . . It was the Right honourable Marcus, Mosiah, Garvey who brought Ethiopia to Jamaica. . . He and H.I.M. Emperor Haile Selassie I are the two great Heroes of the Black / African Revival that is inevitably leading to I n I Redemption. (Jah Bones 1985:12f.)

Many Rastafari regarded Marcus Garvey as a prophet. They considered the coronation of Haile Selassie as the King of Kings in Addis Abeba as the fulfillment of a prophecy attributed to Garvey, according to which enthroning an African king marked the beginning of the liberation of all Africans (Tafari 1985:21). There is a direct link between the veneration of Haile Selassie as a God and redeemer of all Africans and the demand for repatriation on Garvey's terms: "The way I n I see it is that repatriation to Africa is a must! It will take time but it is inevitable. . . One central fact about Rasta livity is that Rastas live in order to give thanks and praises to Jah Rastafari, Haile Selassie I and to go 'back' to Africa. . . To say Africa to the Rasta is like saying God, Selassie I, Power, Good and all that. . . The continent of Africa is a giant piece of magnet, it keeps magnetizing I n I. I n I are drawn to Africa as if by some great magnetizing power and one finds that one is getting closer until one is right there in Africa" (Jah Bones 1985:70).

The two major premises of Rastafari philosophy—the divinity of Haile Selassie and the reality of physical repatriation—were perpetual objects of criticism by outsiders. Despite repeated attempts to "deprogram" Rastafari, the latter clung to their pan-African orientation in harmony with Marcus Garvey's "prophecy." There is no discrepancy between their call for repatriation and political action in the diaspora, although they have often been accused of escapism. "What I see is Rastas fighting for justice and rights wherever I n I live but the ultimate goal is still repatriation. . . every Rasta man and woman knows that Africa is the headquarters of all blackness and the long-term objective is to get Rastafari fully established in Mother Africa!" (Jah Bones 1985:71).

Rastafari reasonings about the necessity for repatriation hark back to the 1930s in Jamaica. With the internationalization of reggae music, performed primarily by Rastas, the doctrine reached millions around the world. Texts such as Bob Marley's worldwide hit "Exodus" (on the LP of the same name, 1977) directly addressed people who shared the historical experience of the diaspora; and indirectly, of course, also those who, independent of their skin color, felt that the time had come for cultural criticism of Europe and the United States.

Bob Marley's rise to international fame paved the way for the solo careers of the other "Wailers" Peter Tosh and Bunny Wailer and for many other singers from Jamaica, notably Burning Spear, Gregory Isaacs, Culture, U-Roy, and Judy Mowatt. African identity, pan-African solidarity (especially with oppressed black South Africans), and African redemption were thematized in hundreds, if not thousands, of texts in the reggae discography. Responsible in part for this enthusiastic reception of Africa by African-Americans was the fact that the singers did not rigidly reproduce Garvey's doctrines. Owing to the dynamic quality of Rasta reasoning, other concepts also found their way into the discourse on Africa. Demands for a cultural orientation to Africa in the spirit of the cultural migration back to Africa that had been formulated by the late Malcolm X did not necessitate physical repatriation: "The experience of being drawn to Africa is something else—it puts one in a situation where one finds oneself constantly thinking, talking, walking, and acting Africa. To the Rasta, most definitely, Africa is no myth; it is the biggest reality that he experiences. It does not matter that the average Rasta does not know Africa, in a physical sense. What really matters is that the average Rasta knows, only too well, Africa in the spiritual and psychological terms" (Jah Bones 1985:70).

Rap and hip-hop function as *the* means to communicate today's ideologies of black nationalism, and are comparable to the significance of the Harlem literary renaissance for the Garvey movement or to an even greater extent to that of reggae for Rastafari. The "Poets of the Hip Hop Nation" reproduce not only the thoughts of the political activists, but also view themselves as educators and think tanks. Nelson and Gonzales (1991:287) write about XClan, the aforementioned messengers of the Blackwatch Movement: "The self-proclaimed 'revolutionists for justice' call their music vainglorious ('the coming of the gods'). They declare they're not in the entertainment business. And they assert they're not rappers but messengers of truth who hung with Biblical figures like Mohammed and Issac. . . XClan. . . is informed by the theories of authors like Martin Bernal and Cheikh Anta Diop, who believe that the roots of civilization as we know it are Black, and that math, the sciences, philosophy and the arts began in Egypt, not Greece."

"XODUS" is the title of an LP publication of XClan. It signifies a radical departure from antagonistic (white) society. X, an omnipresent symbol for black nationalism and Afrocentricity in the African-American community, replaces Anglo-American "slave names" and is used to draw attention to the fact that African names were taken away. The name XODUS indicates a desire to separate the descendants of enslaved Africans from the children of slaveowners.[189] Bob Marley's Exodus and XClan's XODUS are by no means identical in their messages, but, to borrow a Rasta phrase, "within one vibe." Afrocentricism, pan-Africanism, and black nationalism in the political contents of hip-hop are certainly not limited to philosophical influences from the Caribbean. I would argue, however, that black discourses in the United States were open to non–African-Americans as well and were often, especially in times of crisis, revived by "Caribbean activists" (see O'Gorman 1987:86).

In addition to ideological participation in the contents of hip-hop, Caribbean influences also contribute to this musical style. Many of the first performers and inventors of hip-hop, such as Afrika Bambaataa and Grandmaster Flash, give the lion's share of the credit for the development of hip-hop to Kool DJ Herc, a Jamaican who moved from Kingston to the Bronx in 1967: "For Grandmaster Flash, whose parents came from Barbados . . . it was the 'monstrous' soundsystem of Kool DJ Herc which dominated hip hop in its formative days. . . . Giant speakers were essential in the competitive world of Jamaican soundsystems (soundsystem battles were and still are central to the reggae scene) and Herc murdered the Bronx opposition with his volume and shattering frequency range" (Toop 1984:18f.; see also 60ff.).

Like Jamaican dance hall culture, rap was a male-dominated form of expression. In the contest of the artistic opponents to win over their audiences, males predominated. With the increasing politicization of rap by groups such as Public Enemy and the development of Afrocentric or Nation Conscious Rap, a flaw of the Black Power movement of the 1960s became evident in retrospect, which Michele Wallace (1991:81) holds responsible for ensuing political setbacks: "Perhaps the single most important reason the Black Movement did not work was that black men did not realize they could not wage struggle without the full involvement of women."

Female rappers Queen Latifah, McLyte, Yoyo, Shelly Thunder, Sister Harmony, and Sister Souljah began to provide a counterbalance to the domain of "Black Male Power." The rap singer Sister Harmony explicitly cites Paula Giddings' book *When and Where I Enter* as the primary inspiration for shaping her historical consciousness as a black woman (Spady 1991:147). Sister Harmony's activities as a rap artist support a central thesis of Giddings (1988:7):

> Throughout their history, Black women also understood the relationship between the progress of the race and their own feminism. Women's rights were an empty promise if Afro-Americans were crushed under the heel of a racist power structure. In times of racial militancy, Black women stepped forward to demand the rights of the race from the broader society, and their rights as women from their men. The latter demand was not seen in the context of race versus sex, but as one where their rights had to be secured in order to assure Black progress.

Afrocentric confirmation of group solidarity as a foundation for the transformation of structures of institutionalized power is the key to the progress made possible for the entire black community by the activist traditions of black feminists (see Collins 1991:141f.). "Black women's experiences and the Afrocentric feminist thought rearticulating them also challenge prevailing definitions of community. Black women's actions in the struggle for group survival suggest a vision of community that stands in opposition to that extant in the dominant culture. . . Afrocentric models of community stress connections, caring, and personal accountability. As cultural workers, African-American women have rejected the generalized ideology of domination advanced by the dominant group in order to conserve Afrocentric conceptualizations of community. . . through daily actions African-American women have created alternative communities that empower" (Collins 1991:223).

In the context of a collective consciousness that allows for the possibility of gender-specific experiences, Afrocentric attitudes gain more power than in the case of individual actions or isolated militant practices. The historical successes of the Maroon communities might also be exemplary here, since they relied far more on practices of nation and community building than on military strategies. Achieving pan-African goals largely depends on solidarity within the black communities in Africa and in the diaspora. A text called "A.F.R.I.C.A." of the "old school" rap group Stetsasonic (1987), which I read in this light, inspired the title of this chapter. The text calls Africa the motherland; proclaims the need for unity of the black African nations and the African diaspora in the fight against apartheid in South Africa; and points out the continuing bondage of slave mentality even in those who are supposedly free.

The one-sided questioning in this chapter notwithstanding, I do not see the interchange about strategies of black liberation—with Africa as a point of reference—as a one-way street from the Caribbean (especially Jamaica) to the United States. A reciprocal exchange of ideas is at work, the intensity of which has continued to increase since the end of slavery in the mid-nineteenth century. In the past decade, the media options, especially in the sphere of popular culture, have introduced a new quality of intercultural exchange and globalization. The examples of reggae and hip-hop allow us to gauge how reciprocal ideological enrichment motivates processes of political consciousness. The fusion of diverse styles with new creative results is extraordinary in the origin of reggae and hip-hop: "Kool DJ Herc is generally acknowledged as the Godfather of Hip Hop. However, he is seldom seen within the broader context of Jamaican and Afro-American DJing. One must be aware that black American rhythm and blues was to Reggae what Herc is to Hip Hop. This area of cross-cultural influences among peoples of African ascent is a challenging area of inquiry" (Spady and Eure 1991:xii).

In responding to this challenge, I have examined certain aspects of the Africa discourses of African-Americans regarding their Caribbean "input." My task, as I understood it, was not to push ahead to a final result. It would of course be correct to assert that the discourses on Africa in the diaspora began with the experiences of black people in the "New World" and have been continuous since then. Yet, assertions of this sort are little more than banalities. To me it seems more important to stress that Africa never, anywhere in the diaspora, presented a coherent and homogenous image in black consciousness. Moreover, the divergent discourses on Africa were the focal point for the collective experience of peoples of African origin, and thus the very starting point for political action.

CONCLUDING REMARKS

The audience at the 1992 Maroon festival in Washington, D.C. eagerly awaited the appearance on stage of the activist, writer, anthropologist, choreographer, and former dancer Katherine Dunham. Two aides helped Ms. Dunham, now over eighty years old and confined to a wheelchair, onto the stage of the festival tent. In her introductory remarks for the dance performances of the Jamaican Maroons, she recalled her experiences more than half a century earlier in Accompong:

> The Maroons gave me a hard time; they were withdrawn, very proud. . . I was totally green when I went there. I mean I knew nothing. . . I was looking for a dance-form that would allow me to train people. . . The Maroons did not show me what I wanted. They swore they knew nothing about it. . . Finally I went to Kingston— great frustration one day—went to the library, looked for sources about Maroons and found some dusty pages, pictures of what was called a gumbe, square drums and various instruments. And went back to the Maroon people, some of my best friends, and said: Look, did you ever hear of these? And they said: Well, you know. . . Little by little the old people. . . I have been there for four weeks before I could force on them some drum beats and some dances. . . And the one I was finally able to find was one that at that time was forbidden, and even now is considered magic. . . I must stop now 'cause I think we are going to see some dancing. . . I will see things that I worked so hard to see and could not. . . Now I will see it for the first time. (Dunham, unpublished speech in August 1992)

Katherine Dunham was allowed to remain on stage as a guest of honor for the presentations of the Jamaican Maroons that followed. In the course of these presentations, she experienced first-hand the dances, songs, and rhythms the Maroons had described to her as forgotten traditions in the 1930s. I am relating this experience, which was quite moving to most people who witnessed it, to call attention once again to what I consider a crucial criterion for interpretations of the history of the Maroons. Their internal social forms of organization, just like the strategies of structuring their external relations, were subject to secrecy, leading outsiders astray, and camouflage. To a certain extent, these strategies still hold today, owing to the continual precariousness of their autonomy status. For the (ethno-)historical interpretation of the cultural and political practices of Maroons this means that looking beneath the verbalized surface of the texts about Maroons is required to reveal their context. In other words, a certain degree of skepticism concerning the historical sources is necessary. This method does not yield *the* correct interpretation of history, but allows for alternative views.

At least one of these views, namely my own, was linked to the communicative experience with Maroons living today, by which I mean the whole arena of personal relations including professional contacts in the context of oral history research. In addition to the so-called oral traditions, as an essential component of Maroon historiography, the practical attitudes, philosophical horizons, and modes of behavior of the Maroons further developed my interpretive framework. In attempting to avoid the trap of simply reading my experiences in the present into the past, I confronted my "ethnographic" perspective with those of the written colonial sources, the secondary literature, and the Maroon historians. Nonetheless, the unbroken proud habitus of today's descendants of the rebels and their identification with the First Time of the freedom fight reinforced my conscious bias for an outlook on Maroon history as an ultimately successful conflict for power. This may sound like a tautology: the Maroons were powerful because they survived and they survived because they were powerful. I would counter with the argument that the apparent contradictions, their often-assailed transformation from freedom fighters to collaborators of the plantocracy, their diplomacy with the various rulers in Jamaica, and their supposed (temporary) losses incurred in attaining their rights and independence. All this reveals a structure behind the actual historical practices of the Maroons until the present day, which can best be described with the expression Malcolm X made popular: "by any means necessary."

Some authors (for instance, Campbell 1990:250ff.) have reached a very different conclusion, namely that the Maroons of Jamaica increasingly fell under the sway of the colonial state once the peace treaties were signed: "In the final analysis, therefore, the Maroon story is a study of colonial power. And it is in this sense that we can see a parallel with the proposed 'indirect rule thesis' as practiced by Britain in colonial Africa." To bolster her interpretation, Campbell (1990:254ff.) looks back to the events preceding the second Maroon war in 1796. She claims that when the Maroon authorities met British Superintendent John James, they readily subjugated themselves to this powerful and effective foreign administrator:

"Maroon officials under James's rule soon lapsed into a state of lethargy, so that by the time of the termination of his tenure the Trelawneys seemed to have lost their fierce independent spirit and their reliance on their own initiative. The colonial-dependency syndrome had begun."

Campbell (1990:255) finds confirmation for her view that the Maroons lost their identity over 200 years ago in the fact that they adopted Anglo-Saxon "slave master names," and that they furthermore asked the colonial power for medical care. Yet another confirmation for her interpretation is found in Dallas's mocking portrait of Colonel Montague as "a pathetic figure of fun": "it could represent the mimicry that can come about when a person or a collective has lost its confidence in its cultural values."

In contrast to this interpretation, an analytical reading of the colonial sources means, in this case, at least leaving open the possibility that within their community, the Maroons continued using (African) Maroon names, just as they practiced herbal medicine and the science of their bush doctors. This view is also supported by fact that even today there are Maroon specialists highly trained in herbal medicine. Moreover, the depiction of the elderly Montague James as an object of ridicule who was subordinate to the white Superintendent John James as Assistant Superintendent of Trelawney Town and received a salary from the British administration was comparable to Dallas's descriptions of the negative, subservient character traits of Colonel Kojo at the signing of the peace treaty in 1739.

The political interests and racist implications behind the reports of that time appear far too evident, but even if we grant the colonial accounts a certain degree of credibility, the question remains as to whether the conditions described actually point up a cultural loss for the Maroons or rather indicate conscious role-playing on the part of the autonomists. What colonial sources depict as the end of autonomy and the beginning of direct domination could just as well have been a deliberate, sly strategy of the Maroons to preserve their ability to function as an independent society. It strongly recalls the trickster stories of Anansi when the Superintendent John James, described as vain by Campbell, supported "his" Maroons considerably in their dealings with the colonial administration and thereby gained them numerous material advantages just for being allowed to perceive himself paternalistically as their white father/ruler. On top of that, Colonel Montague James received payment (albeit somewhat sporadic) from the colonial administration for his function as the Maroon chief. If the apparent subordination vis-à-vis the

British authorities is seen as a trickster strategy that brought the Maroons more advantages than disadvantages, the rejection of the weak successor of John James, Thomas Craskell, also seems understandable. Maroon history has numerous examples of creative manipulation of external relations to protect social and cultural integrity and substantial political autonomy; Katherine Dunham's experiences in Accompong belong in this category.

In my view, scholarly interpretations that use the data to infer a loss or surrender of the proud cultural heritage of the Maroons ignore the ways in which Maroons, in reproducing political relations, also modify them in the process. The example chosen by Campbell (1990:254) is a fitting illustration: "Their attitude to James Craskell, James's successor, is instructive. Here was a young man, weak and ineffective, who should, in fact, have been the perfect choice for the Maroons had they had the same pre-Treaty robust confidence in their ability to conduct their own affairs. But in fact, they found him unacceptable precisely because he was too weak and not able to govern them as did James." In contrast to this interpretation, I find that the rejection of the new superintendent by the Maroons was caused not by his weakness at governing, but by his uselessness as a buffer to the plantocracy and as an attorney for the Maroons, functions that John James had obviously exercised.

The peace treaty did in fact alter the foundations of Maroon existence; it is precisely for this reason that the descendants of the freedom fighters consider this document sacrosanct. Once the armed conflict had been settled, diplomacy replaced the earlier military strategies. Maroon independence and self-determination did, however, remain vulnerable, albeit in a different way. To defend them "by any means necessary," "diplomatic" political practices were most likely inescapable, much as they may appear opportunistic from today's perspective. However, this type of assessment posits an incorrect dualism between the fighting "idealistic" rebels before the treaties and the "opportunistic" Maroons afterwards. How could we explain, for example, that soon after the change of superintendents, the opportunistic "buffoon" Montague James, whom Dallas compares to an old woman, could lead the Maroons of Trelawney Town in a war (1795–1796) that once again resulted in a peace treaty and not a military defeat for the guerrillas? This same Montague James stayed on as Colonel after the colonial rulers broke the treaty and the Trelawney Maroons were deported to Nova Scotia and subsequently to Sierra Leone.

In the closing sentence of her book, Campbell (1990:260) carries her insistence on the loss of culture and identity by the "colonial-dependency syndrome" in the post-treaty era to its logical conclusion by describing the Maroon communities of today as an anachronism:

> That some of the Maroon communities exist today. . . is due to atavistic stubbornness. When in the 1840s the government tried to encompass them into the wider political system of the island, which, to official thinking, was the logical things to do—considering how their powers had been whittled away—the Maroons stoutly refused. The Maroons have their own reality carved out of their history. It is the abstract notion of this history exemplified by their treaties and lands, sacrosanct to them and inalienable, that has fed this stubbornness. It has given them a perception of themselves that borders on 'the chosen.'

The archival sources convey several erroneous impressions, which was precisely the intention of the (European) creators of these sources. Uncritical readers could easily conclude that in the eighteenth century, Maroon traditional values simply disintegrated and Maroons surrended both their identity and desire for self-determination. If this contention were true, the continued existence of the Maroons today would be utterly incomprehensible or at best a sign of primitive and anachronistic stubbornness on the part of the living descendants of the black freedom fighters. Moreover, a dualistic viewpoint—resistance vs. collaboration or "fighting idealists" vs. "broken opportunists"—requires splitting Maroon history into two seemingly diametrical epochs: one before and one after the treaty. This interpretation contradicts fundamentally the orally transmitted Maroon perspective, as was discussed in the chapters on the interactions between living and dead Maroons and the quality of the peace treaty. It also negates, at least implicitly, a history of Maroon political achievement in defending their autonomy against the various attempts of the colonial power to subjugate them, including enacting laws for a unilateral invalidation of the treaties, economic boycotts, and attempts at religious, cultural, and judicial infiltration.

European observers of the time, whether they be colonial rulers, official chroniclers, or travelers, painted a picture of the Maroons guided by their own views and interests. As a massively defamatory construction, it can obscure the true essence of Maroon history. With some considerations of plausibility that at times relied more on analogic insertions than on "hard" facts, I have attempted to open up a possible interpretive route of entry. I see the historical and symbolic significance of the Maroons con-

241

firmed in their continual striving for national independence. In order to create and defend "their" nation, they employed diverse strategies and practices that accorded with this primary goal, even if they were not always immediately successful. To observers from the outside, the politics of the Maroons may appear idealist at one point and opportunistic at another, alternating between revolutionary and counterrevolutionary. In my opinion, such categories are useless. Maroons themselves have most likely devoted little thought to these kinds of questions. Instead, they have focused on devising appropriate actions in given situations to secure their status as a sovereign community with a common political and cultural experience.

Many of today's descendants of Africans enslaved and transported in the diaspora see a link to their own history and a symbol for their future in the success of "separatist" politics resulting from black resistance to oppression. However, the accomplishments of the Maroons during the entire colonial period also deserve recognition and respect from people who do not share the same historical experience. It has been the intention of this book to contribute to that goal.

NOTES

1. "First Nations" is a designation that has become increasingly common in the United States and Canada owing to pressure brought to bear by the original inhabitants of America. In its legal and anthropological implications, it asserts their prior territorial right. This designation is used in preference to the term "indigenous peoples," which has problematic connotations of "primitivity," and the term "Indian tribes," with its racist overtones.

2. The question of how many Africans were forcibly brought to the "New World" is one of the favorite "numbers games" of research on slavery. There is a huge discrepancy between the conservative estimates of scholars, usually ranging from ten to thirty million slaves (see Curtin 1969:3ff.), and the calculations of black activists, who, following Malcolm X, claim up to two hundred million fatalities from slavery (see Spady and Eure 1991:165ff.).

3. I do not intend these statements as a general attack on the methods of archival research. Without archival research, the state of conflict between Africans and Europeans could only be reconstructed from one angle. I object only to reductive positivistic approaches. Even a compilation of source material can, of course, be quite valuable as long as it does not claim to provide a comprehensive picture of social reality.

4. This version of Nanny's descent was unknown to me from either the literature or the oral traditions of the Maroons. As improbable as the assertion may appear at first glance, written sources indicate that it cannot simply be dismissed as a Maroon myth. In the 1670s and 1680s, English buccaneers led by Henry Morgan were retained to fight the Maroons. Their assignment may have been to induce Lubolo, who led the Maroons at the time, to negotiate: "Conceivably, therefore, the Buccaneers were employed to treat with, if possible, and not to fight Lubolo, promising him amnesty, freedom, and lands for settlement if he would submit to the British authority" (Campbell 1990:21).

5. Treating historical issues also necessitates a critique of current socioeconomic structures. Slavery provides the metaphor for today's living conditions and new dependency relationships in the post-colonial Caribbean nations. "It jus' slavery, man, modern slavery," is how sugar cane workers characterized their working conditions when I filmed "Accompong" (see Zips 1991a).

6. A Jamaican law of 1674 contains a legal definition verifying the slaves' status as commodities and determining that they be considered movable property (Acts of Jamaica 1674, 4, C.O.139/65). For a general comparison of colonial slave legislation, especially in the so-called West Indies of the 18th century, see Goveia (1970).

7. Sugar cane must be squeezed out very soon after it is cut; otherwise part of it is lost and the process of fermentation sets in. Slaves were therefore forced to work at night by torch light (see Hart 1980:16 and Augier/Gordon/Hall/Reckord 1986:84).

8. The numbers games so beloved to some researchers were used to determine the life expectancy of slaves. The contradictory data show the unreliability of the sources that were used (usually records of overseers and caretakers of the plantations). There is no doubt that slaves in general had an extremely brief life expectancy, although it did vary greatly from one island to the next and even from one plantation to another. The type and extent of forced labor was an important factor as well. "House slaves," for example, generally lived longer than "field slaves" (see Hart 1980:106; also Greenwood/Hamber 1980:19).

9. There are numerous parallels between ancient (Greco-Roman) and "modern" (transatlantic) slavery. In both periods, the slave had the judicial status of a "res" (object); the crucial difference was that in ancient Roman law, there was no racially defined slave class or caste, whereas in the colonies the terms "slave" and "Negro" were used interchangeably—which is one of the reasons that this latter term now has decidedly negative connotations (see Edmondson 1976:8ff.; Dunn 1972:225). Thus, in Jamaica the *praesumtio iuris* (refutable assumption) that every black person was a slave also applied (Patterson 1973:90).

10. "Tourist ghettos" (particular secluded beaches and hotels) with their apartheid-like division between foreigners and natives are a contributing factor, as is the preference for "foreign" culture over local talent in the state-run mass media (see Wendt/Linares 1983:16).

11. The slaves were fully aware of this contradiction, as their typical justification for theft shows: "What I take from my master, being for my use, who am his slave, or property, he loses nothing by its transfer" (Anonymous; in Stewart, quoted in Patterson 1973:222).

12. Maroon communities were not limited to the Caribbean islands; they existed in North America, Brazil, Colombia, Venezuela, Ecuador, Suriname, and Mexico.

13. An exception is Haiti, in which the only successful revolution took place. Two studies, of the Haitian Maroons by Fouchard (1981) and of the Haitian revolution by C.L.R. James (1963), describe in detail how an ultimately successful slave revolt all across the island developed from the resistance of individual Maroon groups.

14. I borrow the notion of guerrilla warfare from its application in later historical contexts in order to highlight differences in military and strategic tactics between the Maroons and the British. It is important to note that the Maroons formed complete societies, which are not reducible to a mere guerrilla.

15. Many English-language works have designated common-law rights over others in African societies as *slavery*. Without going into further detail on the inadequacy of this notion, which carries the connotation of the American plantation, for inner-African relationships of dependence, I will only point out that there was a defined system of reciprocal rights and obligations in those societies, which allowed its underlings to marry, to own property or to act as witnesses in court (see Hart 1980:6ff.; Morrish 1982; Rattray 1929:38).

16. For a discussion of the question of the extent to which the notion of "African paganism" encouraged racial enslavement, see Edmondson (1976:11f.).

17. With the Declaration of Independence of the United States of America and the simultaneous stimulus of the Industrial Revolution, mercantile monopolies in general and the West Indian trade monopoly in particular became anachronisms from an economic point of view (see Williams 1983:126ff.).

18. One passage from the most frequently quoted contemporary commentator on the Maroon wars, Dallas (1803:cvi), affords a revealing insight into the mental attitudes of the early 19th century: "The general treatment of the negroes on this island is temperate and human." Some modern authors have accepted Dallas as an eyewitness of events far too uncritically, which has led to glaring errors in interpretion, as will be discussed in the chapters to come.

19. Many plantation owners preferred living in London or Liverpool as eminent members of British society and having their business in Jamaica conducted by an attorney. They were happy to deal with sugar only when sweetening their tea and fattening up their bank accounts. Patterson (1973:33ff. and 1983:249) has used the notorious absenteeism of the white masters as the basis for his hypothesis of the absentee society, according to which the very lack of a plantocratic elite led to a complete breakdown of religion and morals as well as social institutions such as marriage, family, and education. According to Patterson, this situation brought about an acute social anomaly. A pseudo-society of forced immigrants (slaves) and those just passing through in search of quick profit led to the dissolution of traditional cultures. There was simply no coherent system of values, norms, and beliefs.

　　For various reasons, which cannot be explored in detail here, Patterson's hypothesis should be rejected due to its apologetic implications for the (absent) plantocratic elite. One aspect, however, should be pursued further: with or without a plantocratic elite, the plantation society was in an anomalous situation. In Jamaica and other colonies, only the Maroons had a cohesive system of values, norms, and beliefs, which could have important implications in addressing current questions of cultural identity in the Caribbean.

20. For a more precise delineation of the plantation hierarchy, which was not simply divided into masters and slaves, see Augier/Gordon/Hall/Reckord (1986:86ff.).

21. In *The Sociology of Slavery* (1973:29ff.), Patterson depicts in detail the political structures of white society.

22. The autobiography of the Cuban cimarrón Esteban Montejo (1968) conveys an impression of the decisions and behavior that a runaway faced. Of course, in evaluating its historical autobiographical information, it is crucial to take into account the circumstances of how this book was put together; the fact that some editions of this book specify Montejo as the author and others name the editor, Miguel Barnet, points up one of the difficulties of this oral and written narration for ethnohistorical interpretation.

23. Many of them quite deliberately undertake to draw parallels between their current situation and that of the slaves in order to demonstrate how little the predominance of the old power structure has changed. There is still social stratification into a small domestic elite that often cooperates with foreign investors, a fairly small middle class, and the great majority of poverty-stricken urban slum dwellers and poor farmers. These social strata still correlate to some extent with skin color, the elite being mostly white or of

Chinese or Indian background, the middle class brown, and the impoverished majority black (see Beckford/Witter 1985:61ff.).

24. As a countersociety, they were not only a proud challenge to the plantocracy; their settlements to some extent became the model for an independent smallholder system to which the freed slaves in the post-emancipation era could turn. Even today this model lies at the basis of existence in the rural regions of Jamaica (see Rubin 1960b:115; also Ward 1985:25). See Besson (1994:304ff.) for an explication of the relationship between Maroons and proto-peasants.

25. In speaking to Jamaican Maroons, I had the impression that they viewed this development with mixed feelings. On the one hand, they value the national recognition they deserve as forerunners of emancipation, on the other the "nationalization" of their history is also interpreted as expropriation of their cultural singularity (Colonel Cawley, conversation of September 28, 1985).

26. As I indicate in several places, Rastafari philosophy has had a leading role in the Back to Africa movement. However, the writings of Rex Nettleford, Richard Hart, Edward Kamau Brathwaite, and Leonard Barrett, among others, should also be emphasized in this regard. They convincingly show that an identity conflict is a social prison that confines thousands of Jamaicans (Barrett 1979:14).

27. The Maroons are a perfect example of how apparently outmoded conduct can be revived even after years of suppression when the cause of their impediment is removed and they are in a position to reinstate it. In the process, the concrete forms can change and only the structures of this conduct appear as a practical expression of a cultural grammar (see Mintz/Price 1976:27).

28. Even clinging to this ethnic identity meant, strictly speaking, deracination from the more narrowly-defined identity of the clan or a particular village community.

29. General notions such as "syncretism" are only applicable at a certain degree of abstraction. They reveal little about whether a culture came into being from counteracculturation to an oppressive ruling culture or from acculturation or accommodation to it (Bastide 1983:199). According to this collective categorization, the culture of the Maroons and of many Africans on the plantations would be "syncretic" more in the first sense of counteracculturation, whereas that of the "Creoles" would fall more into the latter category of accommodation (see Schuler 1970:384).

30. In Jamaica today, which has so very many Christian churches, it is evident how religious activity was relegated to the churches, separated from everyday life and essentially limited to brief moments on Saturdays or Sundays. In stark contrast are the Rastafari, who view their culture as African and reject any dichotomy between the secular and spiritual spheres.

31. Diverse ethnic heritage was not an automatic ground for exclusion if other circumstances applied, such as the solidarity that grew from enduring middle passage together or working on the same plantation; as a rule, however, a great many revolts were ethnically determined. In Jamaica and Suriname, for example, they were usually initiated by Akan under the leadership of

246

those who in Africa had already held a position of authority on the basis of their genealogy or ritual capabilities (see Schuler 1970:382f.).

32. Crahan/Knight (1979a:xi), referring to new forms of artistic expression in the Caribbean, have noted in this regard: "Africa is the integral link in the fraternal chain that unites all the oppressed and exploited nations of the world."

33. Patterson (1973:174ff.) provides an overview of the character traits that white authors ascribed to the "Quashee" personality based on the written historical sources. He appends to this an analysis of the reasons this stereotype arose, taking into account the active role of the slaves who sought to dupe their masters.

34. The literature has time and again resorted to these categorizations; see, for example, Patterson (1973:260ff.), who distinguishes between active and passive resistance, and Lewis (1983:175ff.), who lists three categories of resistance, but does note that these categories overlap significantly.

35. One of the inventive variants for getting away with a minimum of work without punishment was feigning a need to relieve oneself and asking permission "to go a bush."

36. The popular Jamaican saying "play fool to catch wise" shows that playing dumb and misunderstanding should be understood as deliberate role playing and as a subtle form of resistance, in contrast to Patterson (1983:275), who rejects psychological modes of explanations for slave resistance. The particular cultural significance of the Anansi stories may also be brought in to bolster this thesis. As an African trickster figure, he/she is the literary embodiment of active role-play with deception, playing dumb, and deliberate swindling. Anansi—who is sometimes human and sometimes a spider—advanced in Jamaica to a cultural hero of the enslaved by providing an orally transmitted model of how the mighty can be outmaneuvered with trickery and deception. Many of the fictional stories lent themselves to identification with the hero, who had mastered the techniques of survival. They originated in the West African stories of the Ashanti, whose heroes were represented by the spider Anansi together with his/her son Ntikuma (Tacooma in Jamaica) (Barrett 1979:32ff.). A selection of the lesser-known Jamaican Anansi stories is found in Beckwith: *Jamaica Anansi Stories* (1924).

37. Sugar cane fields and houses constructed of wood were the main targets of this form of sabotage (Mathurin 1975:19).

38. It was all the more painful for the slaves when the Maroons were obliged by the terms of the peace treaties with the colonial rulers not only not to recruit new members but even to capture or kill all future runaways. On the causes and consequences of this treaty agreement, see chapter four.

39. His name was Europeanized by the English, first to Luyola, then to Juan de Bolas; some earlier writings use the latter spelling (Hart 1985:6).

40. According to a rough estimate by Schafer (1973:50), one quarter of the enslaved Africans in Jamaica came from each of the following areas: Senegambia/Sierra Leone, the Windward Coast, the Gold Coast, and Whydah on the Slave Coast. In the decisive original phase of Jamaican Maroon communities (from 1655–1720), prisoners of the wars between Akan

groups, as well as from the Ga and Andagme peoples constituted the majority (up to perhaps two thirds) of the slaves. They were all referred to as Coromantees in Jamaica; later mainly Guang and Fanti from other regions of the Gold Coast (Ghana today) were enslaved; additionally, the Ewe-speaking inhabitants of the Slave Coast as well as Ibo and Yoruba from Nigeria (see Hall 1982:57; a more precise enumeration by time periods is found in Patterson 1973:127ff.).

41. The name Kojo has an African counterpart, Kwadwo, in the Ashanti and Akim term for "Monday." The Fanti use the word Kojo. Kwako (Quaco) is the counterpart of Kwaku ("Wednesday") among the Ashanti and Akim; the Fanti word is Kweku. Some Maroon names, however, can be traced back to the naming system of the Ga. Kishee (a Windward Maroon leader), for example, derives from the Ga name Kushi (see the chart in Hart 1985:11).

42. The British slaveholders seem to have had a particular aversion to Ibos, who frequently reacted to enslavement by committing suicide, especially when they had enjoyed high social status in their homeland. Even today, suicides in Jamaica are sometimes described with the phrase "Him Iboed himself."

43. The Papaws had a similar background. They came from the Dahomey empire, which had produced equally strong military traditions in the course of their attempts at imperial expansion. However, very little is known about their participation in rebellions (see Patterson 1983:263, 283).

44. Contemporary chroniclers (especially Knight [n.d.]; Dallas [1803]; and Edwards [1796]), who wrote as supporters of slavery, described the internal organization of the Maroons through the lens of their colonial perspective and in accordance with their own prejudices. Lacking other source material, most modern authors have turned to these writings for their information, which they often simply repeat without taking a critical stance. In this chapter, therefore, several alternative interpretations are provided, which have at least some degree of plausibility. Perhaps oral history research can introduce new perspectives. The outstanding work by Richard Price (1983b) on the early history of the Saramaka Maroons of Suriname points at such an outlook.

45. Because of their preference for pork, the Maroons used to be known as "hoghunters" (Dallas 1803:26).

46. Even today, most Maroons of Scott's Hall claim to be Ashanti. When asked about their cultural identity, they say: "We live Ashanti." Warriors from the Ashanti empire enjoyed great respect among the Africans. Many of them identified with this reference group and could thereby gain acceptance in a rebel group that had originated as an ethnically cohesive unit (see Genovese 1981:100).

47. Reggae singer and Rastafari Winston Rodney (known by his professional name Burning Spear) made scathing remarks on the legend of the discovery of Jamaica by Columbus (on the LP Hail H.I.M., 1980, in the song "Columbus") by calling Columbus a liar who could not possibly have discovered Jamaica because the Arawaks had been living on the island long before his arrival.

48. First Nations that belong to the language family of the Arawaks are the Guajiro and Pataujano, who still reside around the border between

Venezuela and Colombia.

49. Brazilian examples of collective black resistance to slavery and assimilation by white culture were *quilombos*, autonomous settlements of runaway slaves that were tantamount to "African states in Brazil" (see Kent 1983; Bastide 1983; Hofbauer 1986).

50. The example of massive migrations to urban areas today, in many Caribbean and African countries (among others), shows how flexible people can be in redefining their ethnic identity when their social environment changes. The new urban community, as a dominant focus of identification, can even surpass older ethnic ties to a village or chieftaincy in the West African context (Kopytoff 1976:34f.). A similar effect is evident in Jamaica, in which many migrants from rural areas consider themselves "Kingstonians" once they have settled down in the city. However, this self-conception is just as flexible and can revert back to "country folk" if they return to "their" people. Even the author of this book has experienced the flattering feeling of being addressed as a "Maroon Townite" after a long stay in Maroon Town and seeing his status as an outsider fade away.

51. The external threat of war was an additional reason for the long duration of the probation, the purpose of which was to bolster the solidarity of the new members and to ascertain their loyalty to the community and its leaders (see Price 1983b:17).

52. Kromanti (Coromantee), most likely a hybrid of several West African languages, remained in use for conventions, festivals, and certain rituals (Bilby 1983b:37ff.).

53. Military confrontations between two rebels groups rarely occurred. The Leeward Maroons under Kojo did, however, at one time subjugate a group of Madagascar Maroons and forced them to integrate after killing their leader in battle—if the historical sources are accurate on this event (Kopytoff 1976:38).

54. Maroons also defied virtually all other European powers of the time and forced peace treaties in Brazil, Colombia, Cuba, Ecuador, Hispaniola, Mexico, and Suriname, among other places (Jones 1981:61).

55. On the basic theoretical problems and methodology of the ethnohistorical approach, which rises above a purely factual analysis, see Wernhart and Zips (1998). Ethnohistory in this conception is informed by praxeological and critical theory (see Zips 1998b:221ff.).

56. In accordance with white accounts of the event, the historian Gardner (1971:117f.; first published 1873) describes the raid on Nanny Town as a triumphant surprise attack. In his depiction, a large number of troops succeeded in reaching the Maroon village with several heavy swivel guns.

57. Given the paucity of scholarly source material, it is of particular value that Miguel Barnet taped, edited, and published the autobiography of the escaped Cuban slave and later cimarrón Esteban Montejo (1968). Richard Price (1983b), who published the "historical vision" of the struggle for freedom of the Saramaka Maroons' ancestors in his book *First-Time*, has also provided an invaluable resource. For a reevaluation of colonial sources, see also

Zips (1998c).

58. The great importance of Rastafari philosophy in this process, which has already been pointed out several times, will be treated in detail in chapter six.

59. On the plantations, a great deal of knowledge was cultivated in secret and orally transmitted, which could raise the suspicions of the white masters. Botanical expertise on the part of slaves seemed suspect to them; they feared, for example, sorcery or poisoning (see Martin 1985:205ff.).

60. Today, fertilizer made from bat droppings is quite valuable for particular cash crops (primarily for export). A layer of manure that can be gathered up and carried away in sacks covers the rocky floors of the bat caves.

61. Vic Reid made the oral tradition of the Maroons of the attack of the English on Nanny Town the backdrop of his novel. A "Maroon Griot" (storyteller) appears as the protagonist to narrate the story, which involves a great deal of historical information and many oral histories researched by the author.

62. In countries with few inaccessible, unpopulated areas, the Maroons proved to be somewhat less successful. Sooner or later, their hiding places were discovered—with typically fatal consequences for the black rebels. North America is an example in which Maroon activities always accompanied slavery but did not lead to enduring semi-autonomous states within states (see Aptheker 1983:151ff.).

63. Apart from these two regions, the natural vegetation of the island was mostly destroyed and deforested except for one third of the total land surface of Jamaica, according to the German Handbook for International Cooperation (HIZ:I Jama 0200; 1987:1ff.).

64. Birds do have a larynx, but it is used only to regulate the flow of air in breathing (Burton 1985:120).

65. This passage refers to the Maroons of Panama. However, other Maroon groups knew this or similar methods of making smokeless fire as a basic component of their defense system.

66. In the reggae song "Slavemaster" (on the LP Mr. Isaacs, 1982), the famous Jamaican singer Gregory Isaacs revives this form of resistance, which was employed not only by Maroons, but also by enslaved people. The singer, already heated with anger, threatens to set fire to the plantations if the slave master doesn't give him what he requires.

67. Although the plantations situated in the backlands were usually fortified with palisades, the attacks often succeeded in occupying the plantations and even holding out against approaching troops (Hart 1985:69).

68. Namba Roy spent his youth in Accompong Town (in Cockpit Country). After World War II, he worked in London as an official representative of the Accompong Town Maroons. He died in 1961, several months after the publication of his novel. Beshoff (1983:34ff.) provides a detailed account of his writings.

69. The use of an (African) tone language such as Yoruba or Akan is essential, since it is the tones that are "translated" into drumbeats (Martin 1985:189).

However, no one single African language was spoken consistently, with the possible exception of some small Maroon groups with a common heritage. Still, most cultural traits show a striking similarity to Akan customs.

70. The Maroons tended to establish their settlements as fortifications in South and Central American regions and in Cuba. They surrounded their fortifications with palisades for protection. These armed villages were called *palenques* in Cuba and Colombia (see esp. La Rosa Corzo 1991; also Perez de la Riva 1983:49ff.; and Escalante 1983:74ff.); in Brazil, they were called *quilombo* (see Kent 1983:170ff; also Hofbauer 1986, both of which treat the most famous quilombo "Palmares") or *mocambo* (see Schwartz 1983:202ff.).

71. An example for the successful employment of this tactic is also found in Schafer (1973:134).

72. The notes of Allen and Peters are not altogether conclusive as to whether they had really occupied Nanny Town or another Maroon village. In any case, with this and other military missions, at least the approximate location of the village must have been known to the colonial militia (see Hart 1985:48ff.,81).

73. Colonel Guthrie encountered a similar situation in his attempt to capture Kojo's Town. Hart (1985:101) writes about this attack: "The Maroons employed their usual guerrilla tactics, abandoning the town to the strong force attacking them, suffering no casualties themselves but from the surrounding bush making the position of their enemies untenable in the open ground."

74. The Journals of Assembly (see Patterson 1973:32,48) reported on the agenda of the legislative assembly.

75. Every healthy male white resident of Jamaica could be drafted into these militias. Their effectiveness dropped sharply in the course of the eighteenth century, when more and more regular troops were "imported" from the homeland of the slaveholders.

76. Miskito had already been brought to Jamaica in 1722 without much success. Just sixteen years later, the plan was taken up again (Hart 1985:27,93).

77. Some colonies (for instance, Saint-Domingue) also used collars to which three to four spikes were attached, each four or five inches long. These collars were humiliating as well as debilitating to those who wore them and generally resulted in their social isolation (Debien 1983:119).

78. According to Simon Vestdijk (1941:40), who bases his account on the notes of the son of the plantation owner Richard Beckford from his stays in Jamaica in 1737 and 1738, hangings in cages were punishments meted out primarily to Kromantis. The rebels or Maroons were clearly visible from their cages, which were suspended from 10-foot-high poles. Their slow death by starvation and dehydration occurred after about a week.

79. Every slave who took part in the rebellion of Bybrook and could not escape the clutches of his pursuers was burned alive, torn apart by dogs, drowned, or drawn and quartered (Dunn 1972:261).

80. Sometimes the threat of these punishments had the opposite effect. If a slave

feared torture or some other punishment for any offense, the decision to seek flight might have come more easily (Martin 1985:22).

81. In return, they enjoyed privileges such as better quarters located near the overseers' residence (Patterson 1973:54).

82. The slaves developed their own version of a divide and rule strategy by seizing every opportunity to sow discord in order to pit masters and overseers against one another (Lewis 1983:180).

83. By "free blacks," only those are meant here who had liberated *themselves.* Freed slaves remained quite dependent on the plantocracy, which makes the notion of freedom only partially valid. Emancipated former slaves sought equality with whites and were hardly interested in cooperating with slaves. Many of them went on to become owners of slaves and land (Hall 1982:45f.). An obvious concurrence of interests with the white slaveowners and landowners was one consequence, which was certainly intended by their former masters to prevent an alliance from forming between emancipated blacks and slaves (Augier/Gordon/Hall/Reckord 1986:163; also Beckford/ Witter 1985:21f.). Their relationship to Maroons was varied and contradictory. Some emancipated slaves maintained trade with the rebels; others used their detailed knowledge of the black freedom fighters to provide information to white slavehunters and the militia (Jones 1981:71). Correspondingly, Maroons pursued a similar strategy to black settlers as they did to whites. They allowed no landowners on their territory and tried to keep an open "buffer zone" around their land with raids on remote properties (see Parris 1981:192).

84. It was not unusual for black women on the plantations to have children by Maroon men. Especially in the post-treaty era, the slaveholders clearly knew about these "liaisons" and paid higher prices for the offspring of these unions, whom they considered stronger and more rugged (Jones 1981:69f.).

85. The naming process refers to the tribal subdivision of the Akan into Ashanti and Fanti. Using these names to derive the original ethnic heritage of the Maroons is not feasible, however, for many reasons, including the fact that the terms are also interchanged occasionally and Nanny is identified with Shanti Rose, while her sister is called Fanti Rose (Bilby 1984:13). Dalby (1971:49f.) views this naming process as a reflection of the traditional hostility between Ashanti and Fanti and a continuation of "tribal animosities" in Jamaica. According to the oral tradition recorded by Dalby, however, Maroons identify themselves as Ashanti, whereas they identify other African-Jamaicans as Fanti.

86. A similar genealogical myth links Accompong Town and Windward Maroons. According to the oral traditions of the Accompong Town Maroons, Nanny was Kojo's sister (Hart 1985:44; also Colonel Cawley, conversation of September 28, 1985). However, it is rather unlikely that Nanny and Kojo were blood relatives. Maroon communities strove to forge symbolic ties to maintain a peaceful coexistence. It is evident from the example of the two Maroon groups of Juan Lubolo and Juan de Serras, who fought against one another in the first years of the British occupation, that Maroons in the same colony also pursued diverse politics. Lubolo, who had reached an agreement with the British, was killed by the Maroons under de Serras during an attack on

his former black allies (Parris 1981:191). For a second time, the "divide and rule" policy resulted in discord among the Maroon groups. In the second Maroon war (1795–1796), the two Leeward Maroon villages fought against one another. The settlers of Accompong Town sided with the English against their former comrades at arms of Trelawney Town (for details, see chapter four).

87. The film *Bongo Man* (starring Jimmy Cliff) shows how ambivalent the relationship between Maroons and non-Maroons remains even today. This film gives due credit to the heroic story of the resistance fighters, but has a Rasta woman accuse them of treachery to those on the plantations.

88. John Guthrie was a local planter and officer of the militia respected by the Maroons for his honesty and ecological expertise (Craton 1982:87).

89. According to the Julian calendar, New Year's Day fell on March 25. Before the Calendar Act of 1751, the "old" year was usually listed with dates between January 1 and March 25 (Hart 1985:129). The old sources (for example, Dallas 1803:58; and Edwards 1983:237) therefore date the peace treaty as March 1, 1738, but most modern authors list it as March 1, 1739. It is interesting to note that the Jamaica National Trust in Accompong Town erected a monument to Kojo that bears the date 1739, although the Maroons go by the Julian Calendar; the date engraved on the abeng that is kept in Colonel Cawley's house is March 1, 1738.

90. The complete text of the peace treaty is found in Dallas (1803:58–65) and in Hart (1985:118–120); it can also be examined in the Public Record Office (CO 137/23, W.4).

91. Dallas' accounts would hardly hold up if other sources were brought into play. When sources are introduced without a critical perspective, which is an essential component of ethnohistorical research (Wernhart 1979:40f.), distortions may continue to be transmitted and appear correct.

92. Hart (1985:121f.) provides the complete text of the fourteen articles of the accord with the Windward Maroons and appends an exhaustive comparative discussion of both treaties.

93. Occasionally they managed to dodge these obligations, according to Bryan Edwards (1983:243), who was an unusually harsh opponent of the Maroons. According to his oft-cited report, Maroon pursuers had let some rebels from Tacky's Revolt escape, and hoodwinked the colonial authorities with the severed ears of rebels who had been killed at some earlier point. Whether we should infer an opportunistic preference for the easy way to get a monetary reward or a deliberate favoring of the resistance fighters is as uncertain as the reliability of the source of this report.

94. According to the conviction of the Maroons even today, not only their sociocultural identity could be transmitted in the blood, but also their distinctive features, stores of knowledge, and abilities. Beckwith (1969:184) reports that as late as the first third of the twentieth century, no non-Maroons were permitted in the settlement unless accompanied by a white person or a Maroon. Not long thereafter, exceptions were beginning to be made: Dunham (1946:121ff.) describes the story of a carpenter who, with the support of the Colonel at that time, was allowed to become a resident of Accompong Town.

Dunham reports that this type of permission had never been granted before.

95. A song by Africans who immigrated voluntarily after the emancipation of the slaves after having participated in the uprising of 1865, deplores the role of black allies (of the colonial authorities): "Oh dem Maroon people a kill out me nation. . . " (Schuler 1980:68). The only reggae song I know that is devoted exclusively to Paul Bogle and his historical role as leader of the oppressed comes (ironically) from the group that calls itself Cimarons in homage to the memory of the first black freedom fighters ("Paul Bogle" on the LP: *On de Rock* part 2, 1983).

96. Kopytoff (1979:60) concluded: "As long as Maroon Society stands, The Treaty stands, and vice versa."

97. At that time, Trelawney Town consisted of two adjacent settlements of which (the new) Furry's Town (named after a Maroon leader) was considered untenable and was therefore set on fire. However, the Maroons also gave up the old town a few days later (Hart 1985:171ff.).

98. It was not the first time that the English colonial ruler had made one Maroon community fight another. Soon after the British occupation of Jamaica, the Maroon followers of Juan Lubolo had reached an accord with the colonial ruler and attacked their former black allies, the Vermahalies rebels of Juan de Serras. After Lubolo had been killed by de Serras in this attempt in 1663, his followers disbanded (Parris 1981:190ff.).

99. Then as now, the English Crown represents the Jamaican head of state. The constitution of 1962 established an independent parliamentary monarchy within the Commonwealth, in which the British Queen is represented by a Governor-General appointed by her.

100. Most Maroon leaders held military titles, such as Captain, Governor, or Colonel (Price 1983a:20). In the sources, Kojo is also sometimes referred to as Captain Kojo (Cudjoe) as well as in the peace treaty of 1738/1739. A recent brochure of the Accompong Maroon State mentions him in the rank of General. See also McFarlane (1977), a born Maroon, who reports on his life. McFarlane's publications are based on the oral traditions of his grandfather.

101. The political structure in the Maroon communities still in existence today in Suriname, according to Price (1983a:295), includes village headmen and assistant headmen, who in turn are responsible to the tribal chief, their superior.

102. Craton (1982:77) erroneously calls the organization of the Windward Maroons "Amerindian-style confederacy."

103. Evidence for this assumption is that Nanny was not mentioned in the peace treaty, which had been negotiated and signed by Kwao (see Robinson 1969:59ff.), but two years later an official document that transferred land rights to the Maroons assigned them to "Nanny and the people residing with her" (Hart 1985:81, 83). For a detailed discussion of Nanny in an African Akan political context, see Zips 1998a.

104. In Moore Town, Colonel Harris, who had been elected at one time, considered himself appointed to office for life, which led to serious internal tensions and open conflicts within the Maroon community. Colonel Harris refused to

hand over the necessary documents and turn over his office when Mr. Sterling was elected as the new Colonel in 1973 (Sterling, conversation of January 5, 1988). Schafer (1973:217) reports concerning Scott's Hall that the former Colonel Euthon Latibaudière derived his legitimacy to rule from his royal ancestry and insisted that his title could be passed from one generation to the next.

105. The last portion of the treaty clause curtailed the Colonel's authority to impose capital punishment in cases of serious violations of the law. These far-reaching terms of punishment arose from the need to enforce quasi-military discipline throughout the community (Genovese 1981:53; also see Hart 1985:64).

106. Maroon groups in colonies other than Jamaica obviously counted more strongly on the "forced redistribution of the wealth amassed by slavery." Schwartz (1983:211) writes about the Mocambos in Bahia (Brazil): "Rather than a return to African pastoral or agricultural pursuits, mocambo economy was parasitic, based on highway theft, cattle rustling, raiding, and extortion." The word "parasitic" must be rejected because of its pejorative connotations in the concrete context. Marshall (1976:27) reports on Dominica on the extent to which this form of economic activity was regularly linked to the ideology of resistance: "Bands of Maroons ranging in numbers from forty to fifty set fire to five estates completely destroying buildings and crops, forcing the whites to retreat to other areas."

107. Bargatzky (1986:111) characterizes the tropical rainforest as "the most generalized and productive, most widely diversified of the natural terrestrial ecosystems." With the technique of food production associated with shifting cultivation, generalized artificial ecosystems could evolve on the cleared areas "that apparently optimally simulate the character of a natural generalized ecosystem" (ibid.:114).

108. Under different conditions and with different techniques, slaves also managed both remote provision grounds (which they called "polincos") and small fruit and vegetable gardens ("kitchen gardens") behind their huts (Patterson 1973:219).

109. It is primarily young men who leave the Maroon villages, thus creating a gender imbalance there (Colonel Cawley reporting on the situation in Accompong, conversation of January 11, 1988).

110. Talent Incorporated is located in Port Antonio, a harbor town near Moore Town.

111. Price (1983a:295) names six Suriname Maroon communities: the Ndjuka and Saramaka, who number approximately 15,000 to 20,000, and the much smaller numbers of Matawai, Aluku, Paramaka, and Kwinti.

112. The *social* reality of this "mere" biotic relationship, which is unlikely to be based in fact, needs to be pointed out again (see Müller 1988:133).

113. When "outsider" women marry into Maroon villages, the Maroons reconstruct a biotic kinship: "When you say outsiders, the Maroons know that the female's parents or foreparents are Maroon; so after they trace it to the truth, they really married to Maroons" (Mrs. Hilda, interview of January 13, 1988).

114. Since most modern cultural descriptions of the Maroons rely on the reports of the colonial historian Dallas, I have used the conditional to indicate a necessary critical stance concerning this information.

115. Dallas (1803:110f.) tells that marriage came about by the simple decision to live together and that the bride was presented with clothing and worthless trinkets at the wedding ceremony, while the groom got hogs, chickens, and other livestock from the relatives of his wife. If the couple was later to separate, these gifts would need to be returned (see also Schafer 1973:69, who restates Dallas' description almost verbatim). We have already referred repeatedly to the degradation of the Maroons to primitives or savages implicit in these textual passages. Constructing analyses of legal ethnology on the basis of contemporary colonial sources—such as investigating dowry as a kind of *dos recepticia* in the light of Roman family law implications—therefore seems untenable from the standpoint of a critical scholarly view.

116. There are isolated scholarly instances in which her very existence has been questioned. We will not be dealing with this hypothesis, which is quite unlikely anyway in light of the extant source material, because the focus of the observations is placed on her position in the minds of people who related to her in various ways and not on the so-called historical facts. Most scholars reject terms such as chieftainess and goddess as inapplicable to her probable status among the Maroons of the early eighteenth century (see, for example, Craton 1982:81 and Hart 1985:59; for another view, see Tuelon 1973), but the terms are used by Maroons today. The term chieftainess, for example, is found on the monument for Nanny in Moore Town on a place called Bump Grave; Captain Willoughby of Moore Town describes Nanny as a goddess in his pamphlet "The Maroons in Chains" (n.d.).

117. Maroons now use obeah and science synonymously; science is the more common term. "Higher science" indicates a higher status in the transcendental hierarchy of power.

118. Cubah, who is mentioned here, had an important role in Tacky's Revolt of 1760. According to the Ashanti tradition of the Queen Mother, she "held court" in Kingston and was to rule after the victory of the rebels (see Craton 1982:132; see also Reynolds 1972:7). The fact that this never came about was in part due to the loyalty of the Maroons, who aided their former British opponents in crushing the revolt in return for mercenary compensation (Hart 1985:147).

119. Caribbean feminist literature is making impressive headway in this endeavor (see, for instance, the novels *Abeng* by Michelle Cliff (1984) and *Télumée* by Simone Schwarz-Bart [1987; orig. 1972]).

120. According to Mathurin (1975:3), the African gendered experience of women who had undergone their initiation contributed to their cultural resistance.

121. Debien (1983:120f.) gives an especially impressive example of the tenacity of an elderly slave woman, who undertook three attempts at flight while deathly ill, before the plantation manager (who wrote the original report) kept her shackled until she died.

122. Their achievements in agricultural production made it possible to break away from any residual dependency on the plantation economy after the

abolition of slavery and to create the basis for further cultural black resistance by establishing a relatively independent sector of small landowners (see Brereton 1985:38ff.).

123. The subject of their largest-scale production to date, *Nana Yah* (1980), was the historical figure of Nanny. The capitalized spelling of Nanny signifies the best-known female leader of the Maroons; the lower-case spelling refers to the historical "black mammy" of the manor (see Sistren 1980; also Schwinghammer 1992:124f.).

124. Since the days of slavery, the internal market system of Jamaica has been run mostly by women. Urban marketing of agricultural products and vending of all types of products are still almost exclusively in the hands of women (see esp. Simmonds 1987:31ff.; Mintz 1955:95ff.; Durant-Gonzalez 1983:2ff.).

125. I have attempted to reproduce Mrs. Foster's very interesting information with the greatest possible authenticity by citing the transcribed text of the interview verbatim. In order to be able to talk with me about myal and obeah forms of religious expression, Mrs. Foster needed Kojo's approval, which he granted her in a ritualized communication, to which Mrs. Foster had invited him by pouring rum. He justified his permission, according to Mrs. Foster, by categorizing my "mission" as that of a "cultural messenger." To facilitate comprehension of these texts by non-specialists, I have translated several recurring expressions into Standard English in the glossary at the end of this book (see also Cassidy 1982 and LePage/Decamp 1960).

126. The Maroons themselves use the term "dead," which is not considered inconsistent with their vital role in the social life of the living.

127. In Accompong, the Kojo Health Clinic of Accompong Town was officially opened on January 6, 1988, the 249th anniversary of independence, by a Christian priest, but was not staffed with medical personnel at this point. All information on these annual ceremonies presented here is based on my personal observations.

128. One of the best known storytellers of Accompong was Namba Roy, who could look back on a 200-year family tradition of storytelling by his male ancestors (Roy 1986:iii). As an official representative of the Maroons of Accompong in England, he died in 1961, several months after the publication of his novel *Black Albino*, which was reissued in 1986 (see Morris 1984:24ff.). He himself attributed his artistic prowess, which also included painting and carving, to his father's and grandfather's training: "I found that I just couldn't work satisfactorily to European standards. . . the art of my forefathers was always crying to come out" (Roy; quoted in Beshoff 1983:38. Beshoff's article includes several color plates of his work).

129. In the story "Anansi and Candlefly," Anansi's greed also destroys his food supply (in Jekyll 1966:86–90).

130. The abeng (derived from Ashanti *aben*: animal horn) is blown through an opening on its concave side, rather than at its end; the opening at the end of the cow horn can be used with the thumb to vary the pitch by about one tone (Cassidy 1982:263; also Dalby 1971:43).

131. After hearing on the radio that her son had been involved in a serious auto-

mobile accident, Mrs. Cawley took comfort in the fact that the abeng was not blown, which would have signalled a fatality (conversation of January 7, 1988).

132. Every January in Moore Town the abeng sounds the call for all able-bodied members of the community to help clean up the village (Schafer 1973:215, who obtained this information from Colonel Harris).

133. In this context, the "Creole language hypothesis" should be mentioned, although it is both controversial and difficult to substantiate. It claims that a "Creole" language had already developed in Africa as a language of trade to communicate between groups who spoke various languages and later became a "basilect" for the enslaved, which they developed into the basic Caribbean idioms through "relexification"—i.e., through a change of vocabulary (see Abrahams 1983a:26).

134. Even today, virtually every non-Maroon who attends a Kromanti dance among the Windward Maroons must take an oath of secrecy. The oath is administered by the granfa, who places the sharp side of the blade of a machete in the mouth of the obroni, recites an incantation, and trickles a liquid made of sugar and water, called *asikere*, over the machete and into the throat of the person taking the oath (Bilby 1981:79).

135. Dalby (1971:41) traces the Maroon word *obroni* back to the Twi term for white man, *o-buro-ni*.

136. Although the term *cotta* is no longer used for drum, *cotta stick* is still used for the percussion stick in the Kumina ceremony (Cassidy 1982:268). Bilby (1984:18ff.) describes Kumina as belonging to the cultural tradition of the *Bongo nation*, whose forefathers immigrated to Jamaica from Africa as contract laborers in 1841 to 1865 and settled near the Maroons. Although there are strong similarities between Kumina and Kromanti, their roots are not the same, as is evident in the different languages they speak. Interceremonial visits create a harmonious basis for interaction between the two "nations," although Maroon granfas also have been known to react aggressively to the "different blood" of the *bongo people*.

137. Here, too, we find a phonetic similarity and a semantic connection to *cottawoods*. The potential communicative connection between the cutting drum as a speaking instrument and the cottawood to conjure up an ancestor can be varied according to the intentions of the drummer. Two forms of "drum communication" can be distinguished according to whether the drummer speaks in prearranged signals that have no linguistic basis or forms the spoken words directly with his drumbeats (Finnegan 1970:481). Whether the cutting drum of the Maroons was indeed capable of communicating quasi-linguistic complex messages by simulating the rhythm and the tones of verbal language cannot be claimed with any certainty. It is also unclear whether the Maroons were like the Akan in having not only a specialized form of military drumming, but also a literary language of drums. In any case, there is no doubt that the Maroons could communicate with their talking drums—albeit perhaps in stereotypical phrases and not using a direct translation of linguistic forms. The link between the cutting drummer and the dancing granfa is both formative and iterative. On the language of drums and drum literature in Africa, see Finnegan 1970:481ff.; also Nketia 1982:73ff.; on the

comparison between various drums and drum styles in Jamaica: Roberts 1924; for a comparison to the voodoo drums of Haiti: Courlander 1960:192f.

138. In the view of the Windward Maroons, which accords with contemporary linguistic theory, the everyday language of the Maroons developed from the "pure" Kromanti of the first (guerrilla) warriors, who were born in Africa, to the "Creole" or "Jamaica talk" that is spoken in Jamaica today (Bilby 1983b:39).

139. Primarily Protestant and Anglican churches, along with a few smaller denominations from the United States, were established in the Maroon villages; in Accompong alone there are seven different churches. On the surface, they determine religious life, but the religious traditions of the Maroons are still cultivated in private and are revealed only minimally to outsiders at the annual festivities. Without giving these up, then, many Maroons practice religious traditions derived from their forefathers alongside Christian forms of worship. Furthermore, the latter are often blended with African religious flavors—a process that might be viewed as a form of recolonization in the religious sphere. Whereas the old traditions are kept quite intact, the European-derived denominations are blended with African concepts and thus become syncretized.

140. The code word has roots in the Ashanti language: *asànteé nkútoo* also means "Ashanti only" (Dalby 1971:41).

141. On the religious conflict surrounding the European mission, which still rages today, Jamaican theology professor Leonard E. Barrett (1979:24f.) writes: "It was there that Europe and Africa met in mortal combat. The teachers and preachers were expatriates, who appeared and disappeared without the consent of the community. . . they were not loved by the common people. If anything, the community feared them. They considered themselves responsible for bringing 'civilization' to the community, which to them meant 'good' religion, 'good' speech and 'good' behaviour." The "Afro-Jamaicans" in "their" communities, says Barrett, preferred instead their own religious ideas and forms of expression over the foreign Christian ones. Kumina (derived from the Twi words *akom* for possession and *ana* for ancestor) and Pukumina, both of which rely on communication with the ancestors during the so-called "possession" (myal), more closely approximated their religious experience.

142. Some people altogether rejected the goal of entering heaven, as the following story of an Indian chief in Hispaniola illustrates: "The story is told. . . of the Indian chieftain, Hatuey, who, doomed to die for resisting the invaders, staunchly refused to accept the Christian faith as the gateway to salvation when he learned that his executioners, too, hoped to go to heaven" (Williams 1983:8).

143. Kremser (1977:14ff.) explores in detail the difficulties of choosing non-Eurocentric terms and the resulting conflict of goals in achieving a comprehensible "translation" of cultural contents from one culture into another. Kremser uses the example of the *Boro Mangu* of the Azande.

144. It is unclear whether this spiritual universe of the Maroons, in which ancestral spirits were at the center of religious practices, included a supreme God and/or lesser deities, as did West African peoples (Parrinder 1980:18).

Evidence for this view are terms from Moore Town, Charles Town, and Accompong: *Yánkipon asási* for "God above" (in Moore Town) and *yan-ke-kom assasi* (in Accompong) for "God and earth," which have Ashanti linguistic counterparts, namely the Akan words *(o-)nyànkopan* for "almighty God" and *asàsé* for "earth" (Dalby 1971:41).

145. Obeah, which is still illegal in Jamaica, is nonetheless an enduring component of religious culture both in the interior of the island and in the modern urban centers, and is often the topic of everyday conversation among friends, although not with strangers. Obeah is the focal point of the plot of the Jamaican feature film *Countryman* (produced by Chris Blackwell in 1982).

146. This reciprocal relationship, usually called "possession," builds a social bridge between life and death, with all of the implications that this expansion of the kinship group entails (Kühnel 1986:144).

147. Cassidy (1982:247) considers the Bube word *dupe* (spirit) the most likely etymological source of *duppy*, but Patterson (1973:204) contends that *duppy* stems from the Adagme word *adope* (old spirits).

148. Maroon funerals, which resemble those of the Akan, not only provide the opportunity for friends and family to pay their respects to the dead, but also to inform their forefathers that a virtuous Maroon is about to enter the other world (Schafer 1973:222). Their veneration of the dead is motivated in part by fear of the potentially negative powers of the deceased. Dunham (1946:91) speculated that the tunnel shape of the grave she saw in Accompong, similar to those of the Maroons of Suriname, was originally intended to confound an evil spirit who wished to bring his body back into this world. Her conjecture was not, however, confirmed by the Maroons; they instead attributed the occasional digging of tunnels to the existence of large stones (see also Schafer 1973:223; also Courlander 1960:30f., who describes supernatural sanctions and acts of revenge against the living by furious "spiritual powers" in Haiti). The Cuban cimarrón Esteban Montejo (1968:132f.) reports on the custom of pasting the eyes of the dead with sperm to prevent their physical return.

149. Reports of ghosts are quite common in the literature on *duppies* in Jamaica. The stones thrown by a "duppy hand" are said to make right-angled hooks and target valuable objects such as clocks, glasses, and mirrors (Williams 1938:219). If a so-called noisy ghost, racketing ghost, or missile-throwing ghost begins a reign of terror against particular individuals, the only remaining option is an appeal to the obeah-man, which is generally quite expensive. Even the obeah-man is not always successful. His intervention might even exacerbate the wrath of the "noisy ghost" and worsen the predicament if he is not able to calm down the duppy (as in the lengthy description of one such instance by Barrett 1979:95ff.).

150. In Jamaica today, *duppy* is used as a general or collective term for spiritual entities in a wide range of guises—not just anthropomorphic. Earlier terminological differentiations between various appearances, which corresponded to the African concept of the multiple or dual soul, now seem forgotten (Cassidy 1982:245). In regard to the Kumina ceremony, Kühnel (1986:142f.) distinguishes between a *nkuyu* aspect of the "soul," which enters into the body of the dancer during the dance, and a "duppy soul," which accompanies the corpse into the grave and is later laid to rest with a second Kumina

burial. The Maroons equate "duppy" with "dead" (spirit of the ancestors); the "shadow" is their designation for the aspect of the soul of a living person that can be nailed to the cotton tree by an obeah specialist and thereby captured (Gladdys Foster, interview of January 10, 1988).

151. It is equally true of other religious forms of worship in Jamaica, such as Kumina and the "convince cult," that the spiritual powers partake in activities that are only possible in "material" bodies. They want to dance, sing, speak, smoke, and engage in human relations or, in the convince cult, even in sexual relations. Hogg (1960:11) quotes from the song of a visitor from the other world, which includes the line: "Pum-pum kill me dead, I make he kill me," which, loosely translated, means: "If sex kills me, let it kill me."

152. The postulated existence of a Maroon supreme God raises the question of some form of relationship between Maroon religious forms and the religion of the missionaries. To all appearances, Christianity, obeah, union with ancestors in the Kromanti ceremony, and other Maroon religious forms coexist (see Schafer 1973:226). Obviously the religious Maroon traditions were protected against the missionary assault because they were cultivated "underground." There are also indications that the "back to the roots" movement initiated primarily by Rastafari triggered contrary trends. In Accompong, some very young people are now involved in the Kromanti ceremony. "In spite of the apparent conversion of all Maroons to Christianity, it appears that the traditional religion continued to be practiced as a separate system" (Bilby 1981:53f.). Although the Kromanti tradition was protected by practicing Maroons from missionary zeal to undermine African religions and thus was hardly in a position to undergo a "syncretic process," the Maroons brought their religious values into the Christian churches and greatly influenced their forms of worship—as can also be observed in the rest of Jamaica. "The Afro-Jamaican religious tradition, then, has consistently reinterpreted Christianity in African, not European cultural terms" (Schuler 1980:69; see also Thomas-Hope 1980:11 and Hogg 1960:6).

153. Calling the visiting or "possessing" ancestor evil or an evil power does not automatically convey a negative connotation. It is just as likely that the "evil temperament" in the sense of wild temperament of the ancestor is intended, or the term is selected as a contrast to the Christian Holy Ghost and is meant purely as a classification. Mrs. Gladdys Foster was not only the leading myal specialist of Accompong, but also the head of an African-Christian Revival church (see McIver 1984:47).

154. "The method of healing in the centre is both ritual and herbal" (Barrett 1979:57). Many Jamaican healers, according to Barrett (1979:103ff.), are specialists in botany and clairvoyance as well as other "supernatural" practices. Their paragnostic powers rely on the ability "to read a patient," that is, to discover the nature of his or her ailments without diagnostic examinations.

155. *Obeah* may be traced back etymologically to the Efik word *ubio* (for objects the obeah-man uses for his "magic") and to the Twi word *bayi* (witchcraft, sorcery) or *o-bayifó* (witch, wizard) (Cassidy 1982:241), but the African source of the word *myal* is uncertain. Cassidy (1982:427) considers a combination of the Ewe words *mayé* (bad, evil) and *lé* (to grasp) possible. Schuler (1979:77) conjectures that Central Africa was the place of origin of *myal*.

156. Obeah is still widespread in the Caribbean today and is part of the religious system of the Ndjuka Maroons of Suriname. "In twentieth-century Djuka society, witchcraft remains a major idiom of social organization" (Van Wetering 1983:387).

157. Obeah began to pose a threat to white rule (Williams 1970:118). One factor may have been the use of obeah by the Maroons to prepare for plantation raids. After they had openly "planted obeah" and thereby driven the black slaves to flee the plantation, they could easily take possession of the livestock and certain items for everyday use (Vestdijk 1941:289f.). The Jamaican proverb "Keep sensay fowl fe pick obeah," which advises keeping fowl in the yard or garden to peck planted obeah out of the ground, refers to the "planting" of obeah to inflict harm (Cassidy 1982:104).

158. With ceremonial religious vows, led by the obeah specialists, the rebels are said to have been united for life to an oath of resistance (Gardner 1971:185). Schuler (1979:383) reports of an obligatory blood oath that involved drinking a mixture of rum, gunpowder, grave dirt, and blood. In the Caribbean and in South America, religious specialists such as obeah and myal men and women, voodoo priests, Nánigos, and Muslim teachers led or inspired one revolt after another (Genovese 1981:28; see also Lewis 1983:191).

159. In his poem "By Any Means Necessary" (on the LP: *Outcry* 1984), the dub poet Mutubaruka revives the spirit of resistance of obeah and voodoo, citing them as among the means that could be used to free South Africa and Namibia.

160. Beckwith (1969:106) declares her support of this view of obeah practices: "Many of these people are 'heathen' still, and obeah is the religion of the shadow world, the religion of fear, suspicion, and revenge."

161. Slow poisonings over the course of months were best able to convey the impression of natural ailments (Williams 1970:137).

162. Price (1983a:21) notes for Maroon communities in the diaspora as a whole: "A complex but integrated system of ritual and belief held an important place in social and political control."

163. Many Jamaicans shy away from even speaking the word obeah; they fear the power of the obeah-man, who could punish the disclosure of his identity. This is one reason for the fact that there are about thirty different synonyms for obeah-man in conversational Jamaican usage. Morrish (1982:43) lists the following: *professor, shadow-catcher, four-eyed man, buzuman,* and *guzuman.* Some of these terms, however, are not used exclusively for obeah specialists. In everyday speech, these terms do not automatically refer to the obeah specialists.

164. The giant silk cotton tree is considered the abode of the dead and is therefore occasionally called "duppy tree" (Barrett 1979:92). Since both obeah and myal rely on communication with the dead, various ceremonies take place at silk cotton trees (see Rashford 1985:55). If a tree is to be cut down to build a canoe, for example, the duppies must first be pacified with rum, otherwise the shipbuilder would stand to be injured with his own tools (interview with boatmaker Eric Kerr, April 6, 1988).

165. The fact that the obeah specialist may both plant an obeah (to put one) and pull it out (to pull one) is evidence for a more complex relationship between obeah and myal than the binary opposition "good and bad medicine" would have us believe. The obeah specialist can both heal and kill (Cassidy 1982:244).

166. The public nature of myalism allowed this African religious tradition to gain a strong following with some syncretic aspects and survive as an essentially independent denomination a full century before the Great Revival (around 1860) (Simpson/Hammond 1960:49). According to Schuler (1979:69,76), myalism was far more relevant to many African-Jamaicans toward the end of the time of slavery than the missionary versions of Christian belief, since myal represented the potential for resistance against the oppression they had experienced: "It attracted new followers on the north coast in the 1830s and 1840s and mounted anti-European offensives in both decades, demonstrating a continued Afro-Jamaican awareness of the major source of their misfortune in the nineteenth century. . . The Myal tradition formed the core of a strong and self-confident counterculture."

167. Williams (1970:155) describes myal shadow catching as a ceremony during which the "duppy tree" is pelted with eggs and decapitated chickens.

168. In addition to its protective functions as an amulet or talisman, amber is also said to have powers as a fetish and a mediator to the exosphere (see Cassidy 1982:249). It can also function as a crystal ball.

169. On this level of analytical conceptualization of the relationship between the two religious subsystems, I have focused exclusively on the religious meaning as transmitted by the narration. An empirical inquiry might reveal new insights into further aspects of social control.

170. In Moore Town, the ceremonies take place in mid-October (normally on October 10); in Accompong, on January 6.

171. Like the Ashanti during their *Afahye* festival, the Maroons cook only unsalted food for the deceased ancestors (Schafer 1973:242). The hog is cut open, deboned, and spread out on the charcoal in the traditional manner. Jerk pork is still considered a Maroon specialty in Port Antonio. The flavor of the charcoal substitutes for salt. Since the ancestors take part in the banquet, the living need to adapt to their habits and taste (see Cassidy 1982:196; also Dallas 1803:90f.).

172. This unity between members of the exosphere and the endosphere is the focus of nearly all African-Jamaican religious observance, which in some respects resembles the Kromanti dance of the Maroons (see Hogg 1960, who writes on the "convince cult"; also Cassidy 1982:239ff.; and Barrett 1979:104ff., who deal with Kumina; also Parrinder 1980:23f.; Brathwaite 1981:16ff.; and Pigou 1987:23ff., who view the African experience as a whole as the underpinning of Jamaican religious observance).

173. In this respect the Maroons of Jamaica differ from their counterparts in Suriname, who in 1986 renewed their military resistance to the government, which they continued even after the November 1987 elections. The altogether different nature of the relationship between the government authority and the Maroons of Suriname or Jamaica can be explained in large part by differ-

ent government policies toward the first free communities within their territory. In contrast to the Suriname military government, the Jamaican government agents have regularly agreed to formal displays of respect and explicit as well as unambiguous recognition of time-honored Maroon rights, which nipped any escalation of tensions in the bud. Nanny was declared the Jamaican national heroine and appeared on the $500 bill. A monument to Kojo was erected by the Jamaican National Trust in Accompong, but he has yet to receive the formal title of Jamaican national hero.

174. These 20,000,000 pounds sterling are being claimed by Rastafari organizations such as the Ethiopia Africa International Congress of King Emmanuel Charles Edward to finance repatriation to Africa (Prophet Don and Prophet Selvin, 1984 reasoning in Bull Bay).

175. A seasonal worker on the plantation who had invited me to tour the factory and furnished me with the opportunity to gain first-hand information about the working and living conditions on Hampden Estate spoke in a similar vein: "You better come on Sundays, that's our slave holiday" (Broggs, 1985 conversation).

176. Yellowman uses the word Jamdung, a pejorative expression for Jamaica, from "jam down."

177. Garvey's explosiveness landed him in jail several times. He was incarcerated for five years in Atlanta, after being found guilty on the thinnest of evidence of using the United States Postal Service to defraud investors with direct-mail advertising for his steamship company's stock (Campbell 1985:62; see also the detailed description of the background of the indictment and trial in Cronon 1981:111ff.; also Garvey's own reports in 1930 and 1931 in Clarke/Garvey 1974:139ff., 189ff.).

178. For an overview of Rastafari philosophy and its emergence and spread within Jamaica, see Chevannes 1994 and 1998; also van Dijk 1993; Bishton 1986; Barrett 1977; and Forsythe 1983).

179. However, Garvey also had his reservations about the role of the Maroons after the peace treaties and their alliance with the colonial power (see A. J. Garvey 1974:30).

180. Several Nyahbinghi elders have taken trips to other Caribbean islands, England, America, and Canada, where they participated in a Rastafari Oral Culture Project to clarify the complex relationship between Rastafari and reggae. The brethren also used the opportunity to demonstrate and account for Nyahbinghi music, culture, and philosophy to an interested public (see Montague and Yawney 1985).

181. Reckord (1977:3ff.) credits the role of Count Ossie, the co-founder of the Rasta commune "Mystic Revelation of Rastafari," in developing true Rasta music, and relates it to other African-Jamaican musical traditions (see also Shibata 1980).

182. Bob Marley himself repeatedly repudiated the term "Third World" and criticized it as an expression of Eurocentric attitudes. Rastas countered these attitudes with their Afrocentric vantage point, in which Africa is accordingly called the First World.

183. For an excellent recent overview of Reggae history, see Chang and Chen (1998). See also Davis and Simon 1977 and 1982; Hebdige 1975; Manuel 1995; and Clarke 1980.

184. I would like to thank Kenneth Bilby for this information, which he contributed in the discussion following my lecture at the 1992 International Caribbean Conference in Utrecht.

185. Garvey was elected "Provisional President of Africa" at the 1920 "First International Convention of the Negro Peoples of the World," which he had organized, and "President General" of the UNIA. His autocratic leadership of the UNIA made this election appear a mere formality (see Martin 1986:12f.).

186. The title "Father of Black Nationalism" refers to Garvey's success in organizing a mass movement. However, his historical forerunners, especially Martin Delany, rightfully deserve this unofficial title for formulating the ideologies of black nationalism (Sterling 1971).

187. In the introduction to the new edition of the volume on the Harlem Renaissance, edited by Alain Locke (1992; orig. 1925), Rampersad (1992:xx) explains, nearly seventy years after the publication of the original edition, the reasons for the ignorance surrounding Garvey's movement in the original volume. According to this source, the original editor (Locke) and most authors of the book were affiliated with the integration-minded NAACP, which sharply criticized Garvey's "Back to Africa" policy.

188. Minister Louis Farrakhan, one of the successors of Malcolm X, advocates these views of Elijah Muhammed in his public appearances (see Eure and Jerome 1989:151).

189. Professor X, one of the messengers of XClan, grew up in the familial milieu of the Black Power movement of the 1960s. His father Sonny Carson was himself an activist of the black nationalist community. Professor X knew Malcolm X personally during his childhood (see Spady and Eure 1991:191ff.).

BIBLIOGRAPHY

Abrahams, Roger D.
1983   *Man of Words in the W.I. Performance and the Emergence of Creole Culture.*
          Baltimore: Johns Hopkins Univ. Press.

Acts of Jamaica
1674   Document of the Public Record Office: CO 139/65. London.

Allen, Robert
1990   *Black Awakening in Capitalist America.* Trenton: Africa World Press.

Alleyne, Roger Fafa
1982   "Oral History." *Arise* (Kingston) 1, no. 1:10–11.

Allison, Judy, and Colonel C.L.G. Harrison
1982   *White is a Part of Maroon.* Kingston: Kingston Publishers.

Aptheker, Herbert
1983   "Maroons within the Present Limits of the United States." In Price
          1983a, 151–67.

Asante, Molefi Kete
1991   *Afrocentricity.* Trenton: Africa World Press.

Augier, F.R., and S.C. Gordon
1962   *Sources of West Indian History.* London: Longman.

Augier, F.R., S.C. Gordon, D.G. Hall, and M. Reckord, eds.
1986   *The Making of the West Indies.* London: Longmans, Green and Co.

Banbury, R. Thomas
1894   *Jamaica Superstition; or the Obeah Book.* Kingston: DeSouza.

Bargatzky, Thomas
1986   *Einführung in die Kulturökologie. Umwelt, Kultur und Gesellschaft.*
          Berlin: Dietrich Reimer.

Barnett, Donald, and Karari Njama
1966   *Mau Mau from Within.* London: Macgibbon and Kee.

Barrett, Leonard E.
1977   *The Rastafarians. The Dreadlocks of Jamaica.* Boston: Beacon Press.
1979   *The Sun and the Drum. African Roots in Jamaican Folk Traditions.*
          Kingston: Sangster's.

Bastide, Roger
1972   *African Civilizations in the New World.* New York: Harper & Row.

266

1983   "The Other Quilombos." In Price 1983a, 191–201.
Beckford, George, and Michael Witter
1985   *Small Garden. . . Bitter Weed: The Political Economy of Struggle and Change in Jamaica.* Morant Bay, Jamaica: Maroon Pub. House.

Beckwith, Martha Warren
1924   *Jamaica Anansi Stories.* New York: American Folklore Society.
1969   *Black Roadways: A Study of Jamaican Folklife.* New York: Greenwood (first published 1929).

Berner, Dominique
1984   "Bericht über die afro-karibische Kultur in Martinique und Guadeloupe im 19. Jahrhundert anhand deutschsprachigen Archiv- und Bibliotheksmaterials im Vergleich zur historisch-französichen Dokumentation. Ein Beitrag zur Ethnohistorie der Karibik." Ph.D. diss, Univ. of Vienna.

Berry, James, ed.
1984   *News for Babylon. The Chatto Book of Westindian-British Poetry.* London: Chatto & Windus.

Beshoff, Pamela
1983   "Namba Roy: Maroon Artist and Writer." *Jamaica Journal* (Kingston) 16, no. 3:34–38.

Bessell, M.J.
1938   "Nyabingi." *Uganda Journal* 1, no. 2:73–86.

Besson, Jean
1994   "Free Villagers, Rastafarians, and Modern Maroons. From Resistance to Identity." In Wim Hoogbergen, ed., *Born out of Resistance. On Caribbean Cultural Creativity*, 301–314. Utrecht: ISOR Publ.
1995   "The Creolization of African-American Slave Kinship in Jamaican Free Village and Maroon Communities." In Palmié 1995, 176–86.

Bilby, Kenneth M.
1979   "Partisan Spirits: Ritual Interaction and Maroon Identity in Eastern Jamaica." M.A. thesis, Wesleyan University.
1981   "The Kromanti Dance of the Windward Maroons of Jamaica." *Nieuwe West-Indische Gids* (Utrecht) 55, nos. 1 & 2:52–101.
1983a   "Black Thoughts from the Caribbean. I-deology at Home and Abroad." *Nieuwe West-Indische Gids* 57, nos. 3 & 4:201–14.
1983b   "How the 'Older Heads' Talk: A Jamaican Maroon Spirit Possession Language and its Relationship to the Creoles of Suriname and Sierra Leone." *Nieuwe West-Indische Gids* 57, nos. 1 & 2:37–88.
1984   "'Two Sister Pikni.' A Historical Tradition of Dual Ethnogenesis in Eastern Jamaica." *Caribbean Quarterly* (Kingston) 30, nos. 3 and 4:10–25.
1985   "The Holy Herb: Notes on the Background of Cannabis in Jamaica." In *Caribbean Quarterly: Rastafari Monograph*, 82–96.
1992   *Drums of Defiance: Maroon Music from the Earliest Free Black Communities of Jamaica.* Washington, D.C.: Smithsonian Folkways Records.

Bilby, Kenneth, and Diana Baird N'Diaye
1992   "Creativity and Resistance: Maroon Culture in the Americas." In Smithsonian Institution, ed., *1992 Festival of American Folklife*, 54–61. Washington, D.C.: Smithsonian Institution.

Bilby, Kenneth, and Filomina Chioma Steady
1981   "Black Women and Survival: a Maroon Case." In Filomina Chioma Steady, ed., *The Black Woman Cross-Culturally*. Cambridge, Mass.: Schenkmann Publishing Company, 451–67.

Binder, Wolfgang, ed.
1993   *Slavery in the Americas*. Würzburg: Königshausen & Neumann.

Birhan, Farika
1980   *The Rasta Dictionary*.
1983   *Haile Selassie I (a collection of Rastafari Poetry from the Theocratic vision of the Nyabinghi Order of the tribe of Judah)*. St. Andrew / Jamaica: Queen Omega Communications.

Bishton, Derek
1986   *Black Heart Man. A Journey into Rasta*. London: Chatto & Windus.

Bitterli, Urs
1976   *Die "Wilden" und die "Zivilisierten". Grundzüge einer Geistes- und Kulturgeschichte der europäisch-überseeischen Begegnung*. Munich: C. H. Beck.

Blackwell, Chris, prod.
1982   *Countryman* (video). London: Island Records.

Black Starliner Inc.
n.d.   *RASTA. Emperor Haile Selassie and the Rastafarians*. Trinidad: Black Starliner, Inc.

Boggs, James
1990   "The Influence of Malcolm X on the Political Consciousness of Black Americans." In J. H. Clarke 1990, 50–55.

Bourdieu, Pierre
1972   *Esquisse d'une théorie de la pratique, précédé de trois études d'ethnologie kabyle*. Paris: Droz.

Bourguignon, E.
1970   "Ritual Dissociation and Possession. Belief in Caribbean Negro Religion." In N.E. Whitten and J.F. Swazed, eds., *Afro-American Anthropology. Contemporary Perspectives*. New York: The Free Press.

Brathwaite, Edward Kamau
1977   *Wars of Respect*. Kingston: Agency for Public Information.
1981   *Folk Cultures of the Slaves in Jamaica*. London: New Beacon Books.
1984   *History of the Voice. The Development of Nation Language in Anglophone Caribbean Poetry*. London: New Beacon Books.

Brereton, Bridget
1985   *Social Life in the Caribbean 1838–1938.* Kingston/London: Heinemann.

Buckley, Roger Norman
1979   *Slaves in Red Coats. The British West India Regiments 1795–1815.* New Haven: Yale Univ. Press.

Burnett, Michael
1982   *Jamaican Music.* Oxford: Oxford Univ. Press.

Burton, Robert
1985   *Bird Behaviour.* London: Granada Publications.

Campbell, Horace
1985   *Rasta and Resistance. From Marcus Garvey to Walter Rodney.* London: A Hansib Publ.

Campbell, Mavis
1990   *The Maroons of Jamaica 1655–1796. A History of Resistance, Collaboration, and Betrayal.* Granby, Mass.: Bergin & Garvey.

Caribbean Quarterly: Rastafari Monograph.
1985   Reprint of *Caribbean Quarterly* 26, no. 4 (December 1980). Kingston: University of the West Indies.

Carrington, Lawrence D., Dennis Craig, and Ramon Todd Pandake, eds.
1983   *Studies in Caribbean Languages.* St. Augustine/Trinidad: Society for Caribbean Linguists.

Cashmore, Ernest
1983   *Rastaman. The Rastafarian Movement in England.* Winchester, Mass.: Allen & Unwin.

Cassidy, Frederic G.
1982   *Jamaica Talk. Three Hundred Years of the English Language in Jamaica.* London: Macmillan (first published 1961).

Chang, Kevin O'Brien, and Wayne Chen
1998   *Reggae Roots. The Story of Jamaican Music.* Kingston, Jamaica: Ian Randle Publ.

Chevannes, Barry
1981   "The Rastafari and the Urban Youth." In C. Stone and A. Brown, eds., *Perspectives on Jamaica in the Seventies.* Kingston: Jamaica Publ. House.
1994   *Rastafari. Roots and Ideology.* New York: Syracuse Univ. Press.
1998   *Rastafari and Other African-Caribbean Worldviews.* New Brunswick: Rutgers Univ. Press.

Clarke, Edith
1966   *My Mother Who Fathered Me.* London: Allen and Unwin.

Clarke, John Henrik
1974   "The Caribbean Antecedents of Marcus Garvey." In J.H. Clarke 1974, 14–28.
1990   *Malcolm X. the Man and His Times.* New York: Macmillan.

Clarke, John Henrik, ed.
1974   *Marcus Garvey and the Vision of Africa.* New York: Vintage Books.

Clarke, Peter B.
1986   *Black Paradise. The Rastafarian Movement.* San Bernadino: The Borgo Press.

Clarke, Sebastian
1980   *Jah Music. The Evolution of the Popular Jamaican Song.* Exeter, N.H.: Heinemann Educational Books.

Cliff, Michelle
1984   *Abeng.* Trumansburg, N.Y.: The Crossing Press.

Collins, John
1985   *African Pop Roots. The Inside Rhythms of Africa.* New York: W. Foulsham & Co.

Collins, Patricia Hill
1991   *Black Feminist Thought. Knowledge, Consciousness, and the Politics of Empowerment.* Boston: Unwin Hyman.

Compton, Jacques
1980   "Africa in the West Indian Consciousness." In Gates 1980, 26–37.

Cone, James
1992   *Martin and Malcolm and America. A Dream or a Nightmare.* New York: Orbis Books.

Cooper, Carolyn
1986   "Chanting Down Babylon: Bob Marley's Song as Literary Text." *Jamaica Journal* (Kingston) 19, no. 4:2–8.
1993   *Noises in the Blood. Orality, Gender, and the 'Vulgar Body' of Jamaican Popular Culture.* London and Basingstoke: Macmillan.

Cordoves, Raul
1984   "The Maroons of Suriname." *tricontinental* no. 91:32–37, Havana.

Courlander, Harold
1960   *The Drum and the Hoe. Life and Lore of the Haitian People.* Berkeley: Univ. of California Press.

Crahan, Margaret E., and Franklin W. Knight, eds.
1979a   *Africa and the Caribbean. The Legacies of a Link.* Baltimore: Johns Hopkins Univ. Press.
1979b   "The African Migration and the Origins of an Afro-American Society and Culture." In Crahan/Knight 1979a, 1–20.

Craton, Michael
1982   *Testing the Chains. Resistance to Slavery in the British West Indies.* Ithaca: Cornell Univ. Press.

Cronon, E. David
1981   *Black Moses. The Story of Marcus Garvey and the Universal Negro Improvement Association.* Madison: Univ. of Wisconsin Press (first published 1955).

Crummey, Donald, ed.
1986   *Banditry, Rebellion, and Social Protest in Africa.* London: James Currey.

Curtin, Philip
1969   *The Atlantic Slave Trade. A Census.* Madison: Univ. of Wisconsin Press.

Dalby, David
1971   "Ashanti Survivals in the Language and Traditions of the Windward Maroons in Jamaica." *African Language Studies* (London) 12:31–51.

Dallas, Robert C.
1803   *The History of the Maroons.* London: T. N. Longman and O. Rees.

Dalphinis, Morgan
1985   *Caribbean and African Languages: Social History, Literature, and Education.* London: Karia Press.

Dauer, Alfons M.
1983   "Zum Bewegungsverhalten afrikanischer Tänzer." In Artur Simon, ed., *Musik in Afrika*, 234–43. Berlin: Museum für Völkerkunde.

Davis, Stephan, and Peter Simon
1977   *Reggae Bloodlines. In Search of the Music and Culture of Jamaica.* Garden City: Anchor Press.
1982   *Reggae International.* New York: Random House.

Debien, Gabriel
1983   "Marronage in the French Caribbean." In Price 1983a, 107–34.

DeGroot, Silvia W.
1983   "The Bush Negro Chiefs Visit Africa: Diary of an Historic Trip." In Price 1983a, 389–98.
1986   "A Comparison between the History of Maroon Communities in Surinam and Jamaica." In Heuman 1986, 173–84.

DeKort, Jacques, and Marie Zwarthoed
1986   *Call for Support for Indian Peoples of Surinam.* Amsterdam: Workgroup for Indigenous Peoples.

Dijk, Frank Jan van
1993   *Jahmaica: Rastafari and Jamaican Society 1930–1990.* Utrecht: ISOR Publ.

271

Dreher, Melanie Creagan
1982   *Working Men and Ganja.*   Philadelphia: Institute for the Study of
          Human Issues.

DuBois, W. E. B.
1974   "Back to Africa." In J.H. Clarke 1974, 105–19.

Dunham, Katherine
1946   *Journey to Accompong.* New York: Henry Holt & Co.

Dunn, Richard S.
1972   *Sugar and Slaves. The Rise of the Planter Class in the English West Indies
          1624–1713.* Chapel Hill: Univ. of North Carolina Press.

Durant-Gonzalez, Victoria
1982   "The Realm of Female Familial Responsibility."   In Massiah 1982a,
          1–27.
1983   "The Occupation of Higglering." *Jamaica Journal* 16, no. 3:2–12.

Edmondson, Lockslay
1976   "Trans-Atlantic Slavery and the Internationalization of Race."
          Caribbean Quarterly 22, nos. 2 & 3: 5–24.

Edwards, Bryan
1796   *The Proceedings of the Governor and Assembly of Jamaica in Regard to the
          Maroon Negroes.* London: John Stockdale.
1983   "Observations on the Disposition, Character, Manners, and Habits of
          Life, of the Maroon Negroes of the Island of Jamaica; and a Detail of
          the Origin, Progress, and Termination of the Late War between those
          People and the White Inhabitants." (first published 1796). In Price
          1983a, 230–45.

Ehrlich, Luke
1983   *Word Soun' 'Ave Power. Reggae Poetry.* Cambridge: Heartbeat Records
          (booklet).

Erskine, Noel Leo
1981   Decolonizing Theology. A Caribbean Perspective. New York: Orbis
          Books.

Escalante, Aquiles
1983   "Palenques in Colombia." In Price 1983a, 74–81.

Ethiopia Africa Black International Congress
n.d.   *Black Supremacy. In Righteousness of Salvation.* Kingston: EABIC.

Eure, Joseph D., and Richard Jerome, eds.
1989   *Back Where We Belong: Selected Speeches by Minister Louis Farrakhan.*
          Philadelphia: PC International Press.

Eure, Joseph D., and James G. Spady, eds.
1991   *Nation Conscious Rap.* Philadelphia: PC International Press.

Fanon, Frantz
1967   *Black Skins, White Masks.* New York: Grove Press.

Faristzaddi, Millard
1982   *Itations of Jamaica and I Rastafari.* Munich: Rogner und Bernhard.

Finnegan, Ruth
1970   *Oral Literature in Africa.* Oxford: The Oxford Library of African Literature.

Fischer, Peter, and Heribert Franz Köck
1980   *Allgemeines Völkerrecht: Ein Grundriß.* Eisenstadt: Prugg.

Forsythe, Dennis
1983   *Rastafari: For the Healing of the Nation.* Kingston: Ziaka Publ.

Fouchard, Jean
1981   *The Haitian Maroons. Liberty or Death.* New York: Edward W. Blyden Press.

Francis, Armet
1985   *The Black Triangle: The People of the African Diaspora.* Phoenix: Seed Publ.

Franklin, John Hope
1981   Foreword to Cronon 1981, xvii–xix.

Fuchs, Werner
1980   "Möglichkeiten der biographischen Methode." In Lutz Niethammer, ed., *Lebenserfahrung und kollektives Gedächtnis*, 323–49. Frankfurt: Suhrkamp.

Galloway, Ernestine Royal
1981   "Religious Beliefs and Practices of Maroon Children of Jamaica." Ph.D. diss, New York Univ.

Gardner, W. J.
1971   *A History of Jamaica. From its Discovery by Christopher Columbus to the Year 1872.* London: T. Fisher Unwin (first published 1873).

Garrison, Len
1973   *Out of Exile: Historical Survey of the Rastafari Movement in Jamaica* (unpublished thesis). Oxford.

Garvey, Amy Jacques
1974   "The Early Years of Marcus Garvey." In J. H. Clarke 1974, 29–39.
1982   *Philosophy and Opinions of Marcus Garvey.* 2 vols. New York: Atheneum (first published 1923).

Garvey, Marcus
1974   "Why the Black Starline Failed" (orig. 1930). In J. H. Clarke 1974, 139-149.

Gaspar, Barry D.
1984   "'To Bring Their Offending Slaves to Justice': Compensation and Slave Resistance in Antigua 1669–1763." *Caribbean Quarterly* 30, nos. 3 & 4:45–60.

Gates, Brian
1980   *Afro-Caribbean Religions.* London: Ward Lock International.

Genovese, Eugene D.
1976   *Roll Jordan Roll: The World the Slaves Made.* New York: Vintage Books.
1981   *From Rebellion to Revolution. Afro-American Slave Revolts in the Making of the Modern World.* New York: Vintage Books.

Giddings, Paula
1988   *When and Where I Enter. The Impact of Black Women on Race and Sex in America.* New York: Morrow.

Goveia, Elsa V.
1970   "The West Indian Slave Laws of the 18th Century." In Douglas Hall, Elsa V. Goveia, and Roy Aupien, eds., *Chapters in Caribbean History,* 9–53. Kingston: Caribbean Universities Press.

Greenwood, R., and S. Hamber
1980   *Emancipation to Emigration. Caribbean Certificate History Book 2.* London/Basingstoke: Macmillan.

Hadel, Richard S. J.
1976   "Black Carib Folk Music." *Caribbean Quarterly* (Kingston) 22, nos. 2 & 3:84–96.

Halcrow, Elizabeth M.
1982   *Canes and Chains. A Study of Sugar and Slavery.* London: Heinemann.

Hall, Douglas
1985   *The Caribbean Experience. A Historical Survey 1450–1960.* Kingston: Heinemann.

Harris, C. L. G. Col.
1992   "The Maroons and Moore Town." In Smithsonian Institution, ed., *1992 Festival of American Folklife,* 73, Washington, D.C.: Smithsonian Institute.

Harris, Roy Nigerian
1988   *Save the Maroons. Save the Black People.* Port Antonio, Jamaica. (pamphlet)

Hart, Richard
1980   *Blacks in Bondage. Slaves Who Abolished Slavery.* Kingston: The Herald.
1985   *Blacks in Rebellion. Slaves Who Abolished Slavery.* Kingston: The Herald.

Hebdige, Dick
1975   "Reggae, Rastas, and Rudies." In Stuart Hall and Tony Jefferson, eds.,

Resistance through Rituals, 135-155. London: Hutchinson University.

Henney, Jeanette Hillman
1968   "Spirit Possession Belief and Trance Behavior in a Religious Group in St. Vincent, British West Indies." Ph.D. diss., Ohio State Univ., Columbus.

Hetzel, Helmut
1990   "Krise Niederlande—Surinam nach Putsch. Regimegegner fürchten blutige Aktionen der Militärregierung." *Die Presse*, Dec. 29, 1990.

Heuman, Gad, ed.
1986   *Out of the House of Bondage. Runaways, Resistance, and Marronage in Africa and the New World.* Totowa, N.J.: Frank Cass & Company.

Higman, B. W.
1979   "African and Creole Slave Family Patterns in Trinidad." In Crahan/Knight 1979a, 41–65.

Hill, Clifford
1980   "Afro-Caribbean Religion in Britain." In Gates 1980, 67–86.

Hine, Darlene C.
1979   "Female Slave Resistance: The Economics of Sex." *The Western Journal of Black Studies* 3:123–27.

HIZ (Handbuch für Internationale Zusammenarbeit), Vereinigung für internationale Zusammenarbeit, ed.
1987   Looseleaf Edition, 239th supplement. Baden-Baden: Nomos Verlagsgesellschaft.

Hoetink, H.
1979   "The Cultural Links." In Crahan/Knight 1979a, 20–41.

Hofbauer, Andreas
1986   "Von Quilombo zum Quilombismo. Historischer Abriß über schwarzen Widerstand in Brasilien mit besonderer Berücksichtigung der Quilombos von Palmares." Ph.D. dissertation, Univ. of Vienna.

Hogg, Donald
1960   "The Convince Cult in Jamaica." In *Yale University Publications in Anthropology* no. 58:3–24.

Jah Bones
1985   *One Love. Rastafari: History, Doctrine, and Livity.* London: Voice of Rasta Publ. House.

James, Cyril Lionel Robert
1963   *The Black Jacobins. Toussaint L'Ouverture and the San Domingo Revolution.* New York: Allison and Busby (first published 1938).
1981   Preface to Fouchard 1981.

James, Preston E.
1960   "Man-Land Relations in the Caribbean Area." In Rubin 1960a, 14–19.

Jekyll, Walter
1966   *Jamaican Song and Story. Anansi Stories, Digging Songs, Ring Tunes, and Dancing Tunes.* New York: Dover.

Jenkins, David
1975   *Black Zion: The Return of Afro-Americans and West Indians to Africa.* London: Wildwood.

Johnson, Howard, and Jim Pines
1982   *Reggae. Deep Roots Music. A Cultural History of Jamaican Popular Music.* London: Proteus Publ.

Johnson, Linton Kwesi
1975   *Dread Beat and Blood.* London: L'Ouverture Publ.

Jones, Rhett S.
1981   "Identity, Self-Concept and Shifting Political Allegiances of Blacks in the Colonial Americas: Maroons against Black Shot." *Western Journal of Black Studies* 5:61–74.

Kapuscinski, Ryszard
1983   *The Emperor.* London: Picador.

Kent, R. K.
1983   "Palmares: An African State in Brazil." In Price 1983a, 170–190.

Kerina, Murumba
1990   "Malcolm X: The Apostle of Defiance—An African View." In J. H. Clarke 1990, 114–119.

Kinfe, Abraham
1991   *Politics of Black Nationalism. From Harlem to Soweto.* Trenton: Africa World Press.

King, Johannes
1983   "Guerrilla Warfare: A Bush Negro View." In Price 1983a, 298–304.

Kitzinger, Sheila
1971   "The Rastafarian Brethren of Jamaica." In Michael Horowitz, ed., *Peoples and Cultures of the Caribbean,* 380–88. New York: The National History Press.

Ki-Zerbo, Joseph
1981   *Die Geschichte Schwarz-Afrikas.* Frankfurt: Fischer.

Knight, Franklin W.
1978   *The Caribbean: The Genesis of a Fragmented Nationalism.* New York: Oxford Univ. Press.

Köbben, A. J. F.
1983   "Unity and Disunity: Cottica Djuka Society as a Kinship Society." In Price 1983a, 320–69.

Kopytoff, Barbara Klamon
1973   "The Maroons of Jamaica: An Ethnohistorical Study of Incomplete Politics 1655–1905." Ph.D. diss., Univ. of Pennsylvania.
1976   "The Development of Jamaican Maroon Ethnicity." *Caribbean Quarterly* 22, nos. 2 & 3:33–50.
1979   "Colonial Treaty as Sacred Charter of the Jamaican Maroons." *Ethnohistory* 26:45–64.

Kossek, Brigitte
1992   "Women Slaves and Rebels in Grenada." In Thomas Bremer and Ulrich Fleischmann, eds., *Alternative Cultures in the Caribbean*, 21–46. Frankfurt: Vervuert.
1993   "Racist and Patriarchal Aspects of Plantation Slavery in Grenada: 'White Ladies,' 'Black Women Slaves,' and 'Rebels.'" In Binder 1993, 277–303.

Kototo, Asanta
1982   "The Maroons of Jamaica." *African-Caribbean Institute of Jamaica Newsletter* (Kingston) 7:3–40.

Kremser, Manfred
1986   "Ethnohistorie und Feldforschung." In Karl R.Wernhart, ed., *Ethnohistorie und Kulturgeschichte*, 147–61. Vienna/Cologne: Bohlau.

Kremser, Manfred, and Karl R. Wernhart, eds.
1986a   *Research in Ethnography and Ethnohistory of St. Lucia.* Wiener Beiträge zur Ethnologie und Anthropologie vol.3. Vienna/Horn: Ferdinand Berger & Söhne.
1986b   "The Scope of the Project: An Introduction." In Kremser/Wernhart 1986a, 11–36.

Kubik, Gerhard
1981   "Extensionen afrikanischer Kulturen in Brasilien." *Wiener Ethnohistorische Blätter* 21:3–75 and 22:3–77.

Kühnel, Annette E.
1986   "Die Ahnen und die Lebenden—Kumina: Eine afrikanische Kult-Religion in Jamaika." *Nachrichten der Deutsch-Venezolanischen Gesellschaft* 4, no. 3:140–44, Munich.

La Rosa Corzo, Gabino
1991   *Los palenques del oriente de Cuba. Resistencia y acoso.* Havana: Editorial Academia.

Lanternari, Vittorio
1965   *The Religions of the Oppressed (A Study of Modern Messianic Cults).* New York: Mentor Books.

Lawrence, Levine
1977   *Black Culture and Black Consciousness.* New York: Oxford Univ. Press.

Laya, Dioulbé, ed.
1972   *La tradition orale problématique et méthodologie des sources de l'histoire africaine.* Niger.

Lee, Barbara Makeda
1981   *Rastafari, The New Creation.* Kingston: Jamaica Media Prod.

LePage, R. B., and David Decamp
1960   *Jamaican Creole: A Historical Introduction to Creole.* London: Macmillan.

Leslie, Charles
1739   *New and Exact Account of Jamaica.* Edinburgh.

Levine, Donald
1974   *Greater Ethiopia. The Evolution of a Multiethnic Society.* Chicago: Univ. of Chicago Press.

Lewis, Gordon
1983   *Main Currents in Caribbean Thought. The Historical Evolution of Caribbean Society in its Ideological Aspects 1492–1900.* Baltimore: Johns Hopkins Univ. Press.

Lincoln, Eric
1991   *The Black Muslims in America.* New York: Kayode Publ.

Locke, Alain, ed.
1992   *The New Negro. Voices of the Harlem Renaissance.* New York: Atheneum (first published 1925).

Loth, Heinrich
1981   *Sklaverei. Die Geschichte des Sklavenhandels zwischen Afrika und Amerika.* Wuppertal: Hammer.

Madhubuti, Haki
1990   *Black Men. Obsolete, Single, Dangerous? The African American Family in Transition.* Chicago: Third World Press.

Malcolm X
1989   *By Any Means Necessary.* New York: Pathfinder (first published 1970).

Malcolm X
1987   *The Autobiography of Malcolm X.* New York: Penguin (first published 1964).

Malinowski, Bronislaw
1930   "Kinship." *Man* 30: 19–29, London.

Mansingh, Ajai and Mansingh, Laxmi
1985   "Hindu Influences on Rastafarianism." In *Caribbean Quarterly.*

Rastafari Monograph, 96–116.

Manuel, Peter
1995   *Caribbean Currents. Caribbean Music from Rumba to Reggae.* Philadelphia: Temple Univ. Press.

Marshall, Bernard A.
1976   "Marronage in Slave Plantation Societies: A Case Study of Dominica 1785–1815." *Caribbean Quarterly* (Kingston) 22, nos. 2 & 3:26–32.

Martin, Peter
1985   *Das rebellische Eigentum. Vom Kampf der Afroamerikaner gegen ihre Versklavung.* Hamburg: Junius.

Martin, Thomas
1973   *Maroon Identity: Processes of Persistence in Moore Town.* Ph.D. diss., University of California at Riverside.

Martin, Tony
1983   *Literary Garveyism.* Dover, Mass.: The Majority Press.
1986   *Race First. The Ideological and Organizational Struggles of Marcus Garvey and the Universal Negro Improvement Association.* Dover, Mass.: The Majority Press.

Massiah, Joycelin, ed.
1982a   *Woman and the Family.* Cave Hill/Barbados: Institute of Social and Economic Research.

Massiah, Joycelin
1982b   "Women who head Households." In Massiah 1982a, 62-130.
1983   *Women as Heads of Households in the Caribbean: Family Structures and Feminine Status.* Paris: Unesco.

Massiah, Joycelin, and Margaret Grill, eds.
1984   *Woman, Work, and Development.* Cave Hill/Barbados: Institute of Social and Economic Research.

Mathurin, Lucille
1975   *The Rebel Woman in the British West Indies during Slavery.* Kingston: African-Caribbean Publications.

Mbiti, John Samuel
1969   *African Religion and Philosophy.* New York: Anchor Books.

McFarlane, Milton
1977   *Cudjoe of Jamaica.* Short Hills, N.J.: Ridley Enslow.

McIver, Ann Borden
1984   "The Roles of Jamaican Maroon Women in a Changing Community." Ph.D. diss., Univ. of North Carolina at Chapel Hill.

McKay, Claude
1928   *"If We Must Die." Harlem Shadows*. New York: Harcourt, Brace and Co.

McKenzie, Hermione
1982   Introduction: "Women and the Family in Caribbean Society." In Massiah 1982a, vii–xi.

McPherson, E. S. P., and Leahcim Tufani Semaj
1985   "Rasta Chronology." In *Caribbean Quarterly, Rastafari Monograph*, 116–20.

Meillassoux, Claude
1991   *The Anthropology of Slavery: The Womb of Iron and Gold*. Chicago: Univ. of Chicago Press.

Michels, Peter M.
1979   *Rastafari*. Munich: Trikont.
1980   *Haiti — Voodoo/Rasta — Jamaica*. Frankfurt: Network Medienkooperative.

Mills, D.
1992   "Sister Souljah's Rebellion Rap. She Screams It Out. Riots were about Revenge and She's got the Beat." *Washington Post*, May 13.

Mintz, Sidney W.
1955   "The Jamaican Internal Marketing System." *Social and Economic Studies* (Jamaica), no. 4:95–103.
1986   *Sweetness and Power. The Place of Sugar in Modern History*. New York: Penguin.

Mintz, Sidney W. and Hall, Douglas
1960   "The Origins of the Jamaican Internal Marketing System." *Yale University Publications in Anthropology*, no. 57.

Mintz, Sidney W. and Price, Richard
1976   *An Anthropological Approach to the Afro-American Past: A Caribbean Perspective*. Philadelphia: ISHI.

Montague, Charmaine, and Carole Yawney
1985   *Voice of Thunder: Dialogue with Nyah Binghi Elders*. Toronto: Massai Productions.

Montejo, Esteban
1968   *The Autobiography of a Runaway Slave*. London: The Bodley Head.

Morris, Mervyn
1984   "'Strange Picni': Namba Roy's Black Albino." *Jamaica Journal* (Kingston), vol. 17, no. 1:24–27.

Morrish, Ivor
1982   *Obeah, Christ, and Rastaman. Jamaica and its Religion.* Cambridge: James Clarke & Co.

Morsley, Leonard
1964   *Haile Selassie: The Conquering Lion.* London: Weidenfeld and Nicolson.

Muhammad, Elijah
1965   *Message to the Blackman in America.* Newport News, Va.: United Brothers Communications Systems.

Müller, Ernst Wilhelm
1988   "Sozioethnologie." In Hans Fischer, ed., *Ethnologie, Einführung und Überblick,* 113–47. Berlin: Dietrich Reimer.

Murra, John
1960   Discussion of "The Family in the Caribbean." In Rubin 1960a, 75–79.

Nagashima, Yoshiko
1984   *Rastafarian Music in Contemporary Jamaica. A Study of Socioreligious Music of the Rastafarian Movement in Jamaica.* Tokyo: Institute for the Study of Languages and Cultures of Asia and Africa.

Naipaul, V. S.
1962   *The Middle Passage.* London: A. Deutsch.

Neher, Andrew
1962   "A Physiological Explanation of Unusual Behavior in Ceremonies Involving Drums." *Human Biology: A Record on Research* 34, no. 2, May 1962.

Nelson, Havelock, and Michael Gonzales
1991   *Bring the Noise. A Guide to Rap Music and Hip Hop.* New York: Harmony Books.

Nettleford, Rex M.
1972   *Identity, Race, and Protest in Jamaica.* New York: William Morrow & Co.
1978   *Caribbean Cultural Identity. The Case of Jamaica.* Los Angeles: Center for Afro-American Studies and UCLA Latin American Center Publications.

Neumann, Peter
1966   "Bemerkungen zu einigen Rechtsauffassungen der Buschneger Surinams." In *Abhandlungen und Berichte des staatlichen Museums für Völkerkunde,* vol. 25, 1–15. Berlin: Akademie Verlag.

Nicholas, Tracy, and Bill Sparrow
1979   *Rastafari. A Way of Life.* New York: Anchor Press.

Nketia, Kwabena J. H.
1982   *The Music of Africa.* London: Victor Gollancz.

O'Gorman, Pamela
1987   "Music: On Reggae and Rastafarianism—and a Garvey Prophecy."
         Jamaica Journal (Kingston) 20, no. 3:85–88.

Owens, Joseph
1976   *Dread. The Rastafarians of Jamaica.*   Exeter, N.H.: Heinemann
         Educational Books.

Padilla, Elena
1960   "Contemporary Social-Rural Types in the Caribbean Region."   In
         Rubin 1960a, 22–28.

Palmié, Stephan, ed.
1995   *Slave Cultures and the Cultures of Slavery.* Knoxville: Univ. of Tennessee
         Press.

Pan African Secretariat Jamaica
n.d.   "The Great Kojo." Nanny of the Maroons. n.p. (pamphlet)

Parkinson, Wenda
1978   *"This Gilded African." Toussaint L'Ouverture. A Biography of the First
         Black Freedom Fighter.* London: Quartet Books.

Parrinder, Geoffrey
1980   "The African Spiritual Universe." In Gates 1980, 16–25.

Parris, Scott V.
1981   "Alliance and Competition: Four Case Studies of Maroon-European
         Relations." *Nieuwe West-Indische Gids* (Utrecht) 55, nos. 3 & 4:174–224.

Patterson, Orlando
1964   *The Children of Sisyphus.* Essex: Longman.
1973   *The Sociology of Slavery.* Rutherford, N.J.: Fairleigh Dickinson Univ.
         Press.
1983   "Slavery and Slave Revolts: A Sociohistorical Analysis of the First
         Maroon War, 1665–1740." In Price 1983a, 246–93.

Perez de la Riva, Francisco
1983   "Cuban Palenques." In Price 1983a, 49–59.

Philipps, J. E. T.
1928   "The Nyabingi." *Congo. Revue Générale de la Colonie Belge* (Congo) 1,
         no. 1:310–21.

Pigou, Elizabeth
1987   "Western Responses to Death in a Jamaican Context." *Jamaica Journal*
         (Kingston) 20, no. 2:12–16.

Pollard, Velma
1983   "The Social History of Dread Talk." In Carrington et al. 1983, 46–62.

Powell, Dorian
1982   "Network Analysis: A Suggested Model for the Study of Woman and the Family in the Caribbean." In Massiah 1982a, 131–61.

Price, Richard
1983b   *First-Time. The Historical Vision of an Afro-American People.* Baltimore: Johns Hopkins Univ. Press.
1990   *Alabi's World.* Baltimore: Johns Hopkins University Press.
1992   "Maroons: Rebel Slaves in the Americas." In Smithsonian Institution, ed., *1992 Festival of American Folklife,* 62–64.
1994   *On the Mall: Presenting Maroon Tradition-Bearers at the 1992 Festival of American Folklore.* Bloomington, Ind.: Folklore Institute, Indiana University, Special Publications no. 4, Indiana Univ. Press.

Price, Richard, ed.
1983a   *Maroon Societies. Rebel Slave Communities in the Americas.* Baltimore: Johns Hopkins Univ. Press.

Price, Sally
1984   *Co-Wives and Calabashes.* Ann Arbor: Univ. of Michigan Press.

Prince Emmanuel Charles Edwards
n.d.   "Black Supremacy." In *Righteousness of Salvation.* Kingston: EABIC.

Rampersad, Arnold
1992   Introduction to A. Locke, ed., *The New Negro. Voices of the Harlem Renaissance,* ix–xxvii. New York: Atheneum.

Rashford, John
1985   "The Cotton Tree and the Spiritual Realm in Jamaica." *Jamaica Journal* (Kingston) 18, no. 1:49–57.

Ras Seko Tafari
1983   *In Memory. A Selection of Poetry.* Belmont/Trinidad: Afroets Press.
1985   *From the Maroons to Marcus Garvey. A Historical Development.* Tunapuna/Trinidad: Research Associates School Times Publications.

Rattray, Robert Sutherland
1929   *Ashanti law and Constitution.* Oxford: Clarendon Press.

Reckord, Verena
1977   "Rastafarian Music. An Introductory Study." *Jamaica Journal* 11, nos. 2 &3:3–17.

Redkey, Edwin
1974   "The Flowering of Black Nationalism: Henry McNeal Turner and Marcus Garvey." In J. H. Clarke 1974, 388–401.

Reid, Vic
1983   *Nanny Town.* Kingston: Jamaica Publishing House.

Reynolds, C. Roy
1972   "Tacky, and the Great Slave Rebellion of 1760." *Jamaica Journal* 6, no. 2:5–8.

Roberts, Helen H.
1924   "Some Drums and Drum Rhythms of Jamaica." *Natural History* 24, no. 2:241–51.
1925   "A Study of Folk Song Variants Based on Field Work in Jamaica." *Journal of American Folklore* 38, no. 148:149–246.

Roberts, George W. and Sinclair, Sonja A.
1978   *Women in Jamaica. Patterns of Reproduction and Family.* New York: Kraus Thomson.

Robertson, Diane
1982   *Jamaican Herbs.* Kingston: Jamaican Herbs Ltd.

Robinson, Carey
1969   *The Fighting Maroons of Jamaica.* Kingston: William Collins & Sangster.

Rodney, Walter
1969   *The Groundings with my Brothers.* London: Bogle-L'Ouverture.
1972   *How Europe Underdeveloped Africa.* London: Bogle-L'Ouverture.

Rouveroy van Nieuwaal, E. Adriaan B. van, and Werner Zips
1998a   E. Adriaan B. van Rouveroy van Nieuwaal and Werner Zips, eds., *Sovereignty, Legitimacy, and Power in West African Societies. Perspectives from Legal Anthropology.* Münster and Hamburg: Lit Verlag.
1998b "Political and Legal Pluralism in West Africa: Introduction and Overview." In van Rouveroy van Nieuwaal / Zips 1998a, ix–xxiii.

Rowe, Maureen
1985   "The Woman in Rastafari." In *Caribbean Quarterly, Rastafari Monograph*, 13–22.

Roy, Namba
1986   *Black Albino.* Essex: Longman (first published 1961).

Rubin, Vera, ed.
1960a   *Caribbean Studies: A Symposium.* Seattle, University of Washington Press.
1960b   "Cultural Studies in Caribbean Research." In Rubin 1960a, 110–22.

Rubin, Vera and Lambros, Comitas
1976   *Ganja in Jamaica.* New York: Anchor Press.

Saakana, Amon Saba
1985   *Blues Dance.* London: Karnak House.

Schafer, Daniel Lee
1973   *The Maroons of Jamaica.* Ph.D. diss., Univ. of Minnesota.

Schomburg, Arthur
1992   "The Negro Digs up His Past." In Locke 1992, 231–37.

Schuler, Monica
1966   "Slave Resistance and Rebellion in the Caribbean during the Eighteenth Century." Ph.D. diss., University of the West Indies.
1970   "Ethnic Slave Rebellions in the Caribbean and the Guianas." *Journal of Social History* 3, 374–85.
1979   "Myalism and the African Religious Tradition in Jamaica." In Crahan/Knight 1979a, 65–80.
1980   *"Alas, Alas, Congo." A Social History of Indentured African Immigration into Jamaica, 1841-1865.* Baltimore: Johns Hopkins Univ. Press.

Schwarz-Bart, Simone
1987   *Télumée.* Wuppertal: Peter Hammer (first published 1972).

Schwartz, Stuart B.
1983   "The Mocambo: Slave Resistance in Colonial Bahia." In Price 1983a 201–26.

Schwinghammer, Susanne
1992   "Töchter Afrikas—Mütter der Diaspora. Ein Beitrag zur weiblichen Geschichte und Widerstandskultur in Jamaika unter besonderer Berücksichtigung der Aktivitäten des Frauentheater-Kollektivs Sistren." M.A. thesis, Univ. of Vienna.

Semaj, Leahcim Tufani
1982   "Rastafarian Critique on Rasta." In *Arise* (Kingston) 1, no. 1:51–55.
1985   "Rastafari: From Religion to Social Theory." In *Caribbean Quarterly, Rastafari Monograph*, 22–32.

Sheridan, Richard B.
1986   "The Maroons of Jamaica 1730–1830. Livelihood, Demography, and Health." In Heuman 1986, 152–72.

Shibata, Yoshiko
1980   *Development of Rastafarian Music, its Growth and Diversification.* Kingston: Caribbean Seminar Series.

Simmonds, Lorna
1987   "Slave Higglering in Jamaica 1780–1834." *Jamaica Journal* (Kingston) 20, no. 1:31–38.

Simpson, George E.
1955   *Political Cultism in West Kingston.* Kingston: Institute of Social and Economic Research 4, no. 2.

Simpson, George E. and Hammond, Peter B.
1960   Discussion of "The African Heritage in the Caribbean." In Rubin 1960a, 46–53.

Sistren
1980   *Nana Yah*. Kingston: unpublished manuscript.

Sistren with Honor Ford-Smith, ed.
1986   *Lionheart Girl. Life Stories of Jamaican Women*. London: The Women's
            Press.
Smith, Michael G.
1960   "The African Heritage in the Caribbean." In Rubin 1960a, 34–45.
1984   *Culture, Race, and Class in the Commonwealth Caribbean*. Kingston:
            Department of Extramural Studies, Univ. of the West Indies.

Smith, Michael G., Roy Augier, and Rex M. Nettleford
1960   *Report on the Rastafari Movement in Kingston*. Kingston: Institute of
            Social and Economic Research.

Smith, Mikey
1985   "Mikey Smith: Dub Poet, interviewed by Mervyn Morris." *Jamaica
            Journal* (Kingston) 1, no. 2.

Spady, James
1991   "When and Where I Enter: Sister Harmony and Black Women
            Rappers." In Eure/Spady 1991, 147–49.

Spence, Balfour A. B.
1985   "The Impact of Modernization on Traditional Farming Communities:
            Case Studies of the Accompong Maroon Village." M.Phil. thesis,
            University of the West Indies.

Stedman, J. G. (Captain)
1983   "Guerrilla Warfare: A European Soldier's View" (first published
            1796). In Price 1983a, 305–11.

Sterling, Dorothy
1971   *The Making of an Afro-American: Martin Delany, 1812–1885*. New York:
            Da Capo Press.

Stewart, J.
1823   *A View of the Past and Present State of the Island of Jamaica*. Edinburgh:
            Oliver and Boyd.

Stewart, Robert
1984   *The 1872 Diary of James Splaine, S.J. Catholic Missionary in Jamaica: A
            Documentary Note*. Kingston.

Stone, Carl, and Aggrey Brown, eds.
1981   *Perspectives on Jamaica in the Seventies*. Kingston: Jamaica Publ. House.

Tafari, Seko
1985   *From the Maroons to Marcus. A Historical Development*. Port of Spain:
            Research Associates School Times Publ.

Tafari I, Jabulani
1985   "The Rastafari Successors of Marcus Garvey." In *Caribbean Quarterly, Rastafari Monograph*, 1–13.

Tanna, Laura
1983   "Anansi—Jamaica's Trickster Hero." *Jamaica Journal* 16, no. 2:20–31.
1984   *Jamaican Folk Tales and Oral History*. Kingston: Institute of Jamaica.
Tannenbaum, Frank
1960   Discussion of "Race Relations in Caribbean Society." In Rubin 1960a, 60–66.

Textor, Robert
1980   *A Handbook on Ethnographic Futures Research*. Stanford: Stanford Univ. Press.

Thelwell, Michael
1980   *The Harder They Come*. New York: Grove Press.

Thicknesse, Philip
1790   *Memoirs and Anecdotes of Philip Thicknesse*. Dublin: William Jones.

Thomas, Michael and Boot, Adrian
1982   *Jah Revenge. Babylon Revisited*. London: Eel Pie Publ.

Thomas-Hope, Elisabeth
1980   "The Pattern of Caribbean Religions." In Gates 1980, 4–15.

Toop, David
1984   *The Rap Attack. African Jive to New York Hip Hop*. London: Pluto Press.

Tuelon, Alan
1973   "Nanny—Maroon Chieftainess." *Caribbean Quarterly* (Kingston) 19:20–27.

Turner, Harold
1980a   "Caribbean Christianity." In Gates 1980, 38–48.
1980b   "New Religious Movements in the Caribbean." In Gates 1980, 49–57.

Van Bladel, Leonie
1987   "French Guyana: Influx of Surinames." In *Refugees*, Feb. 1987, 9–10.

van Dijk: see Dijk, Frank Jan van

van Rouveroy van Nieuwaal: see Rouveroy van Nieuwaal, E. Adriaan B. van.

Van Wetering, W.
1983   "Witchcraft among the Tapanahoni Djuka." In Price 1983a, 370–88.

Vernon, Diane
1980   "Bakuu: Possessing Spirits of Witchcraft in the Tapanahony." *Nieuwe West-Indische Gids* (Utrecht) 54, no. 1.

Vestdijk, Simon
1941   *Die Fahrt nach Jamaika. Aus den Papieren Richard Beckfords, die von seinen Erlebnissen auf dieser Insel in den Jahren 1737 und 1738 berichten.* Brünn: Rudolf M. Rohrer Verlag.

Viola, Herman
1992   "Seeds of Change." In C. Margolis and H. J. Viola, eds. *Seeds of Change. Five Hundred Years since Columbus*, 11–16. Washington: Smithsonian Institution Press.

Wagley, Charles
1960   "Plantation America: A Culture Sphere." In Rubin 1960a, 3–13.

Wallace, Anthony F. C.
1956 "Revitalization Movements." *American Anthropologist* 58:264–81.

Wallace, Michele
1991   *Black Macho and the Myth of the Superwoman.* London: Verso.

Walne, Peter, ed.
1973   *A Guide to Manuscript Sources for the History of Latin America and the Caribbean in the British Isles.* London: Oxford Univ. Press.

Ward, J. R.
1985   *Poverty and Progress in the Caribbean 1800–1960.* Basingstoke: Macmillan.

Warner-Lewis, Maureen
1979   "The African Impact on Language and Literature in the English-Speaking Caribbean." In Crahan/Knight 1979a, 101–24.

Waters, Anita
1985   *Race, Class, and Political Symbols.* New Brunswick: Transaction Books.

Wendt, Doug, and Lance Linares
1983   "Reggae and Radio." *Reggae and African Beat*, Sept./Oct., 16–19, Los Angeles.

Wernhart, Karl R.
1979   "Die Bedeutung des sozialwissenschaftlichen Ansatzes für Geschichtswissenschaft und Ethnohistorie." *Wiener Ethnohistorische Blätter* 18:39–76.
1980   "Auswirkungen der Zivilisationstätigkeit und Missionierung in den Kulturen der Autochthonen. Am Beispiel der Gesellschaftsinseln." In Klingenstein, Grete et al., eds., *Europäisierung der Erde? Studien zur Einwirkung Europas auf die außereuropäische Welt.* Wiener Beiträge zur Geschichte der Neuzeit, 120–46. Vienna: Verlag für Geschichte und Politik Wien.
1986a   *Ethnohistorie und Kulturgeschichte.* Vienna: Bohlau.
1986b   "Ethnohistorical Research in St. Lucia: Theoretical Positions and Methodology." In Kremser/Wernhart 1986a, 147–54.

Wernhart, Karl R., and Werner Zips
1993   "Ethnohistorie und Kulturgeschichte. Diskussion der theoretischen
        und methodologischen Grundlagen." In Wolfdietrich Schmied-
        Kowarzik and Justin Stagl, eds., *Grundfragen der Ethnologie. Beiträge
        zur gegenwärtigen Theorie-Diskussion*, 255–72. Berlin: Dietrich Reimer.
1998   *Ethnohistorie. Rekonstruktion und Kulturkritik. Eine Einführung.*
        Vienna: Promedia.

White, Timothy
1983   *Catch a Fire. The Life of Bob Marley.* New York: Holt, Rinehart &
        Winston.

Whitney, Malika Lee, and Dermott Hussey
1984   *Bob Marley: Reggae King of the World.* London: Plexus.

Whyte, Daisy
1974   "The Death of Marcus Garvey." In J. H. Clarke 1974, 342–44.

Williams, Eric
1960   "Race Relations in Caribbean Society." In Rubin 1960a, 54–60.
1983   *Capitalism and Slavery.* London: Andre Deutsch (first published 1964).

Williams, J. J.
1938   "The Maroons of Jamaica." *Anthropological Series of the Boston Graduate
        School* 3, 318–471.
1970   *Voodoos and Obeahs: Phases of West Indian Witchcraft.* London: Dial
        Press (first published 1932).

Willoughby, A. B.
n.d.   *The Maroons in Chains.* n.p.

Wilmore, Gayrard S.
1983   *Black Religion and Black Radicalism. An Interpretation of the Religious
        History of Afro-American People.* New York: Orbis Books.

Yawney, Carole
1972   *Herb and the Chalice: The Symbolic Life of the Children of Slaves in Jamaica.*
        Toronto: York University.
1978   "Lions in Babylon: The Rastafarians of Jamaica as a Visionary
        Movement." Ph.D. diss., McGill Univ.
1985   "Strictly Ital: Rastafari Livity and Holistic Health." Unpublished
        paper presented at the Ninth Annual Meeting for Caribbean Studies,
        Ontario.
1993   "Rasta Mek a Trod. Symbolic Ambiguity in a Globalizing Religion."
        In Thomas Bremer and Ulrich Fleischmann, eds., *Alternative Cultures
        in the Caribbean*, 161–68. Frankfurt: Vervuert.

Zindi, Fred
1985   *Roots Rocking in Zimbabwe.* Gweru/Zimbabwe: Mambo Press.

Zips, Werner
1986   "Geschichte von drüben? Gedanken zu kommunikativen

Forschungsansätzen in der Geschichtswissenschaft und ihrer Praktikabilität für die ethnologische Feldforschung." *Wiener Ethnohistorische Blätter* no. 30, 3–35.

1987a   "'Sie hören die Gewehre des Krieges.' Schwarzer Widerstand in Surinam." *Entwicklungspolitische Nachrichten* no. 4, 7–9, Vienna.

1987b   "'They were Children in the Forest but we were Children of the Forest.' Kulturökologische Aspekte des Befreiungskampfes der Maroons von Jamaica." *Mitteilungen der Anthropologischen Gesellschaft in Wien* 117:113–23, Vienna.

1991a   "Accompong—Schwarze Rebellen in Jamaica." Film C2281 des ÖWF. In *Wiss. Film* 42:129–33, Vienna.

1991b   "Widerstand in Jamaica/Staatsoberhäupter—Statement von Colonels und des Staatssekretärs." Film C2281/6 des ÖWF. In *Wiss. Film* 43:71–72, Vienna.

1993   "We are at war. Schwarzer Nationalismus in den USA im 20. Jahrhundert." In Thomas Fillitz, André Gingrich, and Gabriele Rasuly-Paleczek, eds., *Kultur, Identität und Macht. Ethnologische Beiträge zu einem Dialog der Kulturen der Welt*, 135–60. Frankfurt: IKO-Verlag für interkulturelle Kommunikation.

1994a   "'To make war with words.' Soziale Organisation und Widerstand in afrikanisch-karibischer Oralliteratur." In Manfred Kremser, ed., *Ay Bobo. Afro-karibische Religionen*. Part III: Rastafari, pp. 119–48. Vienna: Wiener Universitätsverlag.

1994b   Rastafari—Eine Kulturrevolution in der Afrikanischen Diaspora. In Manfred Kremser, ed., *"Ay Bobo." Afrokaribische Religionen*, Part III: *Rastafari*, 15–31. Vienna: Wiener Universitätsverlag.

1997   "Injustice done to the Maroons. A Comment." *The Gleaner* (Kingston, Jamaica) 163, no. 53 (March 5), p. 8A.

1998a   "Nanny: Nana of the Maroons? Some Comparative Thoughts on Queen Mothers in Akan and Jamaican Maroon Societies." In van Rouveroy van Nieuwaal/Zips 1998a, 191–227.

1998b   "'The Good, the Bad, and the Ugly.' Habitus, Feld, Kapital im (Feld des) jamaikanischen Reggae." In Wernhart/ Zips 1998, 221–38.

1998c   "Obscured by Colonial Stories. An Alternative Historical Outline of Chieftaincy in Jamaican Maroon Societies." In E. Adriaan B. van Rouveroy van Nieuwaal and R. van Dijk, eds., *African Chieftaincy in a New Socio-Political Landscape*, 205–37. Münster and Hamburg: Lit Verlag.

GLOSSARY

a: is, be, am, are, it is, there are, to, of, in, at
an': and
anyting: anything
'ave: have
bokkle: bottle
bredda=br'er=bro: brother
cyaan=cyaan't: can't, cannot
dat: that
dawg: dog
de: the
deh: there
desso: there
dem: them (also as a plural marker; e.g., de man dem: the men, the people)
dey: they
dideh: there
dis: this
djink: drink
dung: down
ebryting: everything
fe (or: fi): for, to
fraid: afraid
gi: give
gwan (or: gwaan): go on, went
groun': ground
haffe: have to
him= 'im: his, her, he, she
i': it
I-sah: allright sir (one of many I-words in Rasta talk, lending a positive connotation)
I-ses: praises
'im= him: him, her, he, she
inna: in the
Jamdung: Jamaica (pejorative neologism in Rasta talk: 'to jam down')

jus': just
lef': left, leave
lick: hit, beat, strike
likkle: little
madda: mother
man: man, woman, men
mawnin: morning
me: I, me, my
mek: make
notting: nothing
nuh: no, not, does not
odder: other
ol': old
ongly: only
oonoo: you
outta: out of
pon: at, upon, on
roun': around
sah: sir (also used to address a woman)
seh: say, that
sen': send
smaddy: somebody
tan deh: stand there (often used as a warning about spirits)
tek: take
thanx: thanks
ting: thing
tun: turn
wah= wha: what
way: away
went: go
wey: which, what, where
wid: with
yah: here
yasso: here
yu: you

PHOTO CREDITS